To Iris
With grateful than
Pamela

elp.

WIGSTON
AT WAR

By Pamela Ward

ISBN 0-9547591-0-9
Copyright © Pamela Ward 2004
First Edition 2004
£12.99

Published By
Pamela Ward
Printed By
Norwood Press
Anstey, Leicester

FOREWORD

Wigston and its surrounding area owe a debt of gratitude to Pamela Ward for her splendid book *Wigston at War*. For the past two and a half years, she has devoted herself to the task of bringing alive the stories of the local men who responded to the call "For King and Country" to defend the freedom which we are able to enjoy today and for which they paid the ultimate sacrifice.

Hardly a family remained untouched by the ravages of the Great War which was followed twenty-one years later by the Second World War, a combined total of ten long years of warfare in which the young and not so young men of Wigston marched, sailed and flew in the various theatres of war across the world.

By dint of meticulous research, carried out with great sensitivity, and respect for the memory of those who died on active service, Pamela has produced a valuable record which will serve as a legacy to their memory. The use of photographs, letters, newspaper cuttings and documents illustrate their deeds and the stories of our fathers, sons and brothers in a way that is both humbling and fills one with a sense of great pride in their courage and determination to preserve our freedom which meant so much to them.

Pamela was inspired to write her book as a result of selling a poppy to the wife of a sailor who did not return. The poppies, that grow in Flanders Fields, have come to symbolise the enormity of the sacrifice made by communities such as Wigston.

Whilst they lie at rest, they will remain forever in our hearts and in the minds of future generations of Wigstonians thanks to *Wigston at War*.

May they rest in peace.

Derek Seaton
Historian and Author

PREFACE

"LEST WE FORGET"

It was early November in the year 2000 when I stood as I had done for countless Novembers' selling poppies on the street in South Wigston for Remembrance Day on the 11th. People put money in to the tin as they passed, gave a cheery greeting or stopped for a few minutes for a chat. I am always heartened by the numbers of children who show interest and want to buy a poppy.

Then almost without me noticing her approach she was there at my side. A tiny little figure whom I guessed to be around five feet tall but with a huge heart as she generously piled the coins into my tin.

"You see", she said, "My husband was killed in the war and I never forget him."

The lady was ninety years old. She had lived a full life eventually remarrying and brought up four sons, but those words stuck in my mind, "I never forget him."

The lady carried on to tell me how her husband had died in the Royal Navy and how they had spent his last leave at home. The presents he had bought for her and their three sons and I felt the lump rising in my throat.

I had been selling poppies since the age of sixteen years and knew exactly why I was selling them but the only knowledge I had of the victims of war in South Wigston were the stories that I had heard from my Mother of the lads that used to live in the village and never came back. I had never before met anyone first hand to tell me of their personal loss.

I realized that whilst I had been selling poppies for years I knew absolutely nothing about the men listed on the South Wigston or Wigston Magna war memorials. The lady's words pounded inside my head. I felt I had to know about the village men who had died for freedom. I was standing where they had stood, I was walking where they had walked, I had to get to know who they were.

My quest began immediately and through the following pages I have come to know them. Come to shed tears for them as each story has unfolded before me, shed tears for the families they left behind, the fatherless children who still cry for the love of a father they were so cruelly deprived of and to know that without their courage and sacrifice life as we know it would never have been. I look at their photographs and for a few moments they are alive again.

Sadly it has not been possible to find descendants of every man who gave his life but all of the men listed on the war memorials in Wigston are listed here even if their stories are yet to be told. There are many and I hope that in the future someone may follow on with them. Stories too of the differing groups of Wigston people who gave dedicated service which have only been lightly touched on here. The Land Army Girls, The ATS. ARP, Civil Defence and many other Wigston organizations.

During the course of my research I have discovered names that are not listed on the Saint Thomas War Memorial or All Saints War Memorial and this I hope may be put right in the future. To date I have been able to see two of the names included on to Saint Thomas War Memorial and fifteen names on to a new Memorial Plaque at the Wigston Memorial Peace Park. This book is dedicated to the memory of all of the men and to Doris Hills, the little lady who without knowing it set me on their trail. It is also dedicated to my Mother whose marvellous memory has helped enormously and to my sister Valerie who tirelessly has driven me miles to collect material and to all the relatives and friends of the war heroes who so generously and trustingly have allowed me to use their treasured photographs. Without their tremendous support this book would never have been written.

It is my hope that when these pages are turned the men of Wigston will come alive again, we will know them and remember their dedication and legacy of freedom they have bequeathed us.

"LEST WE FORGET."

Pamela Ward
May 2003

ACKNOWLEDGEMENTS

My grateful thanks extend to all the families and friends who have so generously loaned precious photographs, letters and documents. Without their valuable information, enthusiasm and interest this book could not have been written.

MRS JEAN ATTON	WIGSTON MAGNA
MRS THEODORA MARY BALL	THURNBY LODGE, LEICESTER
MR DEREK BARRATT	WIGSTON MAGNA
MRS MARION BARTHOLOMEW	OADBY
MR MICHAEL W BEATTIE	WIGSTON MAGNA
MR MERVYN BEEBY	SOUTH WIGSTON
MR TERRENCE BIRKIN	WIGSTON MAGNA
MRS CHRISTINA BERRILL	MELTON MOWBRAY
CAPTAIN DAVID BERRY	LUTTERWORTH
MRS TRISHA BERRY	WIGSTON MAGNA
MRS FREDA BODICOAT	SOUTH WIGSTON
MRS IRIS BOWN	MARKFIELD
MR MARTIN BRADLEY	GLEN PARVA
MRS FREDA BRAKER	SOUTH WIGSTON
MR ANTHONY BRIGGS	RATBY
MR JAMES BRIGGS	RATBY
MRS ANN BROMLEY	GLEN PARVA
MRS ETHEL BRYANT	MARKET HARBOROUGH
MRS IRIS CALOW	MOUNTSORREL
MRS SHELAGH CLARK	THURNBY LODGE
MRS HELEN CLAY	LEICESTER
MR PATRICK CLOSE	WIGSTON MAGNA
MR CLIFFORD ELLIOTT	WIGSTON MAGNA
MR VICTOR FOULSTON	WIGSTON MAGNA
MRS YVONNE GRAY	SOUTH WIGSTON
MR JOHN GRECH	
MISS ROSEMARY HALL	WHETSTONE
MR GEORGE HANDS	CROFT
MRS AUDREY HICKFORD	WIGSTON MAGNA
MRS DORIS HILLS	SOUTH WIGSTON
MR MARK HINCKS	SINGAPORE
REVD. DR. PETER HOLMES	GLEN PARVA
MR DAVID HUMBERSTON	LEICESTER
MR DESMOND JARVIS	NARBOROUGH
MRS JANICE JARVIS	ANSTEY HEIGHTS, LEICESTER
MRS JESSIE LEWIS	WIGSTON MAGNA
MRS ANNETTE MASON	SOUTH WIGSTON
MRS MADELINE MARQUES	WIGSTON MAGNA
MRS EILEEN MAWBY	WIGSTON MAGNA
MRS MAVIS MEAD	WIGSTON MAGNA
MRS ELSIE MEARS	WIGSTON MAGNA
MR ROBERT P MOORE	WIGSTON MAGNA
MR KENNETH MUNDIN	WIGSTON MAGNA

MISS MARGARET NOBBS	SOUTH WIGSTON
MRS MAY NOBBS	SOUTH WIGSTON
MRS JANE PITCHES	MANCHESTER
MRS KATHLEEN POTTS	MARKFIELD
MR JOHN PURKISS	MARKET HARBOROUGH
MR PETER REEVES	WIGSTON MAGNA
MR IAN RICHARDSON	WIGSTON MAGNA
MRS HAZEL RUDKIN	SOUTH WIGSTON
MRS EILEEN SALES	WIGSTON MAGNA
MRS HENRIETTA SCHULTKA	COUNTESTHORPE
MRS MARY SHARMAN	WIGSTON MAGNA
MRS DORIS STATHAM	WIGSTON MAGNA
MRS PAULINE STONE	WIGSTON MAGNA
MRS EDNA SUMMERLAND	WIGSTON MAGNA
MR GRAHAM TAYLOR	WIGSTON MAGNA
MISS NORMA THOMPSON	LEICESTER
MRS EILEEN THOMSON	SOUTH WIGSTON
MR CLIFFORD WALKER	RINGWAY, LEICESTER
MR HOWARD WARE	WIGSTON MAGNA
MR DEREK WATTS	AMESBURY, WILTSHIRE
MRS JUDITH WATTS	FLECKNEY
MR VICTOR WATTS	FLECKNEY
MRS JANET WILLIAMS	MARKET HARBOROUGH
MRS MAHALA WILKINS	WIGSTON MAGNA
MR DAVID WINFIELD	NEW PARKS
MRS BARBARA WOODWARD	WHETSTONE

APPRECIATION

I would like to thank most sincerely the following people for their willingness to help when needed.

Mrs Violet E Ward for her marvellous memory and support.

Mrs Valerie de Soto for tirelessly driving me to collect material at a moment's notice and for valuable time freely given in preparing finished documents for the printer.

Samuel Edward de Soto for his help with the scanning programme

Mr Alan May of Mays Computers, Churchgate, Leicester for his expertise.

Mr John Winfield of New Parks, Leicester for his specialised help with computers in getting me started and Mr Gordon Macdonald for his assistance.

Revd. Dr. Peter Holmes for the use of his computer at the beginning

Mr Michael Walton of Cheshire for his dedication and patience with my computer problems

Simon Ford, Radio Leicester Publicity
John Florance and Chris Highton, Radio Leicester

Nick Ridley, Editor, Leicester Mercury

Mr Derek Seaton for expert help and advice with publishing.

Jess Jenkins and Aubrey Stevenson, Record Office Wigston. Arranging for me to view Wigston disks at Leicester Reference Library

Mr Martin Bradley. Enthusiasm and willingness to supply Blaby and Cosby names.

Victor and Audrey Foulston, Valerie de Soto and Janet Bradley for invaluable help with researching epitaphs on the gravestones at Wigston Cemetery.

Mrs Doris Statham. Enthusiastic encouragement and interest.

BIBLIOGRAPHY

War Memorial South Wigston

War Memorials Wigston Magna

War Memorial Blaby. Names supplied by Mr Martin Bradley

War Memorial Cosby. Names supplied by Mr Martin Bradley

War Memorial Countesthorpe

War Memorial Oadby

War Memorial Whetstone

Croft Information – supplied by Mr George Hands

Families and Friends of men lost 1914-1918 and 1939-1945

Mr Dean Allen, Oadby and Wigston Borough Council. Access to official archives.

The Commonwealth War Graves Commission

The Naval and Military Press provided by Sqn. Ldr. R L Stanley MBE

Mrs Jean Atton. Access to The Royal British Legion Records

Pam Howells, Reference Library, Leicester

Kew Record Office

Trinity House

Registry of Ships and Seamen – Cardiff

The Leicester Mail

The Leicester Daily Mercury

Leicester Chronicle and Leicester Mercury

Leicestershire Mercury

'The Established and the Outsiders'. Norbert Ellis and John L Scotson

Daily Express Encyclopaedia

The Life and Times of Winston Churchill. M Thomson

English History. A J P Taylor

A Dictionary of Modern History. A W Palmer

A Short History of the Second World War. Basil Collier

The Timetables of History. Bernard Grun

Checking Various History on Line articles via the Internet

CONTENTS

FOR THE FALLEN

They shall grow not old, as we that are left grow old;

Age shall not weary them, nor the years condemn.

At the going down of the sun and in the morning

We will remember them.

Laurence Binyon
1869-1943

KOHIMA EPITAPH

"When you go home, tell them of us and say,

For their tomorrow, we gave our today"

John Maxwell Edmonds
1875-1958

WIGSTON AT WAR

PART ONE

1914 - 1918

The First Great War began on the 28 July 1914 with the declaration of war by Austria upon Serbia. Until it ended on the 11 November 1918 the greater part of the war was waged by land armies led by Germany and Austria, the Central Powers against France, Russia, Great Britain and America, and the Allied and associated Powers. totaling twenty six million men.

Alliances linking countries drew them into war rather than preventing it. The Austro–German Alliance was bound in 1879, whilst England was still embroiled in the Zulu War. The Triple Alliance was in place between Italy, Austria and Germany in 1882 and Russia was allied with France in 1883. In the early part of the twentieth century England had formed an alliance with Japan and Entente Cordiale with France and Russia.

Germany's rise and a national desire to dominate other nations, rivalry and mistrust by Austria of Russian policies in the Balkans, Serbian aspirations, conflicted with political ideals of free thinking nations and all served to promote war. Britain's support of France was viewed with suspicion by some nations, the widening of the Kiel canal and the build up of the German Navy saw Britain strengthen its naval power also; but in the sweltering summer of 1914 Britain was viewed by Germany as emersed only with Ireland's problems dismissing their strength as of little consequence. The assassination on 28 June 1914 by the Serbian, Prinzip, of the Arch Duke Francis Ferdinand, heir to the Austrian throne, and his wife, in Sarajevo, fuelled the anger of the German Emperor, William II who ordered preparations for war. Eventually more countries became embroiled in conflict and inevitably neutral countries were caught up in it too. Britain's entry into the war was sealed by Germany's refusal to recall their invading troops from Belgium.

In Leicester the holiday mood was changing. June and July 1914 were memorable months in the county. From Glen Parva Barracks in South Wigston, detachments went on parade at Victoria Park in Leicester to join a battalion with band and drums heralding recruitment. In contrast, in the Town Hall Square, a requiem was held for the soldiers killed in South Africa and at Blaby suffragettes were burning down the railway station whilst others were tying themselves to chairs in St Paul's Cathedral in London. Meanwhile King George V and Winston Churchill, First Lord of the Admiralty, were inspecting warships at Spithead.

The Royal Horse Artillery housed in Hazel Street School in Leicester began training on the recreation ground at Filbert Street whilst in Western Park one thousand men were being drilled. Drivers were needed to become driving instructors, men for mine laying and fuse setting and battery gun drill.

At the end of July The Leicester Daily Mercury was reporting on 'Gossip from the Capital'.

'Partial mobilisation of Austria', 'Russia mobilising', 'German fleet ordered to gather off the Norwegian Coast'.

At the beginning of August the British fleet was cleared for action in response to the seizure of British ships in the Keil Canal and in Leicester the Automobile Club appealed for patriotism to car owners to give up their motor cycles and mechanically propelled commercial vehicles whenever they should be needed.

On the 4th August 1914 The Leicester Daily Mercury reported the news,

'BRITISH ULTIMATUM, EXPIRING AT MIDNIGHT, REJECTED IN ADVANCE BY GERMANS INVADING BELGIUM, BOMBS DROPPED ON FRENCH TOWNS'.

A report on Wednesday 5th August 1914 headlined, 'ENGLAND AT WAR, AWAITING NEWS FROM THE FLEET'.

Action followed swiftly.
'British Army mobilising', 'Government to take control of the railways', Admiral Jellicoe proclaims, 'Your country needs you, Answer your country's call'.

In Leicester the military were purchasing horses and the Co-operative Society announced that the delivery of provisions could not be guaranteed now due to the lack of horses. The society urged their customers to fetch their own goods.

On the 6th August 1914 the British cruiser HMS Amphion was the first casualty of naval warfare with the loss of over one hundred British sailors. The vessel hit mines which had been laid by the German minelayer, Konigin Luise as it steamed South in the North Sea to lay mines in the Thames Estuary. HMS Amphion had sunk the minelayer the day before rescuing some of her crew but the German sailors died with their rescuers.

Peace was at an end in England and three days later on the 10th August 1914 The Leicester Mail was reporting on events in South Wigston.

'RESERVISTS LEAVE GLEN PARVA DEPOT'.
'At midnight on Saturday about 800 reservists paraded at Glen Parva Barracks and marched to the railway station, entraining in two specials for, it was stated, Portsmouth. They were given a hearty send-off by a large crowd – their relatives and friends having been permitted by the officers and staff to assemble at the barracks in the afternoon. On Sunday evening more reservists left the Depot, to the strains of Mr Charles Moore's Temperance Band and ringing cheers from the onlookers.
Fifty horses which had been commandeered were paraded on the green on Saturday and taken away for transport duty'.

Recruiting at Glen Parva for Lord Kitchener's Army was averaging one hundred a day being drafted to Aldershot.

The 12th August saw the funeral of William Dunmore, Dunmore's Biscuits, Canal Street, South Wigston and at Saint Thomas Church the Voluntary Aid for Sick and Wounded was established. The first of a course of lectures delivered by Miss Courtey, Superintendant of the County Nursing Association, preceded a working party formed to make clothing for Arthur W Faire's Voluntary hospitals and various local centres.

The era of invention had begun and brought new technology and mass destruction with it. Submarines, torpedoes and mine laying at sea and on land coupled with developing aircraft, the tank and poison gas claimed many lives.

The first German Zeppelin raid on England in January 1915 put fear into the civilian population on the coast and in London until later in October 1917 a raid over the Midlands in bad weather was considered to be a complete failure. This virtually marked the end of the airship's power as the Germans returned to the use of other aircraft.

In May 1915 the sinking of RMS Lusitania caused the death of 1,198 passengers which included many children, and crew. The liner returning to Britain from New York was thought to be carrying small arms for Kitchener's Army. The Germans had threatened to sink the Lusitania but it was regarded by many as propaganda. By the end of 1915 it was calculated that the loss to Britain's merchant shipping was 100,000 tons.

In 1916 on the Western Front two million men died at Verdun and the Battle of the Somme alone and in 1917 Britain suffered a further loss of four million tons of Britain's merchant shipping. In 1918 a severe food shortage in Britain necessitated the establishment of national food kitchens and rationing.

In South Wigston and Wigston Magna lives would be shattered for ever as in every other village in Leicestershire men responded to their country's call. The horrors of this new age were unfolding and families would pay a high price for peace throughout England the effects of which are still evident today. Wigston men died in battle and from disease in the field and when peace was almost secured in 1918 their loved ones died at home from the ravages of the first major influenza epidemic followed by the second in 1919. By 1920 it is estimated that twenty two million people died in the epidemic worldwide. South Wigston and Wigston Magna graves are stark epitaphs in Wigston cemetery as the war graves are sad reminders of the harsh reality of their lives. Wigston fathers died in the Great War of 1914 – 1918 and their sons died in the second war of 1939 - 1945.

Back in 1914 in Wigston, at the outbreak of war, despite the overcrowding housing problems and the pollution of the River Sense; organisations were soon springing into action to provide help wherever they could to assist the war effort and on the 19th August 1914 at the Co-operative Hall, The Leicester Mail reported that the Wigston Aid Committee had been formed. The meeting organised by the Reverend T W Wright and attended by over a hundred residents formed the society to aid provision of articles required by the Red Cross Society. Mrs Owston was appointed president and the committee consisted of twenty-seven ladies.

Every able bodied man in towns and villages in England was called upon by the War Minister Earl Kitchener to enlist for service to King and country and The Leicester Mail on 31st August 1914 was reporting on
'RECRUITING AT WIGSTON', AN EXAMPLE TO EMPLOYERS AND EMPLOYEES'.
'Following an earnest appeal by Mr E Lee, managing director of Two Steeples Ltd. Wigston. a recruiting campaign took place in the factory and twenty-two gave in their names for enlistment including Mr F W Lee, the youngest son of the head of the firm. All the men have been promised underwear by the firm while they are away, and reinstatement on their return'. In South Wigston at the Barracks on Saturday evening 'a series of concerts was held in the dance rooms, Sergeant Major Cattell presiding, the idea being to entertain recruits and their friends. The artistes were; Messrs Fred Asher, Countesthorpe, W Taylor, C Bass, L Burley, T Paxton, H Moore, (clarionet) C Moore, (cello)

Miss Lockton with Mr H J Heaton as accompanists. The Temperance Silver Prize Band and Male Voice Choir gave a concert. Mr C Moore conducting on the Green on Sunday afternoon when £9-12s-6d was collected for the National Relief Fund. In the evening the Band assisted at a service in the Barrack square, Mr A E Porter conducting: St Woolstan's choir led the singing. Mr H E Smith, Leicester YMCA, secretary, gave a stirring address. The YMCA have volunteered to erect a large tent on the green at the Barracks for the use of recruits. The evening's collection amounted to the sum of £1-5s-4d.'

Thursday 3rd September 1914 The Leicester Daily Mercury readers learned about the, 'DEPARTURE OF DRAFTS FROM GLEN PARVA'.
'This morning about 240 drafts left to join the 3rd Battalion, all looking fit and well. They were followed by a party of 16 from The Two Steeples Ltd, Wigston. to join the 6th Battalion, (Kitchener's) Battalion. The party was under the command of Colour-Sergeant Gurr who was employed by the firm, and had re-joined the colours. They met with a great reception, the female employees accompanying them en masse, many of them carrying flags. They were played to the station by Mr Chas. Moore's Band. This morning there were still about 1,850 recruits at the Depot, and more are expected during the day. Last evening a concert was given at the Barracks in the YMCA marquee which was crowded to overflowing with recruits and their friends'.

On the 8th September 1914 The Leicester Daily Mercury printed a 'shabby letter' written from —-the present headquarters of the 4th Leicester (Territorial) Battalion. Private H W Parsons, late of Wigston. says. 'This newly appointed military centre is almost another Leicester. My home being at Wigston I know very few Leicester boys but I have been simply astonished to find so many I know from Wigston. I walked along the main street in town here the other night and suddenly heard a cry of 'GOOD OLD WIGSTON' and at least a dozen of the boys came across to shake hands. I have met many more since, many of them belonging to the football clubs, and the same old spirit that was shown when Wigston United won the cup is strikingly apparent when Old Wigstonians get together. We are all billeted with the townspeople, and most of the boys are getting an excellent domestic in addition to military training. We are all pledged for foreign service, but of course we are in the hands of the military authorities. I am staying in the same house as another boy from Leicester, who has nine other brothers serving his country. Three of them are with the Fleet, two are with the Expeditionary Force in France and the other five are with Kitchener's second army. Bye the bye, the 4th Leicesters played the Lincolns last week at 'Soccer' and lost 4 – 0 but I think if we can arrange another match we shall reverse that score. We have challenged them at 'Rugger' but they won't face it. 'Kindest Regards'

On the 12 September 1914 The Leicester Chronicle and Leicestershire Mercury reported on a 'Patriotic Meeting at Wigston Magna'.
It was held in aid of the Red Cross Fund on the Banks, Bell Street. Mr H T Hincks presided. 'Stirring speeches were delivered by Councillor A S Payne, Mr Pochin, Mr J D Broughton and Mr F Simpson all of whom impressed upon the young men the duty of coming forward in the defence of their country's honour and rights of liberty of the civilised world. It was a time when every man who could bear arms should come forward and join one or other of the various branches of the services and give their names in as recruits'. Once again Mr Charles Moore conducting the Silver Prize Band had paraded through the village collecting over £11-00 for the fund.

Reports continued to reach the press on varying activities in support of the war effort. A dance was held in South Wigston at the Girls' School in mid September in aid of the Prince of Wales Relief

Fund. With a hundred people in attendance it was a great success and the music was provided again by Charles Moore and the Silver Prize Band.

The monthly school managers meeting was held in the Council Chamber and Miss Eva A Veasey was appointed as student teacher to the South Wigston School as vacancies had occurred due to four of the male staff, (F Broacher, E Powdrill, Aspell and Wallace) enlisting in Kitchener's Army. Low attendance at the Boys' school was thought to be caused by many of the children waiting out to see the soldiers. However, the managers recognised the high number of children obtaining scholarships at South Wigston. Mr Payne and Mr Black had approached the Commanding Officer at the Depot regarding the opening of the schools for sleeping purposes for the recruits. The officer thought that the men had better remain in barracks as he did not have sufficient supply of NCOs to look after them. It was agreed that dances would be held every Saturday evening in the school to raise money for the National Relief Fund.

A dance was held in aid of the Prince of Wales fund in the Clarence Assembly Rooms in 1914 and also in South Wigston residents had a thousand soldiers billeted on them. This step was taken to accommodate the increasing flow of recruits daily enlisting. The allowance made by the military authorities for each man was two shillings a day for food and lodging. It was understood that a number of the borough and county police were at the barracks acting as drill instructors. Large drafts of men were frequently being forwarded to military centres in readiness for whatever duties they may be called upon to perform.

With the barracks on Saffron Road, South Wigston had become an important centre on the military map and soldiers would be marched from their quarters to the garrison church of Saint Thomas for the Sunday services.

Wigston people supported the war effort wherever they could. The once sleepy villages came alive bursting with activity but inevitably sadness overshadowed the community as by Christmas of 1914 families in Bassett Street, Garden Street, Park Road, Kirkdale Road and Central Avenue were being informed that their men were listed as some of the first casualties of war dying in France and Belgium. Some were just teenagers only eighteen years old and so it went on for the next four years, young boys knowing nothing of war from every corner of Wigston patriotically marching away to fight. Not all of them returned. Many who did, died from their wounds in battle but on the 17th April 1915 'a curious and touching scene' was reported by The Leicestershire Mercury as 'Miss Vesta Tilley', music hall star, sang to the wounded in Leicester. Men in the 5th Northern Hospital with arms in slings, some on crutches, others borne in on stretchers propped up with pillows and cushions by the nursing staff, watched enthralled as Miss Tilley dressed in khaki uniform burst into song with 'The Army of Today's Alright'. Miss Tilley accompanied by Mr John W Lowe, conductor of the Palace orchestra, marched up and down and 'gave it as she had never given it before'. Poignantly, 'Wan faces flushed and the more lusty cheered'.

Back in Wigston fund raising continued to support the needy as Flag Days for the Red Cross and Saint John of Jerusalem were being held. In September and October of 1915, £66-17-9d was raised for the Serbian Relief Fund and £100 for the Red Cross. On Christmas Day a house to house collection raised £45 for the Belgian Relief Fund.

Flag Days were popular in raising money for charity as in 1916 funds for soldiers and sailors were collected. On Emblem Day proceeds of £31-15-0d was given to the Leicester Nursing Association. People were actively posting information throughout the district in Wigston for the Relief of Belgium.

On the 31 May the Battle of Jutland was in progress off Denmark and lasted into the first day of June. The short sea battle between the British and German fleets was significant as it was believed to be indecisive. Both sides claimed victory. The destroyer H.M.S Shark, with the fourth flotilla, was put out of action coming under German fire whilst attacking the German battle cruiser squadron. H.M.S. Shark did fire a torpedo but out of ninety two officers and ratings only six of her crew survived. Able Seaman George Henry Dewick on active duty on H.M.S. Shark, whose wife lived in Moat Street, Wigston Magna, lost his life. Four days later on the 5 June 1916 the Secretary of State for War, Earl Kitchener, was travelling on H.M.S Hampshire on a mission to Russia. The vessel struck a mine off the Orkneys and with most of the crew the man who had recruited and organised three million men for 'Kitchener's Voluntary Army', drowned.

In February 1917 the German Navy had sunk over two hundred ships bringing food and supplies to Britain. Although in 1917 it was reported that Britain's wheat harvest had been the best in living memory, due to panic buying; it did become necessary to introduce food rationing. Bread was rationed and then sugar late in 1917 whilst butter, margarine, lard, jam and some meats were not rationed until the middle of July 1918. Some of these items continued on ration into 1919 and 1920.

In the Spring of 1917 the Mayor of Leicester approached the Wigston Magna Urban District Council by letter to request their help in raising funds for the benefit of disabled soldiers and sailors. The county target was set at £100,000. After consideration and agreement that Wigston's disabled men would be included in the scheme, the Mayor estimated that Wigston's contribution should be set at approximately £600.

It was further agreed that Lady Pearson should be informed that the Council would be pleased to assist in arranging two concerts to help raise funds for blind soldiers. One would be held in Great Wigston in June 1918 and one in South Wigston. If the weather was fine they would take place in the open air. Duly two concerts were held for Saint Dunstan's blind soldiers and sailors.

In 1918 in South Wigston the Gas Company were extending their mains along Countesthorpe Road. This was excellent news for Crow Mills Pumping Station in providing power and lighting for their operations to be more efficiently carried out.

Not such good news for an improved mail service was at hand as the Postmaster at Leicester expressed his view that it was not possible to have a Sunday delivery due to the circumstances of war. On weekdays an earlier service could not be promised either due to the late running of trains and trams.

In Bassett Street Schools in South Wigston and Long Street School at Wigston Magna demonstrations were taking place on how to bottle and preserve fruit and in July the Council received communication from the National Salvage Council promoting patriotism as they urged the general public to save their fruit stones and nut shells. The War Office sanctioned the disclosure of this need stating that the items were required for 'gas masks'. The collection was expected to be small but it was stressed that the need was great. It was therefore decided that head teachers would take responsibility for arranging collection of these valued articles. Nut shells and fruit stones must be kept separate and labels could be applied for.

The horrors of battle warfare in the trenches was felt deeply at South Wigston and Wigston Magna as the names of those who died continued to be mourned. Arras, Ypres, the Somme, France and Flanders, all had become familiar household names. When the wounded soldiers, many of whom suffered with 'Trench Foot', were brought from the railway station, temporarily to Saint Thomas's Hall before their final journey to the Barrack Infirmary on Saffron Road; the mutilation of war was seen face to face . On these occasions a local girl Doris Dunn who was a member of Violet Moore's Ladies Choir, left her job at John Black's shoe factory in her lunch breaks, to sing to them.

On the 7th November 1918 in a railway carriage at Rethondes a German armistice delegation met with Marshal Foch and Admiral Wemyss. In the early hours of the 11th November 1918 the armistice was signed and came into force at 11-00am. On the same afternoon Lloyd George, the British Prime Minister, read out the terms of the armistice in the House of Commons.

The war graves at Welford Road Cemetery at Wigston Magna can be seen today evoking thoughts of barbaric warfare and the price those men paid for peace. Worse, the agony of those lost who have no known grave. No place for families to mourn.

For all of them in 1919 the clock on Saint Thomas's Church Tower in South Wigston was installed as part of a village's remembrance to its fallen soldiers. A swimming bath given by Mr Dunmore in memory of those who died was situated by the locks on the Grand Union Canal at South Wigston.

To celebrate the end of hostilities, at Bassett Street School, a place where so many of the young boys lost had only read of war, a public tea was held.

In 1923 the first war memorial to commemorate the dead was erected in South Wigston and further extended to include the casualties of 1939 – 1945. A memorial board at All Saints Church in Wigston Magna commemorates the victims of 1914 – 1918 and latterly a new plaque in the Peace Memorial Park at Wigston Magna includes also the men of 1939-1945.

The following pages record a part of the lives of some of those brave men who for one brief moment come alive again. To see them is to know them and to remember that as we walk the streets of Wigston we are walking in their shadows.

A post card found at a sale by Mr Tony Briggs of Ratby, Leicestershire.

TRANSCRIPT

POST CARD SENT TO MRS A VANN
26 PADDOCK STREET, WIGSTON

Dear Mother and Dad
We have just seen Harry moved out of one ward in another / he has moved in 22A so he has only gone up one, are you pleased. I saw the Doctor / If I had not done so he would have been at Cardiff today. I am pleased to say he is getting on fine, have you heard from Oswin today if so let me know, there was another train came in this morning some bad cases —————- say hope you and Dad are well with best love from
Maria or Marcia or Martha

UNSURE OF THE SIGNATURE

ERNEST EDWARD DANIEL JOHNSON

Ernest Edward Daniel Johnson was born in 1890 the son of Daniel and Ada Johnson and lived at 10 Newgate End, Wigston Magna, Leicestershire. His father served as a Liberal Councillor for Wigston and in 1910 was the council chairman.

On leaving school Ernest became a butcher working for the Co-operative Society. The shop was situated in Bull Head Street in Wigston Magna and had a shoe repairing business at the back in the yard. Later it may have served as a baker's as a Hovis sign was displayed. The shop was demolished in the 1970's to make way for a by-pass.

*Ernest Edward Daniel Johnson
Butcher at the Co-Operative Society,
Bull Head Street, Wigston.*

Ernest joined the Leicestershire Yeomanry (Territorial Army) before the First World War. It was a mounted regiment and he would attend annual camp taking with him one of the horses from the farm which was his family home. Being in the Territorial Army meant that Ernest was called to service early after the outbreak of war. He was just twenty five years old when he died at Ypres, West Flanders in Belgium on Thursday 13 May 1915. He would have known the horrors of the trenches which were dug out by both sides and extended from Nieuport on the Belgian coast, through Ypres to Verdun. Poison gas was first used by the Germans at Ypres in April 1915 but it took a period of four years, 1914 – 1918 with neither side gaining much ground before the Germans were forced back along the Western Front.

Ernest's body was never recovered. Like thousands of others he has no known grave and his name is commemorated on the Menin Gate Memorial. The memorial is dedicated to the soldiers who lost their lives in defence of the Ypres Salient.

Above: Ernest Edward Daniel Johnson
Below: Ypres (Menin Gate) Memorial - Leper West - Viaanderen Belgium

PRIVATE GEORGE TATTERSHALL

George Tattershall was born in 1888 in South Wigston in Leicestershire. He was the son of George (originally from Rotherham) and Eliza of 92 Countesthorpe Road in South Wigston and later 37 Orange Street. His father was employed at the foundry in Canal Street, South Wigston as a stove grate fitter. The family consisted of George, sisters, Blanche and Gertrude, who as a young woman worked at the Railway Hotel on the Spion Kop at Wigston helping to stoke the fires. His brothers were Joseph Absalom, Vallie and baby Reginald who died after a few days following the death of his mother in childbirth in 1907.

George was with the 2nd Battalion, Leicestershire Regiment, when at the age of twenty seven years he died on Saturday 25 September 1915. His name is commemorated on the Loos Memorial, Pas de Calais, France. The memorial commemorates over twenty thousand men who have no known graves, who fell in the Battle of Loos in 1915 to the Armistice in 1918.

Private George Tattershall

Pictures of the Loos Memorial Pas de Calais France

LANCE CORPORAL CECIL CHAPMAN

Cecil Chapman was born in 1895. He was the second son of John and Sarah Ann of 13 Long Street, Wigston Magna, Leicestershire. His parents later moved to Kilby Bridge at Wigston where his father was the lock house keeper.

Cecil had two brothers, (see William Thomas 1916 and Arthur Edward Chapman 1917). All three died in the Great War. One can only imagine the parents grief at the loss of three sons.

Cecil was with the 1st and 4th Battalion, Leicestershire Regiment and was just twenty years old when he died on Wednesday 13 October 1915. His name is commemorated on the Loos Memorial, Pas de Calais, France. The Loos Memorial forms the side and back of Dud Corner Cemetery where 1,700 men are buried.

Pictures of the Loos Memorial, Pas de Calais, France

Cecil Chapman

PRIVATE WILLIAM FREDERICK FRANKLIN

William Frederick Franklin was born in 1898 at Wigston Magna in Leicestershire. He was the son of William and Annie Franklin of 2 Midland Cottages, Wigston.   He was one of thirteen children having six sisters, Elsie, Evelyn, Jess, Annie, Agnes and Freda and two brothers Albert and Arthur. Arthur and Agnes were twins.   Sadly the other children died in infancy.   The family lived for a time in Bushloe End in Wigston Magna before moving to Midland Cottages.

The children all attended the local schools until William Frederick joined the Army.   He was serving with 'C Coy. 4th Battalion Leicestershire Regiment.

On the 21st April 1916, William just eighteen years old, was killed in action at Souchez a village in France.   Suchez in the department of Pas de Calais, on the Bethune-Arras Road was situated between the ridges of Vimy and Notre Dame de Lorette.   Suchez was the centre of fierce fighting between the French and Germans and along with other villages in the Great War was obliterated. Funds subscribed by Kensington in London helped to rebuild Suchez in 1922.

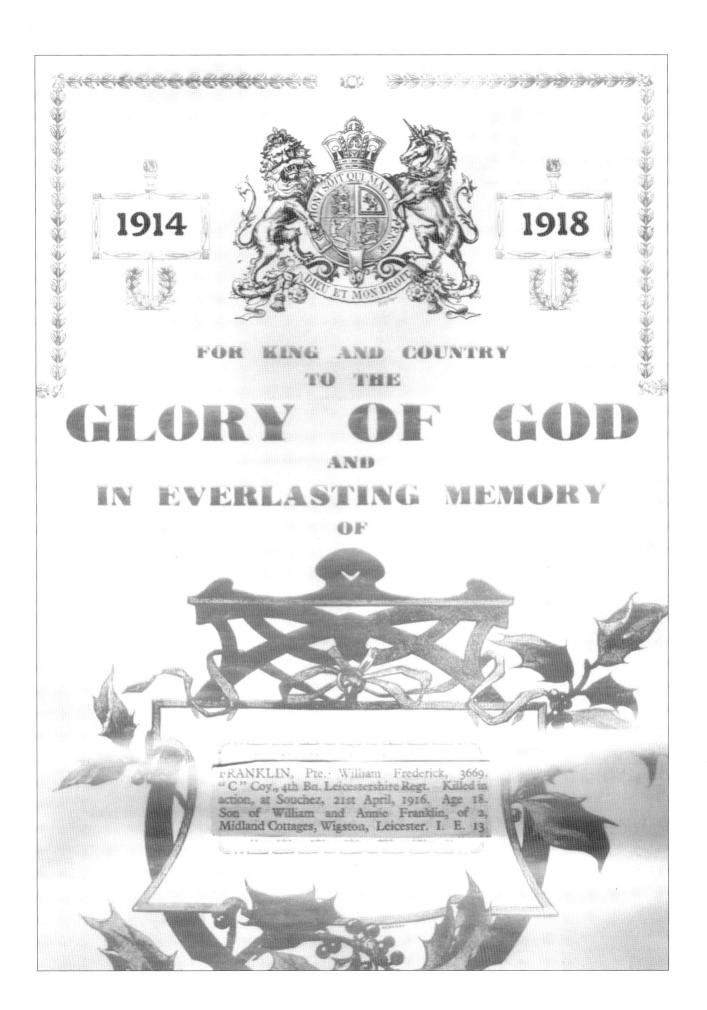

1914 1918

FOR KING AND COUNTRY

TO THE

GLORY OF GOD

AND

IN EVERLASTING MEMORY

OF

FRANKLIN, Pte. William Frederick, 3669, "C" Coy., 4th Bn. Leicestershire Regt. Killed in action, at Souchez, 21st April, 1916. Age 18. Son of William and Annie Franklin, of 2, Midland Cottages, Wigston, Leicester. I. E. 13.

SERGEANT WILLIAM JOHN GURR

William John Gurr was born in 1871 at St. Olaves, Surrey, London and became a regular soldier in the Army.

He lived at Midland Cottages in Wigston before his marriage and was employed at The Two Steeples hosiery factory in Wigston Magna, Leicestershire. He re-joined the colours at the outbreak of the First World War.

With his wife May and baby daughter Irene, William continued to live in Wigston and on Thursday 3rd September 1914 the Leicester Daily Mercury reported on the 'Departure of Drafts from Glen Parva'. The party of 240 drafts left Glen Parva Barracks in South Wigston and were followed by 16 from The Two Steeples Factory. They were all under the command of Colour-Seargeant Gurr and were leaving to join the 3rd Battalion and the 6th Battalion, (Kitchener's Battalion). They were followed by female employees en masse many of them carrying flags. They were played to the railway station by Charles Moore's band.

William John Gurr was with 'A' Coy. 2nd Battalion. Leicestershire Regiment, Depot when he died on Thursday 6 July 1916 at the age of forty five years. His grave is in Wigston cemetery.

Above: Sergeant William John Gurr

Right: Sergeant William John Gurr with Wife May and baby Irene

PRIVATE ALEXANDER CHRISTIE

Alexander Christie was born in Aberdeen in Scotland and lived at 409 Holburn Street.

During his life he was a tailor in the Salvation Army before he came to the Glen Parva Barracks in South Wigston, in Leicestershire. He married Ada Hemmings from Glen Gate in South Wigston and their daughter was named Ivy.

Alexander was with the 12th Battalion, Royal Scots and died on Saturday 8th July 1916. His name is commemorated on Thiepval Memorial, Somme, France.

Thiepval Memorial designed by Edwin Lutyens commemorates 73,357 names of men from Britain, South Africa, Australia, Canada, India and New Zealand who died at the Battle of the Somme. The battle raged from 1st July 1916 to 18 November 1916. Many of the casualties have no known graves but an accompanying cemetery holds British and French graves. Men died on the battlefields and their bodies were pulverized into the earth with the first use of tanks in September 1916. Others died in field hospitals or clearing stations from their wounds whilst many lucky enough to return home died there from wounds received.

Above:
Private Alexander Christie

Left:
Theipval Memorial
Somme, France

WILLIAM BEATTIE

William Beattie

William Beattie was born in 1879 the son of William Bell Beattie and Robina Beattie, nee Dickson at Bowhill Cottage, Kelhead, Annan, Dunfriesshire. He was one of twelve children having six brothers, and five sisters. His brothers, four of whom died young, were named George, Dave, Robert, David, John and Richard and his sisters named Jean, Meg, Mary, Agnes and Janet. William Bell Beattie worked as a ploughman.

As a young man William Beattie moved from Scotland to Wigston Magna in Leicestershire. On the 24th February 1900 he married Mary Whyatt at the Independent Chapel in Wigston Magna, the service conducted by the Minister, Mr Deeming. At this time William was employed by the Midland Railway Company as an engine cleaner based at the Engine Sheds at Wigston. Later he worked as a commercial tea seller.

Living with his wife at 19 Bushloe End, William and Mary had two children, a son, William Zadok and a daughter Robina but William fiercely proud of his Scottish birth moved back to his homeland before the birth of his own son. William Zadok was baptised in Scotland in October 1912.

Whilst in Scotland William was employed as a lime stone quarryman also working for a time as a kennel man. Moving back to Wigston Magna in Leicestershire the family settled at 21 Bushloe End the house next door to their original home. Numbers 19 and 21 Bushloe End were both family homes of the Beattie/Whyatt families.

At the outbreak of war William in true Scottish tradition travelled to Scotland to volunteer to join what he hoped would be a kilted regiment but was drafted into the 15th Battalion of the Royal Scots which was not as the men wore trews.

On Friday 14th July 1916 whilst serving as a Private with the 11TH

Family group, from left to right, Wife Mary, Daughter Robina, William Beattie and Son William Zadok

Battalion, Royal Scots, William Beattie lost his life on the Somme. He was thirty eight years old. In total William is commemorated on eight war memorials. He is named on the Thiepval Memorial, Somme, France, known also as The Memorial to the Missing of the Somme. His name can be seen within the stained glass window in the Church of Scotland building at Kelhead. The War Memorial in the town square at Annan, Scotland bears his name and the memorial at Cummertrees, a little village just outside Annan. William is remembered on the Scottish National War Memorial at Edinburgh, on the inside and outside memorials at All Saints Church at Wigston Magna and the Peace Memorial Park at Wigston Magna, Leicestershire.

William Beattie with his sister Agnes and daughter Robina

15ᵀᴴ Battalion Royal Scots - taken at Troon Higher Grade Grammar School

Somewhere in Scotland - A few Royal Scots enjoying 'Good old English beer'

Top Left; Thiepval Memorial Somme, France - Top Right; Scottish National War Memorial

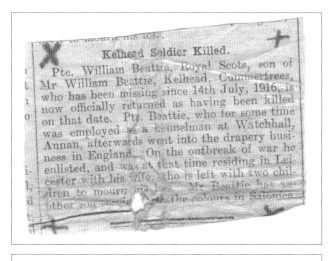

Left; Leicester Mercury 17TH October 1916
Above; Annan News

We often sit and think, dear,
And wonder how you died ;
With no one near who loved you so,
Before you closed your eyes.

In Affectionate Remembrance of

William Beattie,

Who fell in action July 14th, 1916,

AGED 38 YEARS.

GONE BUT NOT FORGOTTEN.

PRIVATE DOUGLAS HOWARD SIBSON

Douglas Howard Sibson was born in 1889 the son of John and Elizabeth Sibson of Wigston Magna. Douglas was one of four sons. His brothers were Leonard, Cecil and Oliver. The four boys were all born at The Craddock Arms in Knighton, Leicestershire where their parents at that time managed the business.

Before the outbreak of the First World War, Douglas went to Canada to join his brother, Leonard. Whilst in Canada Douglas joined the 1st Canadian Mounted Rifles, (Saskatchewan Regiment}.
He died on Friday 15 September 1916 at the age of twenty seven.

Douglas has no known grave and is commemorated at the Vimy Memorial, Pas de Calais, France. The names of eleven thousand Canadian soldiers are inscribed on the memorial.

Children of John and Elizabeth Sibson
Back row from left to right: Leonard, Cecil and Oliver - Front row: Douglas Howard Sibson

PRIVATE WILLIAM THOMAS CHAPMAN

William Thomas Chapman was born in 1887 the eldest son of John and Sarah Chapman of Kilby Bridge, Wigston, Leicestershire. (See brothers Cecil Chapman 1915 and Arthur Edward Chapman 1917).

William served with the 3rd Battalion, Dorsetshire Regiment attd. 7th Battalion, Royal Munster Fusiliers.

Salonika was occupied in 1915 by invitation from M. Venizelos by three French Divisions and the 10th Irish Division from Gallipoli. Other French and British forces landed during the year and in the summer of 1916 Italian and Russian troops joined them. In August of that year a Greek revolution broke out at Salonika causing the Greek National Army to join the allies in the conflict. The town was the base of the British Salonika force containing General and Stationary Hospitals

William was twenty nine years old when he died in the Dardanelles, Gallipoli on Monday 23rd October 1916. He was originally buried at Gallipoli but wild animals interfered with the grave. He was moved to Mikra British Cemetery, Kalamaria, Greece.

Mikra British Cemetery contains many graves which were brought in from other burial grounds and the memorial commemorates nurses, officers and men of the forces of the Empire some of whom were lost in the Mediterranean.

William Thomas Chapman

ARUANA, Waiter Paul, 44. 1st Bn. Maltese
abour Corps. 3rd Feb., 1919. Age 24. Son of
losè and Carmela Caruana, of 8, Strada Reale,
isal Lia, Malta. Also served in Mercantile
arine. Born at Musta, Malta. 1224.

RWAY, Pte. W. H., 27789. 2nd Bn. Norfolk
gt. 8th Feb., 1919. Husband of Ida May
rway, of 22, King St., Bradley. 1262.

SE, Spr. Montague Vaughan, 51561. XVI
rps Signals, Royal Engineers. Died of pneu-
nia 18th Nov., 1918. Son of the late William
tjamin and Sarah Marion Elizabeth Case, of
I St., Poole. 841.

SSAR, Labourer Edgard, 7522. 2nd Bn.
tese Labour Corps. Died of malaria 15th
I., 1918. Age 17. Son of Saverio and Elvira
ar, of 62B, Sda Reale, St. Paul's Bay, Malta.

TLE, Spr. James Arthur, 58257. 139th
y Troops Coy. Royal Engineers. Died of
twater fever 2nd April, 1918. Age 36.
and of Caroline Castle, of 12, Lockwood's
, Upperhead Row, Huddersfield. 246.

TO, Pte. A. A., M2/200430. 708th Coy.
l Army Service Corps. 2nd Nov., 1918.
of Francis Catto, of Knockethie, Ellon;
nd of Jessie S. Catto, of Pluscarden
, 14, Ythan Terrace, Ellon, Aberdeen-
1616.

HI, Pte. Ignazio, M./373835. 781st Mech-
Transport Coy. Royal Army Service Corps.
March, 1919. Age 20. Son of Guisseppi
i, of 3, Nicolo, Strada Reale, Tebley,
1322.

AWAY, Pte. T., 204262. 8th Bn. Oxf. and
Light Inf. 18th Dec., 1917. Age 20.
Edwin Chadaway, of 41, Taunton Rd.,
rook, Birmingham. 189.

WICK, Spr. Albert, 173204. Railway
ortation Establishment, Royal Engineers.
., 1917. Age 43. Son of Thomas and
Chadwick; husband of Edith Chadwick,
Vaverley Rd., Dane Rd., Sale, Manchester.

CHALMERS, Lt. Archibald Douglas
Argyll and Sutherland Highlanders.
enteric 9th Dec., 1918. Age 29.
Mrs. A. J. Chalmers, of Hartley, Ayr, ai
Archibald Chalmers, of Kipp, Dalbeatti

CHAMBERLAIN, Rfn. William, 2079.
Bn. The Rifle Brigade. 25th Oct., 1918.
Son of John George and Sarah E. Cha
of Lidstone, Enstone, Oxford. 673.

CHAMBERS, Pte. Cecil Frank, 242175.
Welch Regt. Died of pneumonia 30th D
Age 21. Son of Henry James and
Chambers, of 45, St. Peter's Place, Cai
1045.

CHAMBERS, Pte. W., DM2/171585.
Mechanical Transport Coy. Royal Army
Corps. 7th Jan., 1919. 1195.

CHANT, Spr. T. H., WR/206817. 19th
Operating Coy. Royal Engineers. Died of.
tal injuries 7th Jan., 1919. Age 29.
Thomas and Elizabeth Ada Chant, of 6, I
Row, South, Hallgate, Doncaster. 1237.

CHANTLER, Spr. T., 67016. 131st Fie
Royal Engineers. 11th Dec., 1918. I
Son of Mrs. Alfred Chantler, of Long
Cheadle; husband of Florence Mabel Chai
45, Warren Rd., Adswood, Stockport. 893

CHAPMAN, Pte. K., 34885. 2nd Bn
Yorkshire Regt. 30th June, 1917. 1818.

CHAPMAN, Pte. William Thomas, 14012
Bn. Dorsetshire Regt., attd. 7th Bn. Royal M
Fusiliers. 23rd Oct., 1916. Age 29. S
John and Sarah Chapman, of Kilby I
Wigston, Leicestershire. 1792.

CHARNLEY, Pte. G. W., M2/119538.
Coy. Royal Army Service Corps. 19th Aug.,
Age 39. Husband of Caroline Charnle
3, Ashton St., Merefield, Rochdale. 1612.

CHERRELL, Pte. Francis, 37096. 9th
South Lancashire Regt. Died of wounds
Sept., 1918. Age 34. Son of Charles Che
of Sheffield; husband of Mary Cherrel
1 Court, 3 House, Headford St., Sheffield.

CHESTERS, Cpl. T. B., T1/1612. Royal A
Service Corps, attd. 97th Coy. Labour C
30th Dec., 1918. 1038.

PRIVATE ARTHUR EDWARD CHAPMAN

Arthur Edward Chapman was the youngest son of John and Sarah Chapman, Kilby Bridge, Wigston, Leicestershire. (See Cecil Chapman, 1915 and William Thomas Chapman, 1916.) The pain of John and Sarah Chapman can well be imagined. They lost a son for each consecutive year 1915, 1916, 1917.

Arthur married Mary Ellen (Nellie) Ward and they lived at 58 Healey Street, South Wigston, Leicestershire. Arthur served with the 1st Battalion, Leicestershire Regiment and was killled in action in France and Flanders on Friday 2nd February 1917. His memorial is at Vermelles British Cemetery, Pas de Calais, France.

Nellie Ward Arthur Chapmans Wife

Arthur Edward Chapman

PRIVATE WILLIAM THOMAS ARTHUR GUDGEON

William Thomas Arthur Gudgeon was the son of George and Mary Gudgeon.   He married Ethel Askin and lived with his wife and three daughters at 49 Glen Gate, South Wigston, Leicestershire. His daughters were Maisie, Vera and Hazel and Hazel was little more than a year old when her father died.

William served with the 1st Battalion, Sherwood Foresters (Notts and Derby Regiment). He died on Sunday 4th March 1917 aged thirty three years.   His name is commemorated on the Theipval Memorial, Pas de Calais, France.

ANTHEM FOR DOOMED YOUTH

WILFRED OWEN

1893 - 1918

What passing-bells for these who die as cattle?
Only the monstrous anger of the guns.
Only the muttering rifles' rapid rattle
Can patter out their hasty orisons.
No mockeries for them; no prayers nor bells.
Nor any voice of mourning save the choirs,-
The shrill, demented choirs of wailing shells;
And bugles calling for them from sad shires.
What candles may be held to speed them all?
Not in the hands of boys, but in their eyes
Shall shine the holy glimmers of good-byes.
The pallor of girls' brows shall be their pall;
Their flowers the tenderness of patient minds,
And each slow dusk a drawing-down of blinds.

William Thomas Arthur Gudgeon

Above: Wedding of William Gudgeon and Ethel Askin
Below: Mrs Gudgeon and their three daughters Vera, Masie and Hazel

PRIVATE ALBERT HURST

Albert Hurst was born in Wigston, Leicestershire in 1885. He was the son of George and Harriet Hurst and was the ninth of eleven children. He was the youngest of his brothers one of whom was Charles. Sadly, no photograph has been found of Albert and his brothers and sisters. One sister's grandson was Alan Wollatt, the Leicester City footballer.

Little is known of Albert's early life but he was a professional soldier in 1914. He served with the 9th Battalion Northumberland Fusiliers and was twice wounded at Ypres. He was a patient at Bury St. Edmunds Hospital before returning to the front line in France.

On the 21st November 1914 'The Leicester Mercury and Leicester Chronicle' reported that;
'Private Albert Hurst of the Northumberland Fusiliers whose home is at Wigston, was wounded in the neck and back at the battle of Ypres and is now in hospital at Ampton Hill, Bury St. Edmunds'.

Two and a half years later on St. George's Day, the 23 April 1917 at the age of thirty two years; Albert died.

He is commemorated at Arras Memorial, Pas de Calais, France. Albert is also remembered on his Mother's and sister's grave in Wigston Cemetery, Leicestershire. A mystery surrounds the grave as his mother is not named on the memorial. Three other people are named but are not in it. The inscription reads,
'Pvt. Albert Hurst.
9th Northumberland Fusiliers
Beloved son of George and Harriet Hurst
Killed in action in France 23rd April 1917 – Aged 32
'He lies away in a far off grave
Amongst the brave and bold
He died by the side of his comrades
And his tale was never told'.

Arras Memorial, Pas de Calais, France

Wigston Cemetery, Wigston, Leicestershire

PRIVATE HAROLD ERNEST BAXTER

Harold Ernest Baxter was born at Wigston Magna in 1894 the son of Abraham and Sarah Baxter of 8 Midland Cottages, Wigston Magna, Leicestershire.   He served with the 2nd and 6th Battalion, Sherwood Foresters (Nottinghamshire and Derbyshire Regiment) and was killed in action in France and Flanders. He died on Friday 29 June 1917 at the age of twenty three years.   His grave is in Metz-En-Couture Communal Cemetery British Extension.   Original burials were made by Field Ambulances and fighting units. Others were added after the Armistice.

Sadly it has not been possible to locate a photograph of Harold Ernest Baxter.   The official post card with suggested sentences sent from him to Mrs M E Baxter, 9 North Street, Wigston Magna was discovered by Mr Tony Briggs of Ratby at Donington and is a poignant reminder of the loneliness so many of the men must have felt.

TRANSCRIPT

'I am very well.'
'I have received no letter from you'
'For a long time'

 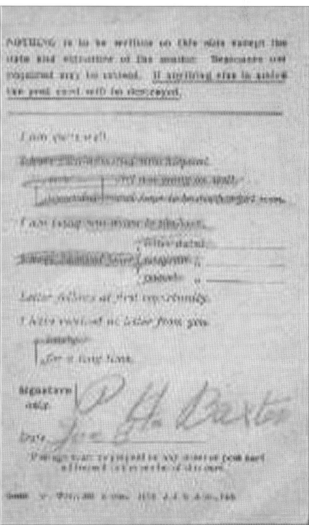

Official Postcard from Harold Ernest Baxter to Mrs M E Baxter

PRIVATE JAMES ROSS WESLEY

James Ross Wesley was born in 1897 the son of Frederick Ernest and Mary Elizabeth Wesley of 26 Station Road, Wigston Magna, Leicestershire. It is possible to piece together part of James's life from documentation which has been preserved in his memory but sadly there are no surviving photograph of him.

James would have been eighteen years old when in September 1915 he was awarded a certificate on completing a course of instruction for first aid at the Leicester Centre of the St. John Ambulance Association and on the 6th October 1915 he was awarded his certificate authorizing him to render first aid to the injured. Photographs survive of his parents and family, cards sent home and a letter dictated by him to a friend for his father. The friend writes that James has been ill and is too weak to write himself but is improving. The day after the letter was written James died of dysentery on the 5th July 1917.

James was serving with 67th Field Ambulance, Royal Army Medical Corps and was twenty years old. He is buried at Mikra British Cemetery, Kalamaria, Greece.

*Mr and Mrs Wesley
James's Parents*

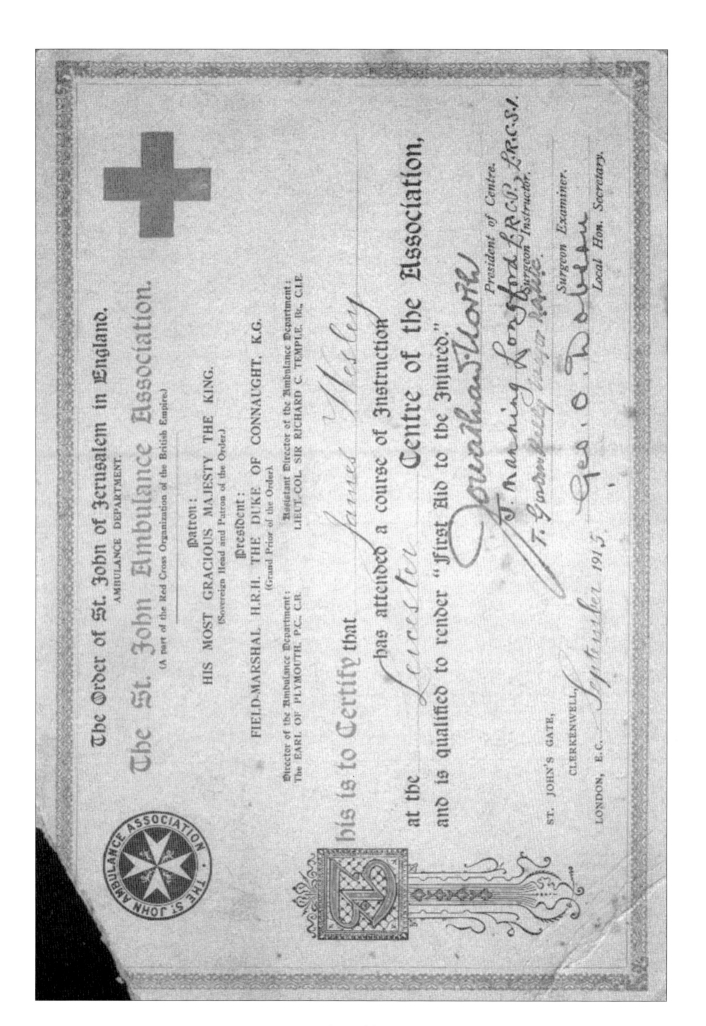

The Order of St. John of Jerusalem in England.
AMBULANCE DEPARTMENT.

The St. John Ambulance Association.
(A part of the Red Cross Organization of the British Empire)

Patron:
HIS MOST GRACIOUS MAJESTY THE KING.
(Sovereign Head and Patron of the Order.)

President:
FIELD-MARSHAL H.R.H. THE DUKE OF CONNAUGHT, K.G.
(Grand Prior of the Order.)

Director of the Ambulance Department: Assistant Director of the Ambulance Department:
The EARL OF PLYMOUTH P.C., C.B.   LIEUT.-COL. SIR RICHARD C. TEMPLE Bt., C.I.E.

This is to Certify that *James Mosley*

has attended a course of Instruction

at the *Leicester* Centre of the Association,

and is qualified to render "First Aid to the Injured."

Jonathan Worth
President of Centre.

F. Manning Forster L.R.C.P., L.R.C.S.I.
Surgeon Instructor.

F. Greenberg Major R.A.M.C.
Surgeon Examiner.

Geo. O. Dobson
Local Hon. Secretary.

ST. JOHN'S GATE,
CLERKENWELL, *September* 1915.
LONDON, E.C.

Page 47

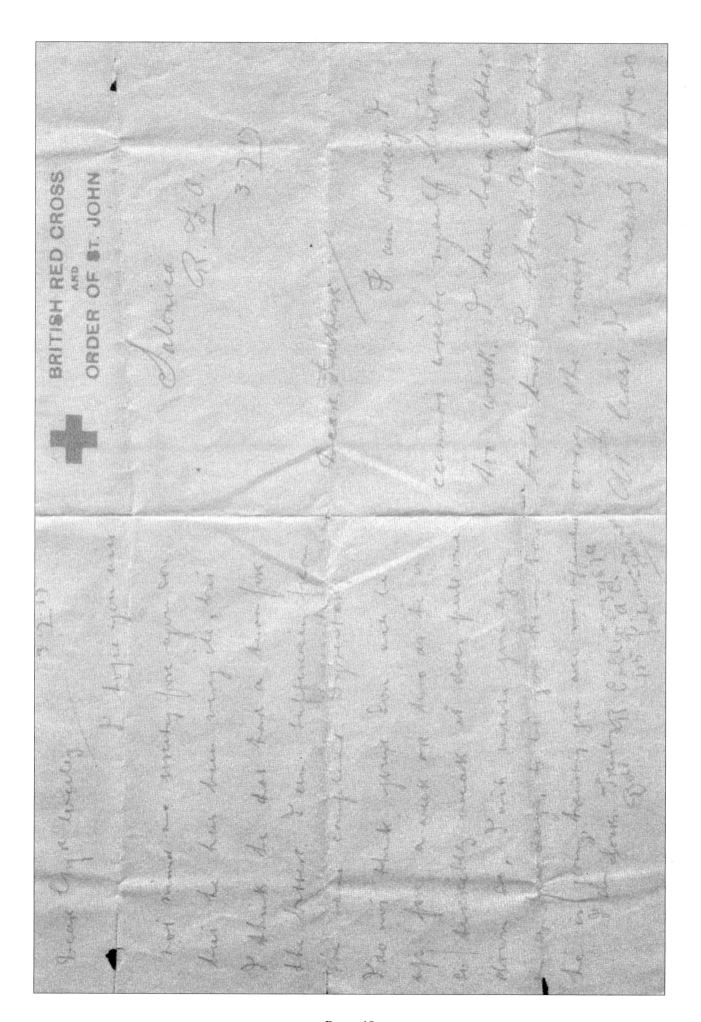

BRITISH RED CROSS
AND
ORDER OF ST. JOHN

No. R.o. 33 8/6/137/14
(If replying, please
quote above No.)

ARMY FORM B. 104—82.

R a m c Record Office,

Woking

9th July 1914

Sir,

It is my painful duty to inform you that a report has been received from the War Office notifying the death of :—

(No.) 103383 (Rank) Private

(Name) James Wesley

(Regiment) Royal Army Medical Corps, 64th Class,

which occurred with the Salonika Expeditionary Force,

on the 5th July 1914.

The report is to the effect that he died of Dysentery

By His Majesty's command I am to forward the enclosed message of sympathy from Their Gracious Majesties the King and Queen. I am at the same time to express the regret of the Army Council at the soldier's death in his Country's service.

3.

I am to add that any information that may be received as to the soldier's burial will be communicated to you in due course. A separate leaflet dealing more fully with this subject is enclosed.

I am,

Sir,

Your obedient Servant,

A. Henderson

Colonel.

Officer in charge of Records.

Mrs. E. Wesley,
26 Station Road,
Syston,
Leicester

18307. Wt. 15148/M 1365. 175M. 2/17. R. & L., Ltd.

P.T.O.

No. 338/C

Army Form B. 104-121.

(If replying, please quote
above No.)

R.A.M.C.   Record Office,

WOKING,

27. 9.   1917.

Sir or Madam,

In continuation of the notification sent to you

regarding the death of the late (No.) 103383 (Rank) Pte

Name   J. Wesley.

Regiment   R.A.M.C.

I beg to inform you that an official report has now been

received that the late soldier is buried at

Mikra British Cemetery, Salonika.

Mr. E. Wesley,   Yours faithfully,
26 Station Rd
Wigston   R.F. Thompson
                                        MAJOR
Leicester   FOR   Officer in charge of Records.

1191 W. W1.2254/H2888 125,000 3/17 J. P.

Record Office,
Woking,
August, 1921.

I am directed to transmit to you the accompanying
British War and Victory Medals
which would have been conferred upon
No. 103383 Private James Wesley, R.A.M.C.
had he lived, in memory of his services with the British
Forces during the Great War.

In forwarding the Decoration I am commanded by
the King to assure you of His Majesty's high appreciation
of the services rendered.

I am to request that you will be so good as to
acknowledge the receipt of the Decoration on the attached
form.

I am,
Your obedient Servant,

Captain,
Officer i/c Records, R.A.M.C.

St. John Ambulance Association
LEICESTER CENTRE.

James Wesley
I have the pleasure to inform you that you
have successfully passed the recent Examination
and that you are considered qualified to render
FIRST AID to the Injured. You will receive
the Certificate of the Association in due course.

6 - OCT 1915   GEO. O. DOBSON, Local Hon. Sec.
268 Welford Road, Clarendon Park.

Page 53

Royal Scots Fusiliers. 29th Oct., 1918. Age 26. Son of James Weir and Sarah Armstrong Weir, of Girvan ; husband of Esther Weir, of 19, Scotlands Close, Kincardine-on-Forth, Fife. 705.

WELHAM, Pte. Thomas Emmanuel, 32199 oth Bn. Hampshire Regt. Died of malaria 5th Sept., 1917. Age 34. Husband of Laura Welham, of 66, Manor Rd., Park Lane, Tottenham, London. 100.

WELLS, Spr. A. J., 506566. 501st Field Coy. Royal Engineers. 6th Jan., 1919. 1188.

WESCOMBE, Pte. E. J., 57283. 82nd Coy. Machine Gun Corps (Inf.). Died of malaria 6th Oct., 1918. Age 25. Son of Mrs. E. Wescombe, of Redfield ; husband of Mrs. B. Wescombe, of 42, Roseberry Rd., Redfield Bristol. 512.

WESLEY, Pte. James Ross, 103383. 67th Field Amb. Royal Army Medical Corps. Died of dysentery 5th July, 1917. Age 20. Son of Frederick Ernest and Mary Elizabeth Wesley, of 26, Station Rd., Wigston Magna, Leicestershire. 5.

WEST, Lce. Cpl. Ernest George, 504055. 500th Wessex Field Coy. Royal Engineers. Died of pneumonia 21st Nov., 1918. Age 25. Son of Samuel and Julia West, of Bath. 913.

WEST, Ord. Smn. E., J/78232. R.N. H.M.S. " Endymion." 30th Aug., 1918. 1784.

WEST, Pte. F., 7548. 3rd Bn. Middlesex Regt. 9th Sept., 1918. Age 40. Husband of E. West, of 13, Tarver Rd., Manor Place, Walworth, London. 384.

WESTGARTH, Pnr. John, 35041. 139th Army Troops Coy. Royal Engineers. 19th Aug., 1918. Age 35. Son of William and Martha Westgarth, of 52, Kirk St., South Byker, Newcastle-on-Tyne. 276.

WESTWATER, Pte. Ebenezer Gardner Templenan, 74330. 82nd Coy. Machine Gun Corps (Inf.). Died of malaria 7th Oct., 1918. Age 24. Son of Mr. and Mrs. Daniel Westwater, of South End Cottages, Balcurine, Windygates, Fifeshire. 533.

Ammunition Col. Royal Field Artillery. 5th Nov., 1918. Age 28. Son of Richard and Emily Whatman, of 1, Hawthorn St., Balls Pond Rd., Islington ; husband of Mrs. Louisa Whatman, of 29, Ramsgate St., Dalston Lane, London. 768.

WHEAT, Pte. F., 4497. 26th Bn. Middlesex Regt. 7th Dec., 1916. Age 19. Son of Mr. and Mrs. Wheat, of 14, Clarence Terrace, Clarence St., Nottingham. 1972.

WHEELER, Pte. H. J., 3379. 16th Bn. Army Cyclist Corps. 24th Feb., 1919. 1282.

WHINCOP, S/Serjt. John Ford, 089021. R.A.S.C. Canteens. 8th Feb., 1917. Age 33. Son of George and Emma Whincop, of Sibton, Suffolk ; husband of Marion J. Whincop, of 10, Smith St., Bainsford, Falkirk. 1822.

WHIPP, Rfn. William, 8916. 3rd Bn. King's Royal Rifle Corps. Died of accidental injuries 5th June, 1917. Age 26. Son of Susanah Whipp, of College Lane, Littlemore, Oxford. 1968.

WHITBREAD, Dvr. H. F., T4/211785. 3rd Base Horse Transport Depot, Royal Army Service Corps. Died of malaria 19th Jan., 1918. Age 29. Son of Frederick and Bridget Whitbread, of 2, Daisy Rd., George Lane, South Woodford, Essex. 212.

WHITCOMB, Pte. E., 6271. 5th Bn. Middlesex Regt., transf. to (587639) 1036th Coy. Labour Corps. 10th Dec., 1918. Age 38. Son of J. Whitcomb ; husband of S. Whitcomb, of 7, Solander St., St. George in the East, London. 894.

WHITCOMBE, Cadet Hugh Donald, Royal Air Force. Croix de Guerre (Belgium). Died of sunstroke 23rd July, 1920. Age 21. Son of John Walker Whitcombe and Louisa Whitcombe, of Dudbrooke, Sevenoaks, Kent. 1556.

WHITE, Gnr. G., 14495. 118th Bty., Royal Field Artillery. 19th Feb., 1919.

WHITE, Pte. J., 31757. 2nd Bn. King's shire Light Inf. Died of malaria 10th Age 26. Son of Mrs. Minnie White, of Court, Hare St., Bethnal Green, London, at Spitalfields. 1264.

Top Photograph:
Frederick Ernest Wesley
Father of James

Bottom three photographs:
Brothers and Sisters of James
at 26 Station Road, Wigston, Leicester

Found with James Ross Wesley's possessions

PRIVATE DAVID SIDNEY WEBB

David Sidney Webb was born in 1895 the son of John E and Sarah Ann Webb of 106 Welford Road, Wigston Magna, Leicestershire. He was one of twelve children, two of the girls were twins. The family also lived in Newton Lane in Wigston.

David Sidney served with the 7th Battalion, Leicestershire Regiment and was just twenty two years old when he died on the 28th July 1917. His grave is at Croisilles British Cemetery, Pas de Calais, France.

Private David Sidney Webb

Private David Sidney Webb from the Train

Above; Brothers Albert, David Sidney and William Webb

Bottom Left; Battle

Bottom Right; William Webb, David's Brother

David Sidney Webb, Mother, Father, Brother and Sisters

CECIL JOHN FREESTON

Cecil John Freeston was born in Leicester. His father was E J Freeston of Conduit Street, Leicester. Cecil married Elsie Bunn of Cook's Lane, Wigston Magna.

Cecil who had reached the rank of Second Lieutenant, was serving with the 7th Battalion, Yorkshire Regiment when on Tuesday 18 September 1917 he was killed. He was twenty eight years old.

Cecil is commemorated at Sunken Road Cemetery, Fampoux, Pas de Calais, France where there are nearly two hundred casualties of the 1914 – 1918 War. Over twenty of the graves are unidentified. Sixteen graves destroyed by shell fire are now represented by special memorials.

The village of Fampoux is situated east of Arras.

Above; Cecil John Freeston

Left; House at Cook's Lane
Cecil with family from left to right
Walter Mason, Edith Mason,
Wilfred Mason, Baby on knee,
Leonard,
Grandma Selina Bunn, Cousin
Connie Sibson,
Cecil Freeston and Wife Elsie
and little Collie dog.

PRIVATE WILLIAM HOLMES

William Holmes was born in Wigston the son of William Holmes the founder of W H Holmes and Son Hosiery Factory in Newton Lane. He was one of eight children. His brother John Henry became an Alderman and Holmes House, a residential home for the elderly in South Wigston, was named in his honour. The six other children were Edward, Mary, Lizzie, Lily, Edith, and Sarah.

William enlisted for service at Market Harborough and served with the 1st Battalion, Grenadier Guards. He was the only Wigston man at that time to serve in the Grenadier Guards. He married and had a son William and a daughter Hilda.

William died on Friday 7th December 1917. His memorial is located at Rocquigny-Equancourt Road British Cemetery, Manancourt, Somme, France.

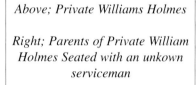

Above; Private Williams Holmes

Right; Parents of Private William Holmes Seated with an unkown serviceman

CORPORAL THOMAS BURDEN

Thomas Burden was born in 1894 the son of George and Susanna Eliza Burden of 49 Shakespeare Street, Knighton Fields, Leicester.

He served with 180th Coy. Machine Gun Corps (Inf) and died at the age of twenty four years on Friday 18th January 1918. His grave is at Alexandria (Hadra) War Memorial Cemetery, Egypt. The original part of the cemetery is built over Roman catacombs and of the 1914 – 1918 war casualties, twenty are unidentified. During the Great War, Alexandria became an Anglo-French camp and hospital centre.

Little is known of Thomas Burden. The photograph of him and his parents was discovered by Mr James Briggs of Ratby at a car boot sale. Research indicates that Thomas's sister, Iris, lived at Avondale Road, Wigston, Leicestershire.

Thomas Burden
Thinks of his parents

SAPPER GEORGE WHYATT

George Whyatt was born at Wigston in 1877. He lived with his wife Mary Ann and their daughter and two sons at 18 Blaby Road, South Wigston, Leicestershire. His baby son Raymond was only six weeks old when he was posted to France. He never saw his family again.

He served with the 231st Coy. Royal Engineers and was killed in action in France and Flanders on Tuesday 9 April 1918. He was forty one years old. He is commemorated at Ploegsteert Memorial, Comines-Warneton, Hainaut, Belgium. The memorial commemorates over 11,000 men who have no known graves.

Ploegstreet Memorial Comines - Warneton Hainaut - Belgium

George Whyatt

PRIVATE ALEC WALTER RICHARDSON

Alec Walter Richardson was born on the 22 January 1893 at East Haddon, which lies between Welford and Daventry in Northamptonshire. His father Thomas, a gardener and mother Mary Ann, a cook, were employed at the ancestral home of the Spencer family at Althorp Hall, in Northamptonshire.

Alec moved with his parents to Wigston shortly after his birth when his father became head gardener at the home of the Owston family at Bushloe House on Station Road. The family home was established at Bushloe Cottages, 19 Manor Street.

Alec grew up in Wigston and after leaving school served an apprenticeship and became a tailor. He married Anne Elizabeth Cobley and they had one daughter, Jean and lived at Broughton Road, Cosby.

Alec joined the Leicestershire Regiment during the Great War and was serving with the 6th Battalion when he was severely wounded in battle and died at the age of twenty six years in a field hospital on the 29th April 1918. He was buried in Esquelbecq Military Cemetery in Belgium.

Top: Alec Walter Richardson
Bottem Left: Alec Walter Richardson with Wife Anne Cobley - Bottom Right: Alec Walter Richardson Grave Stone

PRIVATE JOHN DAYKIN BROUGHTON

John Daykin Broughton was born on the 12th October 1898 at Wigston Magna in Leicestershire and was the son of Ernest and Elizabeth Ann Broughton (nee Forryan) of Elm House, 82 Bull Head Street, (now the Liberal Club). He was one of four children having two brothers, Ernest Alfred and Edwin Forryan and a sister, Edith Emma.

John Daykin was named after his grandfather who founded a noteable hosiery factory in Bell Street, Wigston Magna. He attended Wyggeston Boys School and was very clever and probably at university when he was called for war service as his occupation was listed as student. He attended the Primitive Methodist Church in Moat Street, Wigston Magna.

John Daykin attested to the Army reserve on 2 October 1916 and was mobilized on 14 February 1917. He was posted to the Royal Army Service Corps as a trainee Caterpillar tractor driver. On the 26 May 1918 he accidentally drowned in the River Euphrates near Ramadi, Mesopotamia. He was nineteen years old.

John Daykin Broughton, 1028th M.T. Coy. Army Service Corps. is commemorated at Baghdad (North Gate) War Cemetery, Iraq.

Above:
Private John Daykin Broughton

Left: Ernest and Elizabeth Broughton and Children

From Left to Right: Ernest Alfred, Edwin Forryan Edith Emma and John Daykin

From Left to Right: John Daykin Broughton, Ernest Alfred Broughton and Emma Broughton

GUNNER ROBERT CARR

Robert Carr was born on the 20th January 1885. He was a journeyman butcher and worked for the Co-operative Society in Wigston. Robert was living at 85 Blaby Road, South Wigston, Leicestershire before his marriage to Lilian Hassall. They were married in 1909 at the Independent Chapel at Wigston Magna. He and his wife lived at 98 Leicester Road, Wigston Magna and had two daughters, Dora and Ena.

Robert served as a gunner with the 23rd T. M. Bty. Royal Field Artillery. He died from his wounds in a field hospital at the age of thirty three years on Monday 14th October 1918. His grave is at Roisel Communal Cemetery Extension, Somme, France.

Robert Carr

ROISEL après la guerre — Cimetière Militaire

Robert Carr

Above; Robert Carr's Wife Lilian and Daughters Dora (sitting) and Ena
Below; Somewhere in Wigston thought to be a Celebration after the War

PRIVATE GEORGE KENT

George Kent was born in 1879. He and his wife Alice, (nee Barker) of 54 Countesthorpe Road, South Wigston, Leicestershire had six children. They were Mary, the eldest, Charles, Kate, Dick, George and Evelyn. George's wife came from a touring theatrical family performing on the stage.

George served with the 1st/3rd (East Lancs) Field Ambulance. Royal Army Medical Corps. He died on Monday 21st October 1918 at the age of thirty nine years. His grave is located at Awoingt British Cemetery, Nord, France.

The great majority of burials were made from the casualties at the hospital clearing stations in the area.

Right: Private George Kent

Below: Mrs George Kent and Daughter Evelyn

COMPANY SERGEANT MAJOR
GEORGE WALTER GOODMAN

George Walter Goodman was born in 1884.
His wife was Grace Goodman of 59 Clifford Street, South Wigston, Leicestershire. They had two daughters and Florence was six years old and her sister just a few months when their father died.

George was wounded in service with the 53rd Battalion. Northumberland Fusiliers and died from pneumonia just over a week after the Armistice was signed on Wednesday 20 November 1918. He was thirty four years old. His military funeral was conducted in the garrison church of St.Thomas in South Wigston prior to burial at Wigston Cemetery, Wigston. Leicestershire.

Company Sergeant Major George Walter Goodman

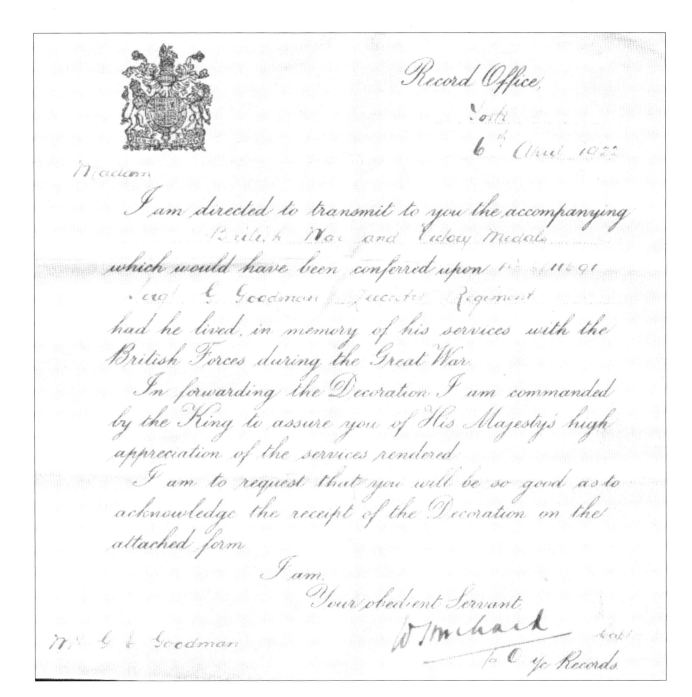

Record Office,
York
6th April 1922

Madam

I am directed to transmit to you the accompanying British War and Victory Medals which would have been conferred upon No. 11691 Serjt. E Goodman Yorkshire Regiment had he lived, in memory of his services with the British Forces during the Great War.

In forwarding the Decoration I am commanded by the King to assure you of His Majesty's high appreciation of the services rendered

I am to request that you will be so good as to acknowledge the receipt of the Decoration on the attached form

I am,
Your obedient Servant,
D Michael Capt.
for O i/c Records

Mrs. G E Goodman

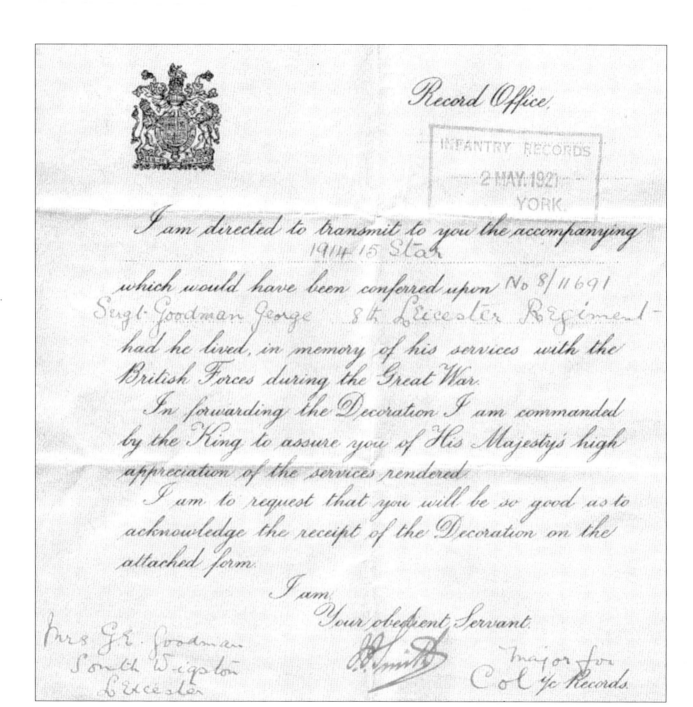

Record Office,

INFANTRY RECORDS
2 MAY 1921
YORK.

I am directed to transmit to you the accompanying
1914 15 Star

which would have been conferred upon No 8/11691
Sergt Goodman George   8th Leicester Regiment

had he lived, in memory of his services with the
British Forces during the Great War.

In forwarding the Decoration I am commanded
by the King to assure you of His Majesty's high
appreciation of the services rendered.

I am to request that you will be so good as to
acknowledge the receipt of the Decoration on the
attached form.

I am,

Your obedient Servant,

Major for
Col i/c Records.

Mrs G.R. Goodman
South Wigston
Leicester

If the deceased soldier is entitled to any other Medals in addition
to the one herewith and you have not received it, or them, it will
not be necessary to communicate with the Office as your address is
registered here and any Medals or decorations to which you may be
entitled will be forwarded there when received.
I would remind you that the number of Medals and Stars authorised
for individuals who served in the Great War amount to many millions.
Every effort is being made to strike, engrave and distribute these
decorations as quickly as possible, but it is evident that the process
will take a considerable time.
If you change your address please notify the Officer in Charge,
Infantry Record Office, YORK, stating Regimental Number, Rank, Name,
Regiment and new address.
Kindly return the receipt in the enclosed envelope.

EX SERVICEMEN ARRV EVALIN COMMITTEE MEMORIAL OPENED IN SOUTH WIGSTON 1923

Top row from left to right;
Mr Bettony, Mr Gothard, Mr Powdrill, Mr Betton, Unkown, Mr Tyres, Mr Medhurst
Bottom row from left to right;
Mr Whyatt, Mr J T S Nobbs, Dr Stedman Poole, Mr C Bass, Mr Bodycote
Below; War Memorial South Wigston, 1923

War Memorial
Blaby Road, South Wigston

TO THE GLORY OF GOD AND IN MEMORY OF THE MEN OF SOUTH
WIGSTON AND GLEN PARVA WHO GAVE THEIR LIVES IN THE WARS
OF 1914 - 1918 AND 1935 - 1945

PART TWO

1939-1945

As September 1939 approached, the atmosphere in England was tense. The Prime Minister, Neville Chamberlain, was persistently and optimistically still trying to convince the population that there would be peace with Germany. By the third day of September he knew that it was impossible to appease Hitler. German troops were invading Poland and bound by 'a pledge of military support' made in March by himself to support Poland in the event of aggression, he had no option but to declare war upon Germany. Despite constant warnings over a long period by Winston Churchill that war was inevitable, England was ill prepared for it and there was little that could be done at that time to save Poland.

On Sunday 3rd September Neville Chamberlain broadcast to the nation that England was at war with Germany and later that day, King George V1 also made a BBC broadcast. The Government formed a special war cabinet consisting of the 'Big Nine'. With Neville Chamberlain as Prime Minister, Winston Churchill became the First Lord of the Admiralty, Sir Kingsley Wood, Air Minister and Leslie Hore Belisha as Secretary For War. The other five posts were filled by Sir John Simon, Chancellor of the Exchequer, Viscount Halifax, Foreign Secretary, Lord Chatfield, Defence Minister, Sir Samuel Hoare, Lord Privy Seal and Minister Without Portfolio, Lord Hankey.

Government plans were instantly put forward for the evacuation of children from major cities at risk from enemy bombing to the countryside and it wasn't long before whole families followed on. With the mass movement of men joining the armed forces, the issue of gas masks, food and petrol rationing, instructions to the public to black out their windows in preparation for the expected bomb attacks, home life in Britain was overturned. News flooded in, France declared war on Germany, Australia, New Zealand and Canada began recruiting and in December 1941 with the bombing of Pearl Harbour by the Japanese, the Americans entered the war. The world was at war and for millions of people, life would never again be the same.

Back in 1939 some people reflected on what they termed the 'phoney war' yet in the summer in Leicester over one thousand officers and men of the 44th Anti Aircraft Battalion were actively training to man search light stations over the county and in the city almost five hundred basements were adapted for air raid shelters. Women of the AuxillaryTerritorial Army, (ATS) left Leicester for a fortnight's training and it was announced that one thousand naval reservists were to be called up. In submarine diving trials in Liverpool Bay, HMS Thetis sank when it was discovered that the torpedo tubes had filled with water.

At Glen Parva Barracks in South Wigston troops were marching from the Depot to the local railway station to join the British Expeditionary Force in France. The village's three railway stations connected to every corner of the country and with the Army based on Saffron Road, South Wigston became a focal point for war preparation. Recruitment and movement of men was an every day ritual. The sound of soldiers feet pounding the parade ground on the barrack square, the bellow of the drill sergeants contrasted with Reveille and the Last Post sending echoes through the nearby village streets.

At the beginning of September an Extraordinary Meeting of the Wigston Urban District Council was held to establish various offices and committees. The Board of Trade with Food Defence Plans instructed the local Food Executive Officer to nominate fifteen members for the control of food for the district. These consisted of Retail Grocers of Provision, Butchers or Fletchers, the Co-operative Society and two of other retail food trades. It is significant to note that one rule insisted that two of the fifteen members must be women.

War Emergency Committees were formed to cover every aspect of war and in due course decisions taken were put into action. The Air Raid Precautions Scheme recruited valued members of the community but the armed forces had the first claim to eligible groups. By this time all street lighting had been extinguished including illuminated public house signs. Road traffic was limited with permits for petrol on strict ration. The A.R.P. was allowed to purchase 3.078 gallons and vehicles were to be at the disposal of the Council first and foremost. Throughout September and October South Wigston and Wigston Magna were actively organizing first aid classes which were well attended and quotations were submitted for Auxillary Fire Service uniforms and equipment. Anti Gas classes were set up, A.R.P. practice exercises carried out, erection of Anderson air raid shelters in the streets, and the need for a temporary mortuary was under discussion. This was eventually established opposite the Council Offices on Station Road. Mr Walker of South Wigston, was allowed to continue using his van for his business with the proviso that the Council would have first claim to it should the need arise for a 'mortuary van'. The culmination of events in 1939 ended in South Wigston with a huge fire at Atkinson's Dyeworks in Canal Street where a number of soldiers were dispatched to cover crowd control.

War tragically was brought home to South Wigston early on in 1939 as the first fatalities of the Royal Navy became known. Four devastated families received news. On the 14th October H.M.S Royal Oak was torpedoed and sunk by the German U Boat 47 at Scapa Flow off the Orkneys. She was carrying the young eighteen year old Raymond Charles Kane of Station Street. On the 23rd November H.M.S Rawalpindi suffered the same fate torpedoed by the Scharnhorst. Cyril Bettoney of Countesthorpe Road lost his life. In the South Atlantic on the 13th December, H.M.S Exeter patrolling with H.M.S Ajax and H.M.S Achilles, suffered extensive fire damage from an attack by the German pocket battleship Admiral Graf Spee. Sixty one lives of Exeter's crew, including Brynmor Richards of South Wigston, were lost. H.M.S Exeter withdrew to the Falkland Islands for repairs. The Admiral Graf Spee in an attempt to avoid the British fleet converging on the River Plate, retreated to Montevideo Harbour. On Christmas Day H.M.S Trawler Loch Doon was believed to have been exploded by magnetic mines off Blyth in the North Sea. This vessel was carrying George Thomas Edwin Walker from Bassett Street. War was very real at South Wigston.

February 1940 saw villagers suffering the effects of scarlet fever. Four cases were reported along with influenzal pneumonia and one case of tuberculosis and later in the Spring came an outbreak of a measles epidemic with ninety one cases being reported. On a lighter note discussions were taking place regarding holding band concerts on the local park and the possibility of opening the cinemas on Sunday evenings for the troops to enjoy. A debate ensued on the possibility of clashing with religious times. The Sunday Entertainment Act became a point of discussion. In May, four band concerts were approved to take place on the park and ice cream was allowed to be sold there. Cricket for the troops was arranged on Aylestone Lane Park.

All committees of the Wigston Council were actively perusing normal everyday problems whilst combating other problems that the inevitable shortages of war inflicted upon everyone. Public Health and Sanitation, Housing, Allotments, Recreation, Rating, Finance and General Purposes meetings still took place regularly. A rescue party depot was established at Newgate End with wardens at South Wigston and Wigston Magna. Wardens regularly patrolled the streets at night checking for lights which had been carelessly left on. Saint Woolstan's House at Wigston Magna had become the headquarters for the South Leicester Civil Defence Unit and at South Wigston Secondary Modern School the clinic was used to accommodate the ARP. Parties would sleep overnight each person with their grey blanket issued and taking their own food to cook. They practised first aid and were ready to move to emergencies at a moments notice. The following evening a different group would take their turn the idea being that a whole contingent of people could share the duties over each week. In Bassett Street Junior School in South Wigston the Saint John Ambulance Brigade met all ready to treat civilian casualties should the need arise.

Government plans for the evacuation of the civil population from London had begun to take effect in many rural areas and Wigston was to become a 'reception area'. When the first designated group de-trained at Wigston Magna railway station thanks were extended to all helpers assisting in the welcoming party. This was to be the start of a mass evacuation to South Wigston and the surrounding areas.

The threat of war was ever present in the country and on the 8th May 1940 Neville Chamberlain resigned. Two days later Winston Churchill was installed as Prime Minister and soon a re-shuffle of the cabinet took place. Winston Churchill remained in the Prime Minister's role throughout the war.

Throughout April and May Germany invaded Denmark, Norway, France, Belgium and the Netherlands and on the 26th May the evacuation of allied troops from Dunkirk began. In June in South Wigston residents saw the effects of war first hand with the return from Dunkirk of many bedraggled and war weary soldiers as they were marched from the railway station back to their barracks on Saffron Road. Italy declared war on Britain in June and the Germans occupied part of the British Isles in the Channel Islands.

In July and early August German fighters were attacking convoys in the English Channel and ports in many coastal towns continuing into September to pound British airfields. In Leicester, bombs practically obliterated Cavendish Road in August and by November one hundred German bombers were devastating many parts of the city with great loss of life. Over a hundred people including soldiers billeted in city homes were killed and many more injured.

The Germans were preparing for their assault on London and British industry in the major cities. Between September and October the Blitz on London was at its height. Day and night raids by the enemy were continuous and the skies were filled with courageous Hurricane and Spitfire fighters in defence of the capital. The Battle of Britain was in progress. By the end of October the Germans were changing their strategy once again to coastal towns but in November the blitz on Coventry devastated that city.

South Wigston's need for an Auxillary Fire Station was under discussion with premises in Canal Street being negotiated with factory owners. A letter was received from a resident requesting the change of Leopold Street's name to Dunkirk Street as King Leopold of the Belgians had become unpopular in many quarters. By September 1940 a letter had been received in the council chamber requesting accommodation for another one thousand evacuees. Many houses on the Hooley Estate were still empty at that time having been built by a private owner. People from other areas had moved there in search of employment but by late 1941 they had soon become occupied by many evacuees from London. Gladys Andrews in South Wigston is remembered for the many occasions in which she provided and hung curtains herself at the windows for the evacuees and on meeting them at the railway station gave her own cardigan to a lady who had very little. Conditions in some houses were very poor as many evacuees were overcrowded and found to be sleeping on floors or with straw palliasses. A meeting decided that beds must be provided in all cases. It is ironic to note here that some people were of the opinion that South Wigston was a likely target for enemy attack due to the presence of the Regimental Depot and the marshalling grounds for the LMS Railway Company in the village.

September saw the Ministry of Agriculture proposing a new scheme be adopted nationwide entitled, 'Dig For Victory'. Every household in Britain was encouraged to grow their own vegetables, to set up allotments and use their gardens to supplement food shortages. With bombardment of merchant shipping supplies of imported goods were under constant attack. This saw the immediate set up in Wigston of the Horticultural Committee. Demonstration plots were found for beginners in the art of producing their own food. The scheme intensified and by 1942 ten million leaflets had been distributed and by the summer of 1943 there were millions of gardeners. At one period, authorized by the War Agricultural Executive Committee, part of South Wigston Park, the Bath Field, was ploughed for the sowing of potatoes and the following year the crop was wheat. The campaign was popular in the country adding vital extra food to the rations dealt out by stores to which each family was required to be registered with.

A Ministry of Information meeting on the 11th January 1941 opened at Long Street School where the speaker was the Parliamentary Secretary, Ronald Tree MP. Colonel Sir Robert Martin chaired the proceedings.

Sandbags were to be issued to every house and senior schoolchildren were to be taught in the use of stirrup pumps. It was decided that new gas curtains were needed in some street shelters and representatives of the Council were to attend lectures at Nottingham University on the 'Treatment And Disposal Of Foodstuffs Contaminated By Gas'. The ARP. would become an invaluable group with knowledge of how to deal with casualties in the event of a gas attack.

In March it was reported that there were now one thousand and eighty evacuees in the Wigston area and at South Wigston a public meeting was arranged with a view to forming an Allotment Association. Furthering the Dig for Victory Campaign the Ministry of Agriculture and Fisheries in their persuit of food production in allotments and gardens were talking of Certificates of Merit.

The Germans were overrunning Greece and London was besieged again with the resumption of enemy bombing. In South Wigston in April news of another tragedy reached a family in Glen Gate. Edward Charles Hickford known as Ted to his friends was killed in an air raid on Exeter Airport.

More was to come. On the 24th May HMS Hood, the pride of the British Navy was sunk in the Atlantic by the German battleship, Bismarck. Leonard Roy Jarvis and Stewart Rendell, both of South Wigston and Walden John Biggenden whose brother Athol lived at Wigston Magna, all sailing on active duty on the Hood lost their lives. The sinking of HMS Hood outraged the nation and inspired the fleet to 'Sink the Bismarck'. This massive undertaking was achieved on the 27th May when nearly two thousand German sailors died with her.

During the Spring the Wigston Urban District Council was kept busy with the day to day running of council business. Highways, Housing, Public Health, Cemetery's, Finance, General Purposes, Wigston Food Control, Evacuation, Civil Defence, all committees meeting regularly to take important decisions and in April, War Weapons Week took place. This was a national drive to raise funds for armaments. One reason for the shortage of arms was given as a consequence of hardware being left behind in Europe during the evacuation of Dunkirk. The scheme proved a great financial success with investments in National Savings. South Wigston and Wigston Magna people took up the cause with enthusiasm. Whist drives, dances, band concerts, gymnastic displays and a football match all served to raise funds. The local schools took part when schoolboys made models of naval vessels. Aero engines as used by RAF bombers and parachutes were exhibited and an open meeting at the Magna Cinema raised £70,000. Wigston's fund raising slogan became. 'A Bomber A Day'. In poor weather every division of local activity paraded the streets inclusive of H.M. Forces, Civil Defence, The St. John Ambulance Service accompanied by the Regimental and Temperance Prize Bands culminating with a Civic Service at Saint Thomas's Church in South Wigston.

Life resumed its daily routine overshadowed by the shortages that war created. The Ministry of Supply were requesting that councils should remove all iron railings from properties and parks for possible melt down for the war effort. During siren control on alert periods the worry that level crossing gates at Wigston South Station may sometimes be closed preventing the movement of essential services became a cause for debate.   Then in the summer a stick of five bombs was dropped by a German aircraft in a line at three hundred yard intervals on Saffron Road to Forryans Farm. Huge craters in the gardens of 134 and 136 Saffron Road were viewed with horror by the community.

News from Leicester reached the public that typhoid cases had been reported and diphtheria was still a threat. Injections were given to schoolchildren but the war carried on. Some factories changed their production lines to munitions one of which was the Premier Drum Company in South Wigston. Great numbers of their workforce were housed in South Wigston having moved from London after the bombing in the blitz of their factory there. In line with the rest of the country, Wigston suffered from the miseries of food rationing. Since 1940 sugar, butter, bacon, meat and paper had been listed. There was an egg shortage but so far there had been no milkless days until later and then even the rationing of onions took hold. Registered customers at stores were required to obtain forms for sugar for fruit preserving but the need for hard cash to support the war effort was unending. The War Fund Committee sanctioned a band concert and gymnastic display to take place in August on South Wigston Park. The Ritz Cinema was a popular venue in 1941.   The summer queues for admittance however caused some traders to complain as their shop doorways became blocked to their customers by the crowds of film goers seeking escapement. This matter was resolved when the suggestion to mark out access areas to shops was taken up.

As the summer ended the threat of coal shortages was becoming evident and the introduction of bins into every street for waste food to be deposited for feeding pigs was on the agenda. Clothes were also hard to replace and some women became expert seamstresses. Ingenious outfits were produced for the many war brides featured in the newspapers as weddings were quickly arranged before the grooms were conscripted into war. Men's trousers were reduced to three buttons and pockets and no turn ups.

The Autumn of 1941 brought more problems to the Council. The influx of evacuees and key workers into varying industries in Wigston saw any available accommodation soon filled. Numerous complaints were received regarding houses on the Hooley Estate. Bug infestation, mice, blocked drains, damp, rotting floors and peeling ceilings were all matters for attention. Besides the everyday mundane duties the Council was responsible for the organization of the Control Room containing maps of the area and each house in the event of any emergency. Residents themselves too were organized in many streets with collections house to house for the purchase of 'street ladders and buckets'. In the event of incendiaries falling in their streets these items were felt to be necessary. Some houses had the added protection of blast walls where it was deemed appropriate. Mr Bates Mission Hut in Leopold Street was used for first aid classes and a headquarters for fire watching parties.

December 1941 saw the call to arms of unmarried women aged between twenty to thirty years and at the barracks on Saffron Road girls who had joined the ATS had already been accommodated there for training and posting, Soon to be established on the corner of Station Road and Clarkes Road in the former Council office and the house next door, was a contingent of fully trained ATS personnel originally members of the Territorial Army. They were a sub station of the large force based at Chilwell in Nottinghamshire and operated from Wigston until the end of the war when the building was taken over as a police station. Some of the forty girls were placed in private billets and many worked in the Loco Sheds based on the Spion Kop at South Wigston. One of their invaluable jobs was to grease the tyre tracks used for tanks ensuring every day that french chalk was rubbed into the tracks. Lorries would be driven back and forth daily to the factories where the tyres and inner tubes were stored ready for collection and dispatch. There were men from the Army Ordnance Depot living in the ballroom above the Clarence Hotel on Blaby Road in South Wigston and at the Elms in Wigston Magna troops of the Royal Engineers were billeted. Girls had joined the WRENS and a great number of Wigston girls had also joined the Land Army, many working as farm hands in neighbouring villages. They tackled any job they were asked to do which included muck spreading. Schoolchildren were also picked up by the lorry load to help with potato picking which in many cases the children enjoyed as much as if it was a holiday.

Japan in its desire to dominate South East Asia and Burma were attacking British and American bases. For a family in North Street, Wigston Magna, tragedy struck again. William Hopkins serving with the Leicestershire Regiment was killed in action. His father had been killed in the First World War.

1942 opened with the capture of Manila in the Philippines followed swiftly by the invasion of Burma and the Solomons by the Japanese. Winston Churchill and President Roosevelt met to agree to a combined Chiefs of Staff the first priority being to defeat Germany. The end of the month saw the first American troops arriving in Britain.

In Wigston the continuing welfare of the children was under discussion. The plan to make available cod liver oil and black currant syrup to under six year olds was soon to be advertised to parents. This measure was seen as a deterrent in the event of scabies scourging the village. In contrast in February the rationing of soap added to the general hardships of the day. Three cases of scarlet fever and two of diphtheria had also been reported and immunization was available in combating the diseases. By September over one hundred requests for the vaccination had been received.

In line with the country's National Savings Campaign another   appeal was launched for a 'National Warship Week'. Wigston planned the 21st to the 28th March to raise funds for their event. The Wigston Temperance Band was to play and a Civic Service was to take place on Sunday 22nd. Consequently enough money was raised for Wigston to adopt the minesweeper, HMS Speedy. A plaque was designed and a presentation was made the following year by the Chairman of the Wigston Urban District Council in conjunction with the local Savings Committee when also the ship's badge was received at Wigston to commemorate its adoption. A photograph of the ship was also to be received later on. In June, HMS Speedy was at sea as part of the Malta convoy, Harpoon, under attack from the air and by Italian shipping at sea.

Also in March the South Wigston Cacklers Club made a request to the local Council for permission to glean the park and recreation ground for corn after the official harvest had been gathered. Historically, gleaning left over ears of corn from the fields was carried out in villages to feed hens.

At the request of the Government Sunday 14 June 1942 was set aside to celebrate United Nations Day. The Civil Defence, service units and other bodies were to participate. In South Wigston a service of dedication took place in the open air on Blaby Road Park led by the local clergy. The Civic address was delivered by the Chairman of the Wigston Urban Council.

A month later in the afternoon of Sunday 19 July a United Children's Service was also held on Blaby Road Park in South Wigston. A week later sweets and chocolate was rationed.

At the end of June in North Africa the first battle of El Alamein had begun. The Eighth Army consisting of British and Commonwealth forces led by General Auchinlech were battling to stop Marshal Rommel commanding German and Italian troops reaching the River Nile. This was achieved by the 25th July. The second battle of El Alamein began on the 23rd October continuing into early November and was led by General Sir Bernard Montgomery. This offensive marked the subsequent advance across Lybia covering fourteen hundred miles in eighteen weeks.

Sunday the 15th November was earmarked by the British Government as Civil Defence Day. It was to be a day of national remembrance for the defeat of German air attacks on England throughout 1940 and 1941 and to honour the work of the Civil Defence services.

In South Wigston on 16th December the British Restaurant at the Grand Hotel in Canal Street was officially opened by the Divisional Food Officer, Ministry of Food. Sixty ladies from the Womens Voluntary Service were on hand to help. British Restaurants had been established nationally to feed the population in times of emergency. Their aim was to provide cheap nourishing food at a fair price and were open to everyone. Office and industrial workers made use of the restaurants and on occasions the Civil Defence and Home Guard also used the facilities as many British Restaurants remained open for long hours.

From the beginning to the end of 1942 South Wigston and Wigston Magna had lost men from all branches of the armed forces; on the land, in the air and at sea.

On the 2nd January 1943 the year began in a festive mood for evacuee children in Wigston when they very much enjoyed a Christmas party which had been arranged for them with the help of billeting officers. Entertainment was provided by the chairman of the Wigston Urban Council and each child received sixpence generously donated by Mr Holmes.

On the same day on the other side of the world, Australian and American forces were fighting back the Japanese in New Guinea and at the end of January over ninety thousand German troops surrendered at Stalingrad.

A month later on the 1st February the first Chindits were moving into Burma in an attempt to repel the Japanese and almost a year later the second force of Chindits fought there in horrific jungle conditions.

In Wigston discussions were afoot to establish an Invasion Committee and the Dig for Victory campaign was still flourishing. The Ministry of Agriculture was again urging amateur gardeners to produce winter vegetables as much as summer produce. Certificates of Merit were being signed by the Ministry as people vied for competition. An appeal by the Ministry of Food to use potatoes in the production of flour saw the Co-operative Society request fifty six pounds of cooked and mashed potato as a daily order being placed at the British Restaurant. It was later agreed that winter wheat would follow the potato crop on the Park Road Recreation Ground in South Wigston and that oats in the Bath Field would be followed by potatoes.

Again a National Savings Campaign was launched and in 1943 it was to raise funds for the Royal Air Force. The Wings for Victory Week encouraged people to organize fund raising events in their villages to meet and exceed financial targets set for them. In Wigston the week was planned for the 20th to the 27th March. The opening ceremony took place on the 20th March and was attended by the Wigston Savings Committee and all heads of service personnel were invited. The Wigston Temperance Band were on hand to play and religious services were conducted. The Wings for Victory Campaign exceeded one hundred thousand pounds.

On Sunday 9th May a Civic Service was conducted by the Reverend Proctor at Saint Thomas Church and in 1943 Whit Monday fell on the 14th June when the Royal British Legion planned for an open air dance to take place in the grounds of Bushloe House.

Blaby Road Park in South Wigston was a popular venue for ceremonial and leisurely events. Major L Browning, Officer commanding the Home Guard suggested that a Drum Head service be held there on the afternoon of Sunday 16th May and the Reverend Proctor of Saint Thomas Church planned for a united Sunday School service for Sunday the 25th July. The following week on the 2nd August, Infirmary Day was planned. Raising funds for the hospital was a well supported event and money was put towards buying new beds. Holiday at Home weeks were planned too for the August Bank Holiday period. With the help of the Holiday at Home Committee, activities on all available parks and recreation grounds were to take place. Free use of cricket grounds, tennis courts and bowling greens was granted and there were to be band concerts in the grounds of Bushloe House.

Early September saw ARP and Civil Defence members test their abilities on an Exercise in Wigston. People were reminded of the seriousness of their services. They included, decontamination of food, mortuary services, provision and care of civilian respirators and certain post air raid services. At the conclusion of the exercise the Womens Royal Voluntary Service ladies served members at a specially prepared meal at the British Restaurant in Canal Street which was very much enjoyed and appreciated.

The search was on for a local venue to hold out of school activities which had become very popular. The previous year needlework classes had been held in Saint Thomas's Hall and at the Methodist Chapel but both premises had been identified as problematic. Two classes had also formed a choir with an accompanying pianist.

It was announced that His Majesty King George V1 had decreed that Civil Defence Day should be combined with the Royal Air Force commemorations for Battle of Britain Day. This was arranged for Sunday 26th September. In Wigston there was to be a local parade assembling and marching from the Bank at Wigston Magna to Blaby Road Park where a service would be held. Two names were put forward to take the salute, the Station Commander of Bruntingthorpe Aerodrome or the Station Commander of RAF. Blaby. Around this time news had broken in South Wigston regarding a resident Flight Sergeant J Queenborough who had been awarded the Distinguished Flying Medal for Gallantry and Devotion to Duty in Air Operations. The importance of the Royal Air Force was never far from people's minds as in July a halt on recruitment of women for the service had been implemented in order that more women were directed into the factories for aircraft production. A Fuel Efficiency Campaign was also a topic for discussion. At the time of the Battle of Britain in 1940, a call to increase the density of 'industrial haze' was being adhered to. Factories belched out as much smoke as possible in the cities the idea being to protect the population from enemy bombing. Smoke abatement regulations were suspended at this time but as the fuel shortages became more and more serious the request was withdrawn by the Ministry of Fuel and Power. Added to that the Air Ministry conceded that too much 'haze' may have been a menace to our own aircraft returning from air raids.

At Wigston South railway station late trains passing through the level crossing were causing dismay as the gates were closed on occasions for lengthy periods. Three minutes had been calculated for a train to travel from Countesthorpe to Wigston South Station but reasons for a twenty minute delay had been explained as fog, engine trouble, freight trains carrying Government traffic, fish supplies sent by passenger train to the NAFFI on Saffron Road and milk to the Co-operative Society and Morrison's Electric Van Company. Passengers too took time alighting and boarding the trains. The railway system however was a vital link at Wigston.

1943 was ending and the Ministry of Agriculture in relentless persuit of the Dig for Victory Campaign were advertising a 'Leicester Back Yard Brains Trust' to take place at De Montfort Hall on Saturday 27th November.

There was a treat in store for Wigston consumers too as a special ration of specified jam was to be available for customers. One pound for each of the three four weekly periods between September and December would be a welcome addition to the pantry for Christmas.

Boxing Day 1943 saw the German battleship Scharnhorst sunk as it stalked the tip of Norway in its quest to halt the Arctic Convoy supply route. Trapped between H.M.S Belfast, H.M.S Sheffield, H.M.S Duke of York, H.M.S Jamaica and H.M.S Norfolk, two thousand German sailors lost their lives.

By the end of December more Wigston families were mourning the tragic loss of their own men also.

New Year's Day 1944 billeting officers helped evacuee children again to enjoy their Christmas party held at the Bassett Street School in South Wigston. In January also Britain witnessed the first Bevin Boys being put to work in the coal mines. Young men between eighteen and twenty five were chosen by ballot according to their registration numbers and forced to work in the mines. This scheme devised by the Minister of Labour, Ernest Bevin, conscripted almost fifty thousand men.

Later that month as the British and the allies entered Italy many of them were taken prisoner by the Germans at the Battle of Anzio. The battle for Cassino followed but it wasn't until June when the goal to liberate Rome was finally achieved.

A national book campaign was launched in February by the Times Book Club. This was quickly taken up by local authorities. In Leicester a meeting was arranged to take place at the County Rooms on Friday 31st March and would be chaired by Sir Robert Martin. An intensive county book and salvage drive was to take place in June in Leicestershire and Rutland. Since the outbreak of war four and a half million tons of salvage and over a million tons of waste paper and books had been collected. These local collections made up for the loss of imports and wood pulp but more was needed. Wigston councilors, salvage officer and librarian were all included in the invitation to attend the conference. One suggestion had been put forward that some benefit may be to help the Duke of Gloucester's Red Cross and Saint John Fund.

Another National Savings Campaign was arranged to take place in Wigston for the 'Salute the Soldier' week. The local Savings Committee set the date for the 15th to the 22nd April and the target to be raised was £100,000.

Ladies classes were flourishing in Wigston. Around twenty met every Wednesday to 'make and mend'. They each took a little tea, milk and cake to share. During one month they made costumes for a local concert and became keen to take part in it too. Life carried on as normal as possible with dances at the Constitutional Hall and Co-operative Hall in Wigston Magna and band concerts, many of which were fund raisers for the troops. Some of the dances were attended by American personnel. Paratroops of the 82nd Airborne Division had been based at the Oadby Racecourse and at Bruntingthorpe Aerodrome and soon became integrated into the surrounding villages.

In Wigston Magna and South Wigston clinics were set up again to immunize the children from the nagging threat of diphtheria.

By June the allied invasion on the Normandy beaches was beginning whilst in the same week the Americans were defeating the Japanese in the Philippine Sea. 1944 was a year for victories with the liberation of Paris in August, in September, Brussels and Antwerp followed by Athens in October.

In London in June, V1 rockets made their first appearance killing many citizens only to be followed later in other towns by V2's. As more evacuation plans were put into effect, billeting officers in Wigston were asked to take a revision of a 1942 survey regarding compulsory billeting for evacuees in to private homes. Morrison shelters were transported to the South of England due to the flying bomb attacks there.

By September some evacuee children were returning to London and life relaxed once more. By October the Invasion Committee had been disbanded, post war housing was on the Council agenda again for discussion with the need to secure land an important topic. Bowls and a garden party was held in the grounds of Bushloe House. The Food Executive Officer was reporting that extra tea rations for Christmas may be available for residents over seventy years old but the WRVS were lamenting the shortage of custard at the Wigston Branch Restaurant.

All allied forces played vital parts in defeating Germany and countries in support of Hitler. By the end of 1944 millions of oppressed people had been liberated but at massive human cost to life and still it was not yet over.

January 1945 began with the American troops landing on the Philippine island of Luzon in persuit of the Japanese. By the end of the month Soviet troops were entering the Auschwitz concentration camp where the discovery of the remains of one million people was made. Others barely alive were liberated from further fear and suffering.

The tide had turned. Germany was losing the battle on all fronts. In February with the bombing of Dresden, over one hundred and thirty thousand people died. Between March and April the bridge at Remegen over the Rhine and Cologne was in allied hands. Mandalay in Burma had fallen, the Rhur and Northern Italy bombarded. Hanover, Vienna, Arnhem all taken by allied forces and by the 23rd April Soviet troops entered Berlin.

Soon the Germans were crushed on all fronts by the allies and it was reported that Benito Mussolini had been executed by Italian anti-fascists. On the last day of April Adolf Hitler and Eva Braun committed suicide. The bodies of Josef Goebbels, his wife and seven children were also discovered in a suicide pact.

The German unconditional surrender was signed on the 7th May 1945. Even before Winston Churchill's public statement to the nation was given in the afternoon, ten thousand people packed the Town Hall Square in Leicester to join in a V E thanksgiving service. Americans, South Africans and Chinese in Leicester all joined in and the Salvation Army were on hand too. The Leicester Mercury described the scene as 'charged with emotion and fervour' as the National Anthem and Rule Britannia echoed in the pouring rain through the gaily decorated square. The Very Reverend H A Jones led the prayers of thanksgiving and the blessing was given by the Bishop of Leicester, Dr.Vernon Smith. For two days Victory in Europe celebrations were everywhere in the county with effigies of Hitler burning on bonfires. In Wigston as in other villages the church bells joyously rang a victory peal, dancing and street parties for the children and festivities in the school halls were soon arranged. Homes were floodlit in South Wigston with gramophones blaring out their music until one and two in the mornings. At the Adult School in Bassett Street in South Wigston on V E night all the local prisoners of war who had recently so far returned were the guests of honour of the South Wigston and Glen Parva Prisoners of War Fund Committee. Thousands of people lined the Bank at Wigston Magna to take part in Victory celebrations organized by the Wigston Squadron of the A.T.C. The proceedings opened with a counter marching display by the Squadron's drum and trumpet band. The crowd were then addressed by Councillor E H Rawson, chairman of the Wigston Urban Council. In Bassett Street, Girls and Boys Schools. South Wigston, parties were held. In the playground at Long Street School in Wigston Magna, children sang and in the grounds of Bushloe House Charles Moore's Silver Prize Band played.

On the 27th May at the Civic Service at Saint Thomas's Church in South Wigston the final standing down parade of all Civil Defence Services took place.

Welfare Officers tasks included informing any evacuees who wished to return to London and were not eligible to travel with any official party that they must inform the London authorities of their housing needs. By July the need to remove street shelters had become urgent as some had become problematic and dangerous. By the end of July the resumption of street lighting and the end of double summertime had been approved.

In mid June nationally, a mass demobilization of men was becoming a reality with thousands of men returning to their homes each week.

The war in the Pacific did not end until August when atomic bombs were dropped on Hiroshima and Nagasaki in Japan. On the 14th August Japan surrendered unconditionally and on the 15th celebrations began.

In Wigston the British Legion made arrangements for a victory celebration party at The Elms for Monday 24th September and in the same month the Food Control Committee still active, were urging the community to eat more fish as due to a wonderful catch at Grimsby a better supply of mackerel could be obtained. Slowly normality was returning.

Amid the celebratory mood the sacrifice of Wigston men would never be forgotten. Poignant too the death of those who died in 1945 when victory was so near or to survive hostilities only to be struck down by illness contracted as a result of war and finally for Leonard Kemp of Wigston Fields who died after the plane which was to bring him home crashed killing all on board. Leonard died from his injuries the next day.

The Remembrance service to all who gave their lives in both world wars took place on the 11th November 1945. In the morning a service was held at All Saints Church in Wigston Magna and in the afternoon at the Garrison Church of Saint Thomas in South Wigston.
Today as then, we will remember them.

MARINE RAYMOND CHARLES KANE

Raymond Charles Kane was born on the 23 January 1921 the son of Charles John and Elsie Kane and baptized at St. Thomas Church in South Wigston, Leicestershire by the Reverend Colin W Weston on the 27th February 1921.

Charles lived at 63 Station Street in South Wigston with his parents and brother William and sisters Doris and Mavis. The four children attended Bassett Street school in the village.

It is significant to note that Charles was described as 'a bright smiling boy' by Lady Castle Stewart who particularly asked for him to be included on a photograph which was taken to celebrate her husband's election victory having being elected as the political representative for the Harborough Division.

Charles was described by his sister Doris as a lively mischievous child remembering the time when she was secretly listening to their neighbour's daughter practising her piano lessons. The children had been forbidden to distract the girl and Charles pushed his sister's head through the window. As the pane cracked Charles made a hasty retreat.

Charles was keen to work having left school at fourteen years old and started out by selling chocolates from a tray round his neck to passengers for the London Midland and Scottish Railway Company at London Road, Leicester. This task on the station platforms proved very profitable for him as passengers not always having the correct change to hand for their purchases; and no time to acquire any; allowed Charles to keep the change for himself. Charles also worked for Dunmore's Biscuit Company in South Wigston by sweeping broken biscuits from the tables.

As a young sixteen year old in 1937, Charles joined the Royal Marines as a boy marine. He trained at the Royal Marine Headquarters, Eastney Barracks at Plymouth. By 1938 Charles was a crew member on the battleship HMS Royal Oak and one of his duties included guarding miscreants on the ship who may have over indulged on shore leave. Charles is remembered for his stories of always 'falling out of his hammock'.

Two months after the declaration of war the Royal Oak was anchored at Scapa Flow off the Orkneys. On Saturday 14th October 1939 Lieutenant-Commander Gunther Prien of the German Navy took the submarine U-47 through the maze of channels considered to be impenetrable. Undetected by the British Home Fleet, three torpedoes were fired. The veteran warship of the First World War, HMS Royal Oak, capsized and sank in thirteen minutes.

Out of twelve hundred officers and crew over eight hundred lives including Charles Kane were lost. Charles was just eighteen years old and the first casualty of the Second World War in South Wigston.

On Lieutenant-Commander Gunther Prien's return to Germany he was congratulated by Adolf Hitler and given a hero's welcome and awarded the Iron Cross.

Raymond Charles Kane is commemorated at Portsmouth Naval Memorial, Hampshire.

Raymond Charles Kane

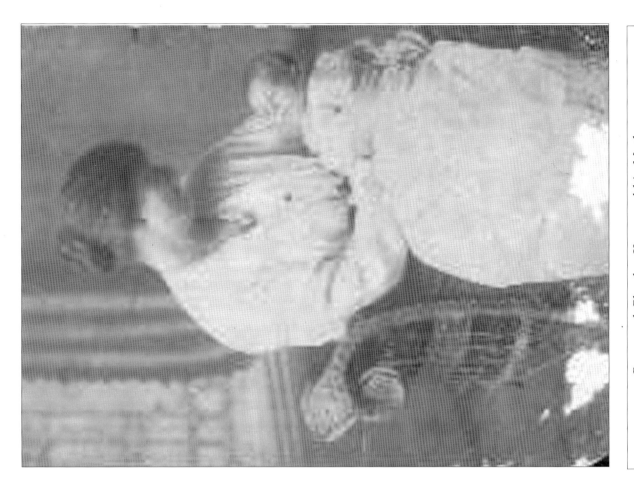

Raymond Charles Kane and his Mother

Mr and Mrs Kane from left to right; Charles, Doris and William

MEDICAL CARD

ISSUED BY THE

LEICESTERSHIRE INSURANCE COMMITTEE,

144 London Road, Leicester.

To
(Full Name) .... Charles Kane. ....

(Address) ...... 63. Station Street. ....

.... South Wigston, Leics. ....

(Society and Branch) .... M.U.O.F. .... 123/.869. .....

(No. on Record Card) .... 353. ....

For Use of Insurance Committee only.   Committee's Stamp.

The above-named is on the list of :—

[Dr.]   J.R.Lund.

In any correspondence with the Committee as to medical benefit this reference
Le..... 150 together with membership number and name of Approved Society
should always be quoted by the insured person.

M05184/5961 3/38 15,000 C&R

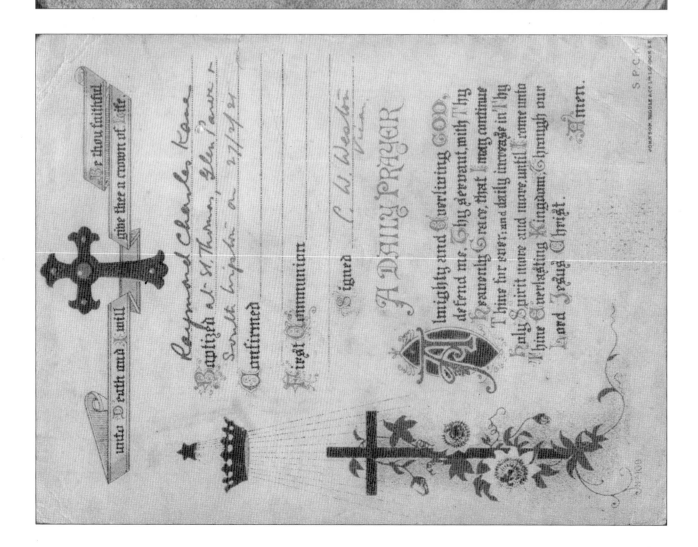

Be thou faithful
give thee a crown of Life
until Death and I will

Received Charles Kane
Baptized at St Thomas, Glen Parva
South Wigston on 27/2/21
Confirmed
First Communion
Signed C. W. Weston
Vicar

A DAILY PRAYER

Almighty and Everlasting GOD,
defend me, Thy servant, with Thy
Heavenly Grace, that I may continue
Thine for ever; and daily increase in Thy
Holy Spirit more and more, until I come unto
Thine Everlasting Kingdom, through our
Lord Jesus Christ.   Amen.

S.P.C.K.

JOHNSON RIDDLE & CO LD LONDON S.E.

Nº 109

Charles Kane in the front holding the poster with Lady Castle Stewart whose husband was elected by a majority of over 3000 to the Harborough division. She asked for 'The bright smiling boy to be on it'

Raymond Charles Kane and Cynthia Bradley

To Wish You all Happiness
on Christmas Day
& throughout the Coming Year.

A kindly wish is mine,
A wish sincere and true,
That every Christmas Day may bring
Increasing joy to you,
True joy that long will stay,
When Christmastide has passed away.

From
Raymond C. Kane

R.M. Barracks,
Plymouth. 1938.

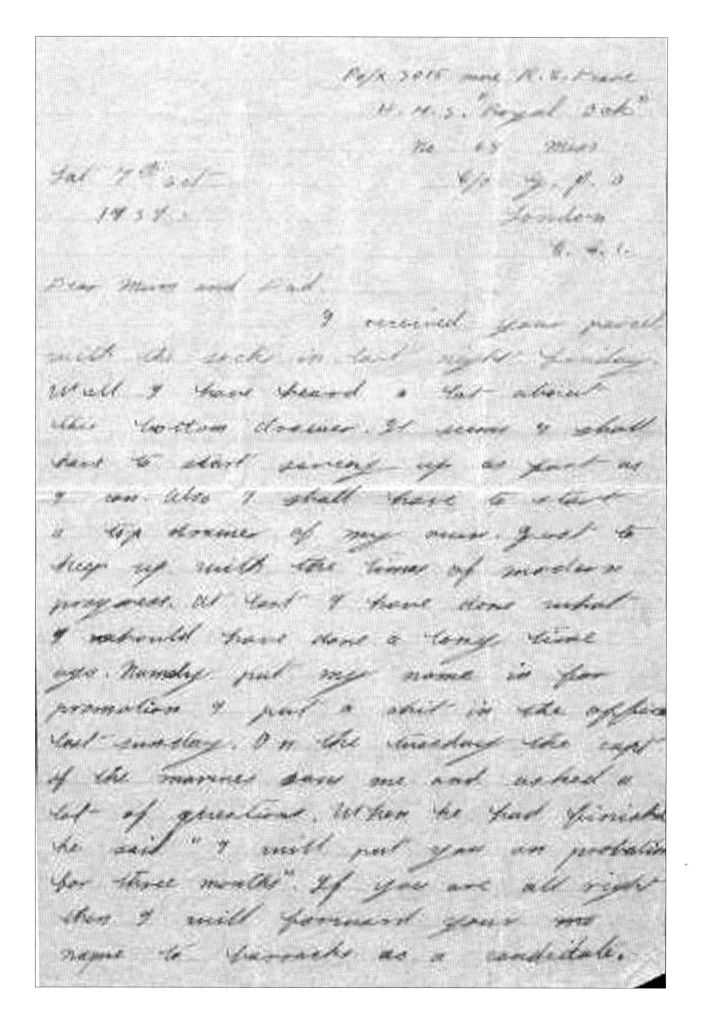

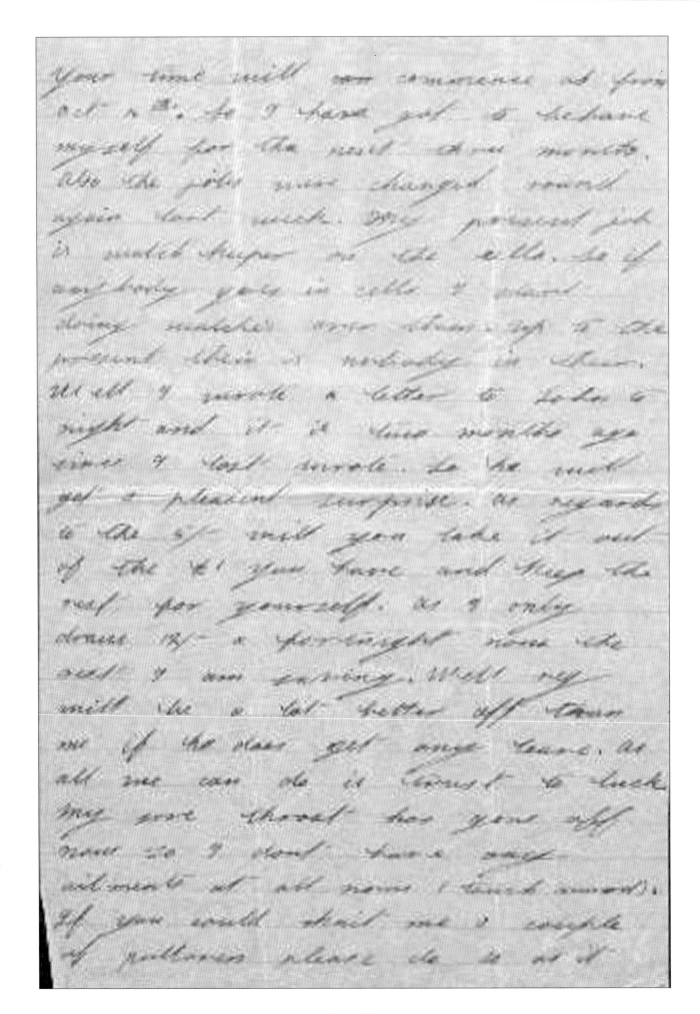

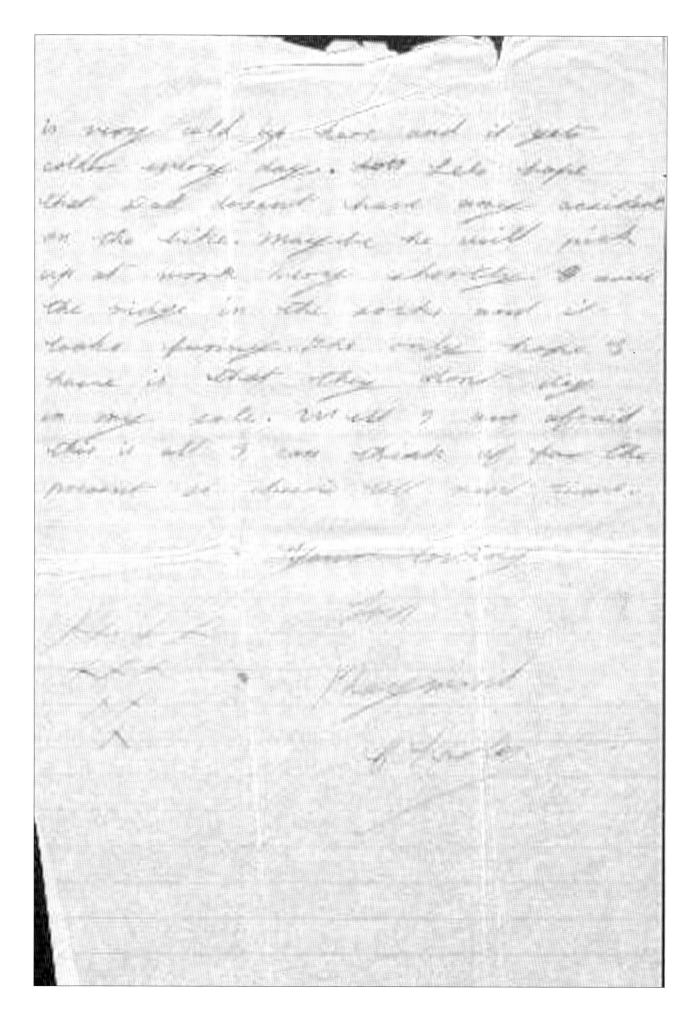

Above; Raymond Charles Kane with Royal Marines
Below; Raymond Charles Kanes with Ship's Company

HMS Royal Oak

Loss of the *Royal Oak*

The numerical odds were too far against the German Navy for there to be any thought of a deliberate engagement with the Allied fleets. Raeder could only wage a guerrilla war – but his U-boats and mine-layers did succeed in drawing blood at the Royal Navy's expense.

Two weeks after Britain had gone to war, on September 17, *U-29* (Lieutenant-Commander Otto Schuhart) sank the first Allied warship to be lost to enemy action in World War II: the elderly aircraft-carrier *Courageous* of 22,500 tons, which was lost with 519 of her crew.

Worse was to come. On the night of October 13–14, under a brilliant display of Northern Lights, Lieutenant-Commander Günther Prien took *U-47* through the maze of channels and currents girdling the stronghold of the British Home Fleet: the vast anchorage of Scapa Flow in the Orkneys, hitherto considered to be im-

penetrable to submarines. Prien found the dog-leg channel in Holm Sound more weakly defended than the others. He fired three torpedoes at the battleship *Royal Oak* (31,200 tons), which capsized and sank in 13 minutes, taking with her Rear-Admiral H. F. C. Blagrove and 832 crew.

The loss of this veteran warship of World War I made little or no difference to the Allies' superiority at sea, but the moral effect was enormous, both in Germany and Great Britain. Prien and his crew were welcomed as heroes in Berlin, and Prien himself was decorated with the Knight's Cross by Hitler. In London, there were wild rumours that the U-boat could only have got into Scapa Flow by treason, and for a while suspicion centred on a Swiss watchmaker in Kirkwall, largest town in the Orkneys. Not until the war was over was it proved for certain that the Scapa Flow feat had been carefully planned from Luftwaffe aerial reconnaissance photographs.

By mid-November the numerous French and British warships in the Atlantic,

△ *Germany's first U-boat ace of the war, Lieutenant-Commander Günther Prien.*
▽ *Prien (in the white cap) with his crew. He was given a hero's welcome on his return from sinking the* Royal Oak *at Scapa Flow.*

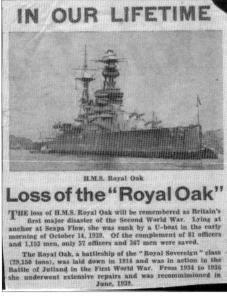

IN OUR LIFETIME

H.M.S. Royal Oak

Loss of the "Royal Oak"

THE loss of H.M.S. Royal Oak will be remembered as Britain's first major disaster of the Second World War. Lying at anchor at Scapa Flow, she was sunk by a U-boat in the early morning of October 14, 1939. Of the complement of 81 officers and 1,153 men, only 57 officers and 367 men were saved.

The Royal Oak, a battleship of the "Royal Sovereign" class (29,150 tons), was laid down in 1914 and was in action in the Battle of Jutland in the First World War. From 1934 to 1936 she underwent extensive repairs and was recommissioned in June, 1935.

hunting what they believed to be two pocket-battleships, led Raeder to order a battle squadron to sail for the North Atlantic on November 21. It was hoped that a demonstration of force in the waters between Scotland and Iceland would draw off some Allied warships from the South Atlantic, easing the problems of *Graf Spee* (still at large). On November 23, the battle-cruisers *Scharnhorst* and *Gneisenau* surprised and obliterated the puny armed merchantman *Rawalpindi* west of the Faeroes.

Admiral Sir Charles Forbes, commanding the Home Fleet, was unable to put to sea and intercept these new raiders. On September 9, he had had to shift his base from Scapa Flow until the defences there – anti-aircraft as well as anti-submarine – had been put to rights. The new anchorages (at Loch Ewe on Scotland's west coast and at Rosyth in the Firth of Forth) were too far to the south to allow sufficient time to intercept German raiders in latitudes so far to the north. The Germans soon got wind of the Home Fleet's change of base and laid magnetic mines in the approaches to Loch Ewe; on December 4, one of them did so much damage to the battleship *Nelson* that she was out of action for several months.

Despite these setbacks, however, the Royal Navy, with the invaluable help of its French ally had, by the end of 1939, apparently achieved its double mission: to safeguard the sea-lanes of the Western Allies, and to cut those belonging to the common enemy. But this satisfactory situation was illusory. The German U-boat fleet was receiving new units at a alarming rate, and in any event was certainly not operating at full stretch. Despite the rapid elimination of *Graf Spee* there was absolutely no guarantee that the Allies could prevent further surface raiders from reaching the Atlantic. And the problem of Germany's inshore supply-routes – those which ran through the territorial waters of Europe's neutral powers – had yet to be tackled.

Grand-Admiral Erich Raeder, here with Himmler on his right, was born in 1876 and entered the German Navy at the age of eighteen. During World War I he was Chief-of-Staff to Admiral Hipper. In 1928 he was made Commander-in-Chief of the Navy.

In October 1939 Raeder was one of the first to realise the strategic importance of Norway, and proposed to Hitler that Germany should acquire bases there. The invasion of Norway on April 9 was the German Navy's first major operation of the war.

Although a believer in waging aggressive war he recognised the difficulty of invading Britain, and after the Luftwaffe had failed to destroy the R.A.F. he persuaded Hitler to shelve the plan.

Germany's continued weakness in big ships led Raeder to concentrate on the production of submarines in an effort to sever Britain's overseas communications, deciding that the most effective way of weakening the U.K. would be to cut her supply lines. This policy at first won many successes, but Raeder was led to resign in January 1943 after Hitler had blamed him for various setbacks. He was replaced by Dönitz. At Nuremberg he was sentenced to life imprisonment, but was released in 1955, and died five years later.

OVER 800 LIVES LOST

H.M.S. Royal Oak.

WHO WAS TO BLAME?

...aster in the history of the Royal Navy.

For six days, beginning at Scapa and ending at Thurso on the 24th, the Board, in committee and sub-committee, studied the evidence, compiled reports, questioned a long parade of witnesses.

The Board found that Captain W. G. Benn and his officers had done all that was possible to save their ship.

Captain Benn had remained in the ship until the last possible moment, until, in fact, the ship left him, and his behaviour was in the best tradition of the service.

Questions

As the testimony further unfolded, it became clear that not only was Scapa Flow not impregnable but it was in fact perhaps one of the places most vulnerable to enemy attack in all of the British Isles.

Faced with the knowledge that a U-Boat had got in, Admiral French, Admiral Commanding Orkney and Shetland, soon was expressing dissatisfaction with almost everything about Scapa's defences.

Blockships alone would not do for the eastern gaps — "we must have lookouts, searchlights and guns at all four entrances."

The questioning moved to the placement of the nets.

"Have you ever heard doubt expressed as to whether the Hoxa boom could keep out a submarine with certainty, even though the foot of the net is some

Prien was congratulated by Hitler.

HERO'S WELCOME

35 feet from the bottom at high water?" Admiral French was asked.

He said, "I am afraid I must acknowledge that I thought the foot of the net was much closer to the bottom because I had been told that the nets had been cut to fit the depth of the water and I naturally assumed that they were right on the bottom."

Although the U-47 had not in fact entered under the net, it was an alarming defence weakness.

Guard ships

French went on to agree that Scapa's defence should be bolstered with Asdic or echo-sounding apparatus, either ashore or afloat.

He had no Asdic ships, no gun defences, apart from 4-inchers in a few guard ships.

He had asked for more patrol vessels — he wanted two at each boom — but never got them.

In effect, French was saying the Admiralty had

not listened to his pleas. He had reported earlier that in his opinion there would be no difficulty for a submarine to come in by either Kirk or Skerry Sounds at slack water, despite the block ships sunk there.

The barriers protecting Scapa Flow were mainly psychological, constructed not of real steel, thick netting, hard blockships, but of threads, imaginary ones, woven out of the belief that what never before had happened never could happen.

Thomas McKenzie, chief salvage officer with a civilian company, whose earlier report warning of the openness of the Sounds to submarine attack had been largely ignored by the Admiralty, now found himself face to face with the generally unseen men of Whitehall.

He could rightly have waved at them the prophetic statement he had made five months earlier, the one containing the words:

NEXT WEEK — U-47's desperate attempts to escape the depth charges from a chasing British destroyer.

The anchorage was thought by many to be impregnable

★ ★ ★

But there were five ways a submarine could have entered

● It is fully recognised that the navigation of the Sounds, even now, presents difficulties, owing to the strong tidal streams and the existing obstructions, but it is safe to assume that an intrepid submarine officer, in war time, would take risks which no discreet mariner would think of taking in peace time.

● The possibility of a hostile submarine entering Scapa Flow, if the Sounds are left as at present, cannot therefore be excluded. The fact that any such craft successful in passing through one of the Sounds could be within torpedo range of capital ships in 15 to 30 minutes, makes it of vital importance that the Sounds should be efficiently blocked.

The Admiralty, having not heeded McKenzie's forewarning, now listened to him explain the situation in impressive detail.

Surprising

"Evidence given to us," the Board lamented in its report, "has suggested that there was room for a small submarine to pass in at certainly five of the seven entrances if the conditions were favourable."

Specific criteria detailing the procedures for defending the Flow had been laid down and yet, the records show the matter was not one of priority, revealing a lack of responsibility that may never be purged from the Royal Navy's history.

Not responsible for prewar planning, Churchill was immune from reproach and ruled out a judicial inquiry which would have assigned blame to individuals because he felt this would impose an additional burden on those engaged in the struggle against Germany.

What is surprising, however, in view of the proof of negligence contained in the records, is that no one in the Navy received so much as a reprimand for one of the worst disasters in its history.

Iron Cross

So the vaunted belief in Scapa Flow, impregnable Scapa Flow, was shattered.

Who was to blame for the weakness of Scapa Flow? The Board of Inquiry made it clear. The Admiralty was to blame; Scapa's commanding officers were to blame; human complacency was to blame.

★ ★ ★

When finally U-47 made fast to her jetty, the top senior officers, including Donitz stepped on to the submarine's narrow deck.

A look of pride sat upon Donitz's face. He listened with deep satisfaction as it was announced that Prien had earned the Ritterkreuz, the coveted Knight's Cross of the Iron Cross.

And every member of the crew was given the Eiserneskruez, Iron Cross, Second Class and told they were to fly that same

Shock for survivors

ON the Tuesday morning after the sinking of the Royal Oak, Scapa Flow had its first air raid of the war and Oak's survivors felt again the threatening, badgering persistence of death.

Four Junkers 88's attacked and a flurry of bombs rained down.

The Germans didn't bomb the hospital ship Abba which had many survivors on board but the planes began their dives over her, using the hospital ship as a screen against fire from British warships.

For the still-shocked men on board, it was a grim experience.

Other survivors suffering from nerves had been landed to go for a calming walk. They threw themselves to the ground as bombs fell and shrapnel slashed around.

And still the solemn threat of death kept shadowing.

Special train

A few nights later after being taken by ship to the mainland, the survivors boarded a special train for the long trip south to Portsmouth barracks.

As Warrant Officer Frank Williams wrote later, "The train left Thurso about 8 p.m.

"At 1 a.m. the train stopped for some reason, waited for five minutes then started again. We had reached probably about twenty miles an hour or less when there was a crash.

"We had run into some stationary coaches on the line. Though nobody was badly hurt, one chap had jumped out and busted his ankle.

"We sorted ourselves out with the help of matches — the lights having failed.

"So ended the unhappy story of the Royal Oak."

afternoon to Kiel, then on to Berlin to meet the Fuhrer.

For Prien, glory had come suddenly.

From then on he was applauded or toasted wherever he went. People wrote him adoring letters, he was in the limelight wherever he went; the mere sight of him in a restaurant or in a train or bus was enough to set people talking.

Prien enjoyed the adulation, yet he wasn't swept off his feet by it; he wasn't a braggart. He told a friend "I am an officer, not a film star."

And, increasingly, the Third Reich's first hero yearned to return to the sea.

MALE SURGICAL WARD 2

"Couldn't you put all my driving instructors in one word to help with my visiting?"

MEN WERE STILL CALLING FOR HELP AS RESCUE VESSEL SAILED AWAY

STRUCK by a broadside of torpedoes from the German submarine U-47, which had stolen undetected into Scapa Flow, the Royal Oak had gone to the bottom. In the water, many men were swimming for their lives.

Warrant Officer Frank Williams could see cliffs about a mile away, and suddenly he remembered a cleft he'd seen the afternoon before when out in one of the Oak's boats.

Williams made for the cleft, using a steady side-stroke but after a minute of this he came upon an upturned boat with some thirty men clinging to it.

"The men were singing and I joined them in both singing and hanging on," he said.

In the water, some distance away, Sergeant George Booth came across another man. They knew each other.

"Let's swim for the shore," Booth called out.

"I can't," came the reply, "my arm's gone."

© Gerald S. Snyder, 1976. From the book, "The Royal Oak Disaster" by Gerald S. Snyder, published by William Kimber & Co., Ltd.

Then Booth heard him say, "C h e e r i o, General," (Booth's nickname).

And his friend sank out of sight.

In this way would life ebb or go on, men die or live to tell their story.

Spar of wood

William Sandifer, exhausted and floating on his back, bumped into a spar of wood, grabbed it, shared it with another officer who swam up, until picked up by the fishing boat Daisy.

The Daisy had been taken over by the Admiralty and, at the time of the attack, had been tied bow and stern to the Royal Oak's port boom.

Frank Williams, in the group of about thirty, still clinging to the upturned boat, too far from the main party of survivors to be picked up by Daisy, after an hour struck out to find the fishing boat, did find her, directed her to the others.

"I have never been so cold before or since," he'd say years later. "The cold seemed to have got right inside my bones somehow and Daisy, with nearly 300 of us aboard, couldn't help to warm us."

Darkness

An unknown rating, rescued by Daisy, jumped overboard three times with a rope's end to save other men; while others on the drifter fished some unconscious from the water.

George Booth felt a pain under his right arm— a boat hook had caught him — the next thing he knew he was being hauled aboard.

The small boat, about a hundred feet long, seventeen feet wide, bounced over the sea, drunken with the weight of men thinking mainly now of keeping warm. "We packed our-selves like sardines and huddled together to try and keep each other warm, as many of us were almost naked," said F. J. C. Hobbs.

"Why doesn't someone come and help us," cried one man, looking out for a ship. "They must know by now that the Oak has gone." But no ship came.

"There was only darkness and cold and death," remembered Taffy Davies.

"And when the Daisy's skipper decided that she was dangerously overloaded and he made his way to the Pegasus, the nearest large ship, I remember the heart-breaking, gut-rending misery we felt when we heard men still calling for help and imploring Daisy not to go; and this was more than two hours after the Oak went down, and still no outside help had arrived."

When the final count was made, it would be found that out of the crew of over 1200 officers and men, 833 were lost.

MORE ON NEXT PAGE

MORE LEICESTERSHIRE NAVAL CASUALTIES

The deaths on war service of more Leicestershire lads in the Royal Navy are revealed to-day.

Marine C. KANE   Boy W. ANDREWS   ...URLEY JOHNSON   Stoker R. BATEMAN (Survivor)

BOY WILFRED E. ANDREWS, aged 17, whose parents, living at Weighbridge House, The Wharf, West Bridge, Leicester, have been notified of his death, was the oldest but one of seven children. When he left Narborough-road School, he worked for a time on the L.M.S. Railway, where his father is employed.

After only six months in the Navy he won a medal for gunnery in the King's Trophy competition.

Another casualty, Thomas Morley Johnson, aged 18, whose parents, Mr. and Mrs. Charles Henry Johnson, now live at Revaside, Queniborough-lane, Queniborough, used to live in Victoria-road North, Leicester. He was educated at Ellis-avenue School, Leicester, and worked for a time at Messrs. Greenless' boot and shoe factory. He had been in the Navy for about 18 months.

In the death of Marine Charles Kane, the 18-year-old son of Mr. and Mrs. C. Kane, of 63, Station-street, South Wigston, the parish has suffered its first wartime loss. Charles went to the South Wigston School, and was a popular boy in South Wigston.

A Survivor

As reported in later editions of the "Leicester Mercury" last evening, Mr. Albert Bateman, of 13, Gwendoline-avenue, Wykin Estate, Hinckley, has received the following telegram:—

"I am pleased to inform you that your son, Stoker Second-Class Robert Bateman, has been saved from the Royal Oak."

Bateman's father told a "Leicester Mercury" representative that his son, who is 19 years of age, had been in the Navy about 12 months. Just before war broke out he visited his home. Before joining the Navy he was employed in the engineering trade in Hinckley.

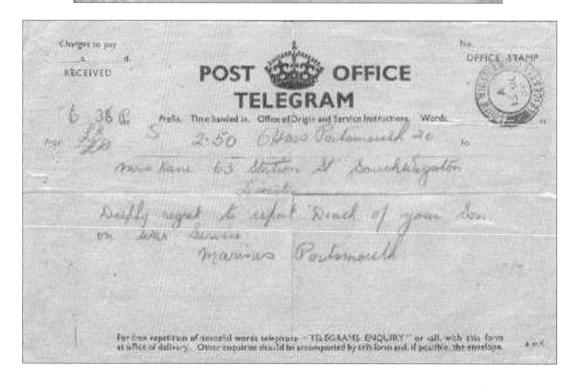

B

Replies should be addressed to :—

The Commandant,
Portsmouth Division, Royal Marines,
Eastney Barracks,
Southea.

EASTNEY BARRACKS,
SOUTHSEA.

Date......15/10/39........

Dear *Mrs Kane*

It is with very deep regret that I learn of the sad death of
your ......*Son*......................

Please allow me to express the sincere sympathy of the
officers and men of the Royal Navy and the Royal Marines.

Yours faithfully,

Mrs Kane
63 *Station Str.*
South Wigston
Leicester

R. Minton

Brigadier,
Commanding Portsmouth Division,
Royal Marines.

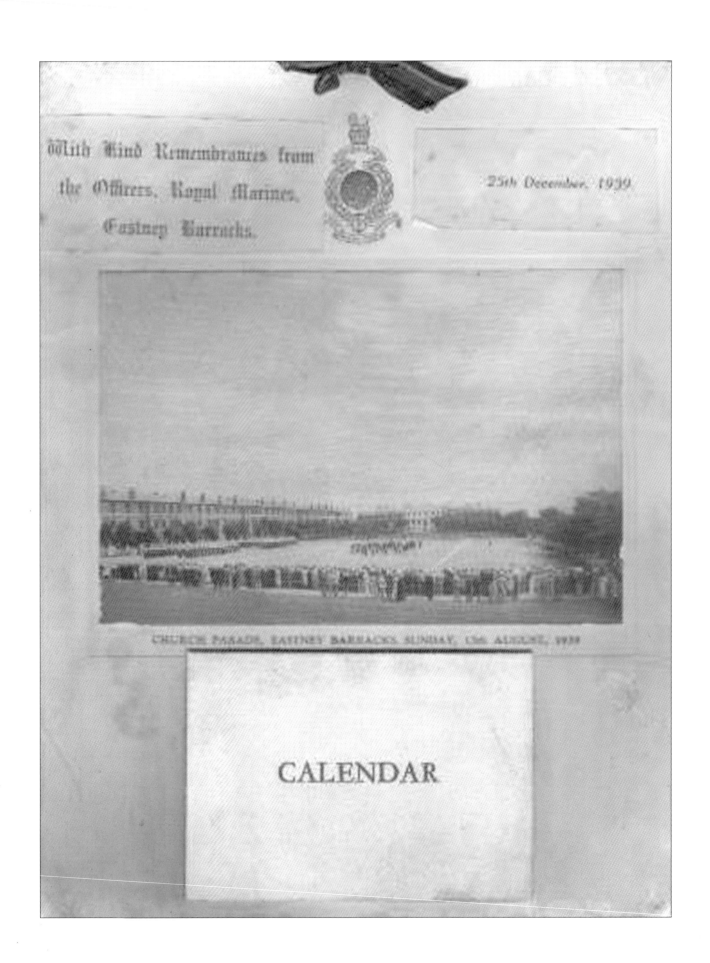

With Kind Remembrances from the Officers, Royal Marines, Eastney Barracks.

25th December, 1939.

CHURCH PARADE, EASTNEY BARRACKS, SUNDAY, 13th AUGUST, 1939

CALENDAR

809 sailors, the Navy pays a most amazing tribute

DOOMED: The battleship Royal Oak

IN MEMORY

IT IS known as Black Saturday . . . the day forty-one years ago when a surprise U-boat attack sank one of Britain's mightiest warships.

Eight hundred and nine men went down with the 29,000 ton battleship Royal Oak, and her supply boat sunk in Scapa Flow, on October 14, 1939.

Every year, in an eerie underwater ceremony, the Royal Navy pays tribute to the men entombed in the wrecks, officially designated a war grave.

Diving at the site, a mile off Orkney, has been banned, to keep away looters seeking relics.

But a Daily Mirror reporter and photographer — both qualified divers — got permission to join the Royal Navy team and photograph this year's unique and moving ceremony . . .

Pictures:
HARRY
PROSSER

Story:
ALISTER
MARTIN

TWO grey seals watch curiously as the Royal Navy's strangest mission reaches its objective . . .

A buoy bobbing forlornly on the wind-whipped waves of Scapa Flow.

It is all that remains to mark the grave of the 510-foot battleship Royal Oak and her 809 crew who went down with her.

All, that is, except the smell of diesel oil, still lingering 41 years after the tragedy.

We made the mile journey from Scapa pier, Orkney, aboard two Navy inflatables — seven frogmen from Rosyth, near Edinburgh, plus photographer Harry Prosser and myself.

The divers led by Lieut. Alan Bayliss, have already placed a wreath of heather, orchids and tulips — tied with red white and blue ribbons — on the buoy.

Now comes the climax to the silent but moving ceremony. .

Wearing a dry-suit and air bottle, Chief Petty Officer John Friar, 33, and Able Seaman Diver Taffy Livingstone dive down 100 feet to the deck of the stricken battleship.

Friar carries a folded White Ensign to replace last year's flag.

Flag

The pair fix the flag between two of the battleship's four-inch anti-aircraft guns.

The once highly polished barrels are now covered in a fungus called dead man's fingers.

Every year, after the underwater tribute, the Navy divers inspect the wreck.

I am taken on a guided

REMEMBERING: Dusty Miller on the marker buoy

The Royal Oak is now a memorial to all British seaman. A flag every year is laid over the wreck of the 'Oak'. Two frogmen lay the wreath and also a service is held and a wreath thrown out to sea

SILENT TRIBUTE: A hundred feet down, the White Ensign is unfurled.

COVERED: A gun wreathed in fungus

tour by Seaman Diver Dusty Miller, 20.

Miller, born in Kirkwall, Orkney, warned me I'd see sights "as spooky as hell." He was right.

Gloom

Swimming through the silent, murky gloom we blunder into the giant rusty coffin.

The leather soles of sailors' shoes litter the sand.

Anti-aircraft guns that could do nothing to save the battleship bristle at all angles.

The mast and bridge festooned with fungus lie shattered on the seabed.

No fish swim around the wreck ... the leaking diesel would poison them.

The stricken vessel, lying on its side, towers 80 feet above us as we swim. At its highest point, it is only a few yards below the surface of the North Sea.

In a secret spot on the Royal Oak I was shown the shape of the ship's bell, buried in sand to foil would-be looters.

The Navy divers want it raised and put on display at St. Magnus' Cathedral, Kirkwall.

"It would be the permanent memorial that the men of the Royal Oak

deserve," said John Friar.

My dive into the depths shed light on the controversy surrounding the Royal Oak's sinking.

Hitler claimed she was a victim of one of his "sea wolves"—U-boat 47—and decorated the captain.

Some British naval experts, however, suspected sabotage.

Thrown

The ragged edges of the holes in the ship's side point inwards—evidence that she was torpedoed. But not necessarily by U-47.

The search for North Sea oil has thrown up yet another equally plausible, theory.

Divers working on a pipeline near the Royal Oak have discovered the wreck of a German U-boat lying not far away.

It now seems certain one of Hitler's sea wolves DID penetrate the closely guarded waters of Scapa Flow.

But after sinking the warship, did the mystery U-boat strike a mine and end up sharing the Royal Oak's last resting place..?

"This marks the wreck of HMS Royal Oak and the grave of her crew. Respect their resting place. Unauthorised diving prohibited."

In 1974, thirty-five years after the Oak went down, a small boat, the RNXS Loyal Proctor, heaved-to above the wreck and while eleven of the 424 men who survived the sinking stood with bowed heads, a bugler sounded "The Last Post."

A piper played "The Flowers o' the Forest," and as the last sad notes of the lament died away a Navy lieutenant representing the Thurso Sea Cadet Company dropped a wreath overboard to float above the Oak's resting place.

Since the tragedy, of the Royal Oak surviv have returned, singly or in groups; while others, never making the trip back, have kept in touch with one another, still discussing details and incidents of the sinking.

But not until twenty-eight years after the disaster, did the British decide on a formal reunion.

It was decided as well to invite the Germans, the remaining crewmen of U 47 who had been posted before the last fatal patrol, and "club together" to help meet the expenses of their former enemies.

For the first time, men from HMS Royal Oak and U-47 met face to face.

The former foes gathered first on 13th October at a social evening at Portsmouth's Royal Navy Association club, then, the next day, they met at the Royal Navy War Memorial in Southsea, at a ceremony to mark the anniversary.

ASSISTANT STEWARD CYRIL EDWARD BETTONEY

Cyril Edward Bettoney was born in 1908 the son of Harry and Sarah Bettoney of 64 Countesthorpe Road, South Wigston, Leicestershire. He was one of three children having a brother Leonard and a sister Eileen. The children attended Bassett Street School.

Cyril left home for London when he became twenty one and had a variety of jobs in the capital and Somerset. Travelling to Ottawa he worked for a time in Government House as a footman but Cyril loved adventure and excitement and his itchy feet were soon tapping again. He moved to Ireland to work as a valet for the 13th Earl of Meath and on his return to London secured a post in Regents Park with the once 'Deb of the Year' Mrs Sweeny, wife of the American financier, Charles Sweeny. Formerly Margaret Whigham, Mrs Sweeny later became the Duchess of Argyll scandalising the nation in the 1960s. Thomas Ades featured that part of her life in the opera 'Powder Her Face'.

After leaving the employ of Mrs Sweeny, Cyril joined the cruise ship, Rawalpindi which sailed between Britain and the Far East. This gave Cyril the opportunity to join the Merchant Navy and at the outbreak of war, Cyril stayed on board. The Rawalpindi was one of the first ships to be converted to an armed merchant cruiser.

On Thursday 23rd November 1939 HMS Rawalpindi was half way between the Faroes and Iceland when Captain Edward Kennedy, (father of Ludovic Kennedy) with his two hundred and eighty men were torpedoed by the German warship, the Scharnhorst. The Rawalpindi was no match for the pride of the German Navy.

Men perished in the horrific fires on board whilst only a handful of men survived the freezing waters but Cyril Bettoney did not. He was thirty three years old and is commemorated at the Liverpool Naval Memorial.

Cyril Edward Bettoney, Assistant Steward, HMS Rawalpindi, Naval Auxiliary Personnel, (MN).

Mr and Mrs Bettoney, Cyril and his brother Leonard

Left: Cryil Bettoney
(Footman)
Right: Cryil Bettoney's
sister Eileen

Margaret Whigham 1912 - 1993
Who became Mrs Charles Sweeny
and later Duchess of Argyll

and all its dangers were or unknown, for, apart from the 50-odd officers and men who had served with the Rawalpindi in her passenger days, the entire crew was composed of R.N.R. men of the Merchant Navy, reservists, pensioners who had come back to the sea after having already completed 22 years in the Navy, and a sprinkling of R.N.V.R.—civilians with the bare essentials of naval training. There was not one active service officer or rating aboard the Rawalpindi.

So Kennedy never reckoned the odds, they were too hopeless to work out. He knew, too, that there was no hope of help from the British Navy, the nearest vessel, the Newcastle, was too far away and could never have stopped the Scharnhorst anyway.

He knew the Rawalpindi could never even think to begin to out-gun or out-run the enemy.

There was no hope. Just no hope in the world, if ever there was a time for despair, this was it.

DECISION

BUT despair could never have touched Edward Kennedy, never have touched Edward Kennedy, for, as it became abundantly clear in the course of the next 40 minutes, he simply did not know the meaning of the word.

The Scharnhorst was closing by the minute and as she sliced her way through another rain-squall her big signalling lamp

What the ringleaders had told him that morning was that not only was the battalion of naval reservists composed, almost to a man, of trade unionists, but that at least 150 of them were miners.

To Kennedy, the prospect of forcing those men to take action against their own kith and kin trade-unionist miners was completely unthinkable.

It wasn't so to the hide-bound Lords of the Admiralty. They called Kennedy's behaviour dereliction of duty, court-martialled him on this grotesquely unfair charge, and, the following year, threw him out of the Navy. But they welcomed him back with open arms when he volunteered his services at the outbreak of war.

★ ★ ★

AND now the moment for the greatest decision of all was here. Again the Scharnhorst blinked out the "Heave-to" signal, and Kennedy knew now there was no time left.

The sensible thing, the wise and politic thing—for which there couldn't possibly have been any reproach—would have been to do as the Scharnhorst ordered.

But with Kennedy, as with most of the great British captains down the centuries, prudence in the face of the enemy was a quality he had never learned, and certainly never inherited. He knew he

THE SUNDAY EXPRESS LONDON JUNE 26 1960

2

A BLAZING WRECK —BUT STILL SHE FOUGHT ON

> The Rawalpindi had no defence against the massive guns of the German warships; but she had a captain to whom surrender was unthinkable. The splendid, hopeless last hour of the Rawalpindi holds a unique place in the annals of the war at sea.

——by Alistair Maclean——

THE cold wind blew steadily from the north. It had come a long way, that wind, from the berg-strewn, fog-shrouded water of the high Arctic, from the unimaginably cold wastes of the Greenland ice-cap.

It was a bitter wind, a wind full of a thousand little knives, and wherever it swept the men in the Northern Contraband Control shrunk from the feathery touch of those icy talons and covered ever deeper in their hooded duffel coats, seeking what shelter they could behind the chilled metal of bridges and open gun-posts.

It blew steadily along the line of the far - spaced vessels of the Contraband Control. It blew across the sleety rain-squalls that were part and parcel of existence in those bleak and unquiet waters, and bridges of three armed merchant cruisers and the eight-inch gun cruisers Norfolk and Suffolk in the Denmark Strait.

It blew across the Newcastle and three older cruisers stretched out between Iceland and the Faroes; and eternally, monotonous, wherever it went men manning bridges and guns cursed the cold and the sub-Arctic and the ill-luck that had brought them this exhausting, uncomfortable and eternally uncomfortable duty in those high latitudes.

THE SHAPE

AND then the wind passed on and blew over the bridge of the armed merchant cruiser Rawalpindi, and here men no longer had any doubts for themselves . . .

GRANDEUR

THE position was almost exactly half-...

...looming ahead through the sleety rain-squalls that were only the tightly identified in as a German pocket battleship, or a German battleship. Twenty seconds passed, thirty, perhaps almost a minute, then the captain of the Rawalpindi lowered his binoculars.

"It's the Deutschland," an unhurried signal, "to the C-in-C."

The speaker, a tall, grey-haired man of 60, was Captain Edward Coverley Kennedy. The time was 3.51 on the afternoon of Thursday, November 23, 1939, a time worth remembering.

PAPER-THIN

AS the Scharnhorst, the massive white water piled high at her bows, smashed her way through the heavy seas and arrived in on him through the gathering gloom, Kennedy couldn't even have stopped to count the odds.

There were no odds. For what had he to offer against this immensely powerful...

was the Scharnhorst, not the Deutschland, but the mistake was one of academic importance only: the tightly identified as a German pocket battleship, or a German battleship... the leviathan... with 11-inch armour plate and nine 11-inch guns, backed up by a secondary armament of 12 5.9-inch guns, capable of delivering an 8,000lb broadside of armour-piercing steel and high explosive.

black, stone, and while were grim, long under a drab coat of battleship grey.

The lavishly furnished interior had been gutted, a main gun and deck fittings removed to make way for ammunition lockers...

Her hastily installed armament—eight old 6-inch guns, four ranged along either side—gave a total 40lb broadside in reply to the Scharnhorst's 8,000. Not that those light 100lb. shells could ever hope to penetrate the Scharnhorst's massive armour anyway.

★ ★ ★

And there had been no time, no option to make any alteration to her unarmoured sides and decks, quite apart from the fact that the hundreds of those was making her decision.

In terms of the penetrating power of modern armour-piercing shells, the hull of the Rawalpindi might as well have been...

...again to stutter out the command "Heave-to"...

...that he is faced with his moment of decision. And for Captain Edward Kennedy the moment of decision had come.

For himself and the 280 men under his command he had to make the decision whether they should live or whether they should die.

It was as simple, as clear-cut as that. And if he had come on the side of life that would have been held him because part from the hopelessness of the situation, Kennedy above all men owed nothing to the world. A Navy and an Admiralty who had ruthlessly, shamefully and utterly, shabbily and utterly... after as a result of another crucial decision he had been compelled to make 18 long years...

In 1921 Britain was torn by industrial strife and the Government called out the Services to deal with the impending trouble. Kennedy at Monmouthshire was one of the... pots and there Kennedy was sent in command of a battalion of naval reservists.

One morning his men refused to parade. Kennedy sought out and spoke to the ring-leaders of the men. He told them that this was tantamount to a mutiny, and was left to make his decision.

He could have made an out-run the Scharnhorst, but twice the height of the tip of the Rawalpindi's main-mast. Kennedy acknowledged the warning by turning even further away from the...

The captain groped through the smoke and flames . . . .

could neither out-fight nor out-run the Scharnhorst, but there were sheltering icebergs and fogbanks near by, and while there remained even one chance in a thousand he was...

...towards this haven. Almost at once the bitter truth struck him, but it was too late now. It would have been too late anyway.

The new arrival was, safely, repre...

....the glorious last hour of ' the Rawalpindi

IN PEACE: The Rawalpindi of palmy days, when she was a crack P. & O. liner plying between Britain and the Far East. She was a stately, luxurious ship—and one of the first to be converted to the role of armed merchant cruiser.

IN WAR: The fighting Rawalpindi. One funnel has been removed, she is painted a drab grey, and many of her deck fittings have been removed to make way for ammunition. But her guns are pitifully inadequate against enemy warships.

Only a handful of men lived at the end

We'll just fight them both, said the captain

© Beaverbrook Newspapers 1960

3

G.R. 4.

Any reply should be addressed to—
THE REGISTRAR GENERAL OF
SHIPPING AND SEAMEN
and the following reference quoted—

Cas.T.124.C.6.

Telegraphic Address :—
REGISTRAR SEAMEN (ALD) LONDON.
Telephone No. :—
ROYAL 5216 (4 lines).

GENERAL REGISTER AND RECORD OFFICE

OF SHIPPING AND SEAMEN,

TOWER HILL, LONDON, E.C.3. XJ.

12th January, 19 40

Dear Madam,

It is with very deep regret that I have to
inform you that it has now become necessary to presume
that your son, Cyril Edward Bettoney, (Asst. Steward)
lost his life when H.M. Armed Merchant Cruiser RAWALPINDI
was sunk in action with a German Warship on the
23rd November last.

This conclusion has been reached, and formal
presumption of death has now been made in view of the
fact that your son's name does not appear among those
of the few prisoners now known to have been taken by the
enemy and because the Admiralty are satisfied that no
further names will now be received.

Please let me express my sincere sympathy with
you in your sad loss, on behalf of the officers and men
of the Royal and Merchant Navies, the high traditions of
which your son has helped to maintain: and my
regret that your long period of anxiety should have
ended so unhappily.

I may, perhaps, add that if for purposes
connected with his estate you should require certificates
relating to your son's death, application should be
made to The Registrar General, General Register Office,
New Cumberland Hotel, North Parade, Blackpool, Lancs.

Yours sincerely,

Mrs S. Bettoney,
    64 Countessthorpe Road,
        South Wigston,
            Leicester.

REGISTRAR GENERAL.

as from Lytchetts
Farnham Common
Bucks

Jan: 5th

Dear Mrs Bellamy,

Please accept my
sincere sympathy in the sad loss
of your son. I met him several
times on board as he was my
husband's personal steward. He
was always so pleasant and so
obliging, and the last time the
ship was in the Clyde we had a
little lunch party, and he managed
everything so nicely - as I told
him afterwards. My husband
liked him so much.
In our sorrow we can take comfort
from the great pride they have left
with us. and I hope these words
of Admiral Horton may help you.
Yours sincerely
Rosalind Kennedy.

H.M.S. RAWALPINDI

an armed Merchant Cruiser which sank off the South-East Coast of
Iceland, on the afternoon of 23rd November 1939, after a naval
engagement with the German Pocket Battleship, *Deutschland* and
another German Warship, resulting in the loss of all but forty-three
of her Officers and Men, twenty-six of whom were taken prisoners
by the Germans.

" . . . she made a most gallant fight against overwhelming
odds and went down with colours flying." (*Admiralty communique*).

ROLL on, proud waves, and icy seas, roll on,
  Where *Rawalpindi* breathed her last. Tell forth
How she despised and scorned the Nazi wrath,
  Roll on, proud waves, where her proud sons have gone.

Tell how beneath the fading Arctic light
  This one-time liner fought with puppet guns
Deutschland, the steel-clad showboat of the Huns,
  The vaunted star of Nazi naval might.

Let there be no regret, nor tears be shed
  By those whose husbands, fathers, sons, have died,
Rather let gladness hearten them, and pride
  In knowing, loving, such immortal dead.

They fought against a foe whose strength whose speed
  Made murder out of honest battle, yet
Although their end they knew, gladly they met
  Defeat, and each man gloried in the deed.

Sailors of England's past, awake, arise,
  Nelson and Hawkins, Rodney, Hood, and Drake,
Grenville and Effingham, arise and take
  These valiant sailors with you to the skies.

Bear them aloft from the deep ocean-bed
  To rest in peace with those of former years
Who held the seas for England. England fears
  No mortal foe, whilst she has these, her dead.
       —LUDOVIC KENNEDY.

ORDINARY SIGNALMAN
GEORGE THOMAS EDWIN WALKER

George Thomas Edwin Walker was born in January 1921 and throughout his life was always known as Eddie. He was the son of Ernest Edwin and Lottie Hannah Beatrix Walker. He lived with his parents and brother Clifford at 27 Bassett Street, South Wigston, Leicestershire. The children attended Bassett Street School and enjoyed happy holidays at Scarborough. His father Ernest was employed at the Constone Cement Works in South Wigston and played football for Leicester City Football Club. His mother worked at Taylor's Dye Works on Saffron Road and Atkinson's Dyeworks in Canal Street, South Wigston.

Eddie left school at fourteen years old and worked for a time in a shoe factory in Leicester. He was laid off in the winter months after the spring styles were completed. He then tried his hand as a motor mechanic but the same situation arose in that trade when work became short.

In 1937 at the age of sixteen, Eddie decided to join the Navy. Land based at Chatham he began his training in seamanship before moving to Pembroke to train as a signalman. His first duty was on HMS Sheffield. He was later transferred to HMT Loch Doon in 1939 which was based at South Shields. The minesweeper commanded by Skipper G.H.A Thompson with fourteen ratings was soon reported missing. HMT Loch Doon was believed to have been exploded by magnetic mines off Blyth in the North Sea.

The official record states that George Thomas Edwin Walker lost his life on the 25th December 1939. (Christmas Day). He was eighteen years old. His name is commemorated on the Chatham Naval Memorial, Kent.

George Thomas Edwin Walker

Mr and Mrs Walker and their two sons

Mrs Walker - Mother

Excuse Short Letter.

22nd Aug.

SSX 23535
19 Mess
H.M.S Sheffield
c/o G.P.O. London

Dear Mam & Dad

I haven't had a
letter since the one on Thursday,
we only had that lot of mail
'cos' of the Plane, as we've been steam
-ing up an' down the North Sea since
last Monday. We're at Invergordon
now by rights we should be at
Hartlepool.

What I really want
to say is — do you reckon you
could let me have 25/- out of my
allotment as we've a kit inspection
coming off, and have a decent amount
of kit to get up to date. I'll let
you know more when we get your
other letter.

Love Ted.

H.M.S. SHEFFIELD

COPYRIGHT   WRIGHT & LOGAN SOUTHSEA

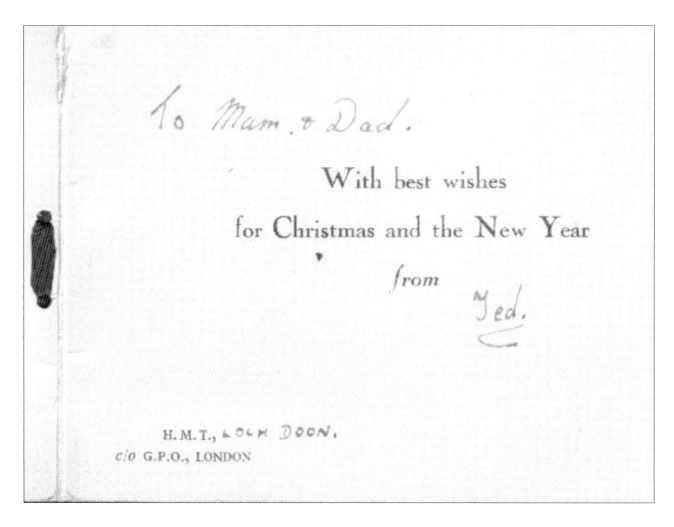

To Mam & Dad.

With best wishes

for Christmas and the New Year

from

Ted.

H.M.T., LOCH DOON,
c/o G.P.O., LONDON

27 Bassett St
South Wigston
Nr Leicester
Tuesday Dec 26th

Dear Ted
               Received your letter & card
yesterday, we were all very pleased with
the card, & we shall be better pleased
when we see you, Roll on January.
& By the way you must not ask
your girl down home yet, for one
thing you dont know wether you
will stick to her or wether she will
stick to you, if you are still going out
with her at Easter, she can come down
then & I shall be at home to look after
her, she could come then wether you
get leave or not. Well Ted I am glad
you got the cake & money O.K. we have
had a very quiet X mas at home, had
a nice turkey & plenty to eat & drink,

Page 127

Cliff been round Pete all the holiday
he is looking forward to you coming
home. Well Ted bring all the washing
you can carry – that will save you
when you get back, We shall set you
up with hair oil, soap, tooth paste etc
so dont buy any before you come
let us have a card if you can
before, to say when you are coming
the last bus leaves Leicester at 10-30
now Charles St a newarkes, Well Ted
I will have to close to catch the post –
   Look after yourself till we see you
  Best love from all at home Hannah

HMT Loch Doon

15 FEARED LOST IN NAVY SHIP

THE Admiralty announced last night that H.M. trawler Loch Doon, commanded by Skipper G. H. A. Thompson, R.N.R., was overdue and must be presumed as lost. The next of kin of the 14 ratings have been informed.

Their names are: Fred Atlass, engine-man; A. T. Cressey, seaman; James Humber, stoker; J. W. Kaveney, seaman; John Mercer, seaman; J. Milne, stoker; William Seymour, seaman.

R. V. Spice, leading seaman; E. Storey, seaman; L. P. Teesdell, seaman cook; Frederick Wadsworth, able seaman; G. T. Walker, ordy. signalman; Richard West, engine-man; and Christopher Wintenny, 2nd hand.

Wedding cake waiting . . . .

Daily Express Correspondent

HULL, Sunday.

ON the sideboard in the home of Nurse Ellen Houldridge in Hamlyn-drive, Hull, a wedding cake stands uncut.

It will be cut on Thursday —if Chief Engineer Fred Atlass of the minesweeper Loch Doon is safe after all.

The minesweeper has been given up by the Admiralty as lost with all hands.

But Nurse Houldridge clings to the hope that Chief Engineer Atlass will return in time for their wedding. She said today :—

"I still think he will come home. He may have been picked up by another ship.

"He has been shipwrecked several times before, and has always had luck with him."

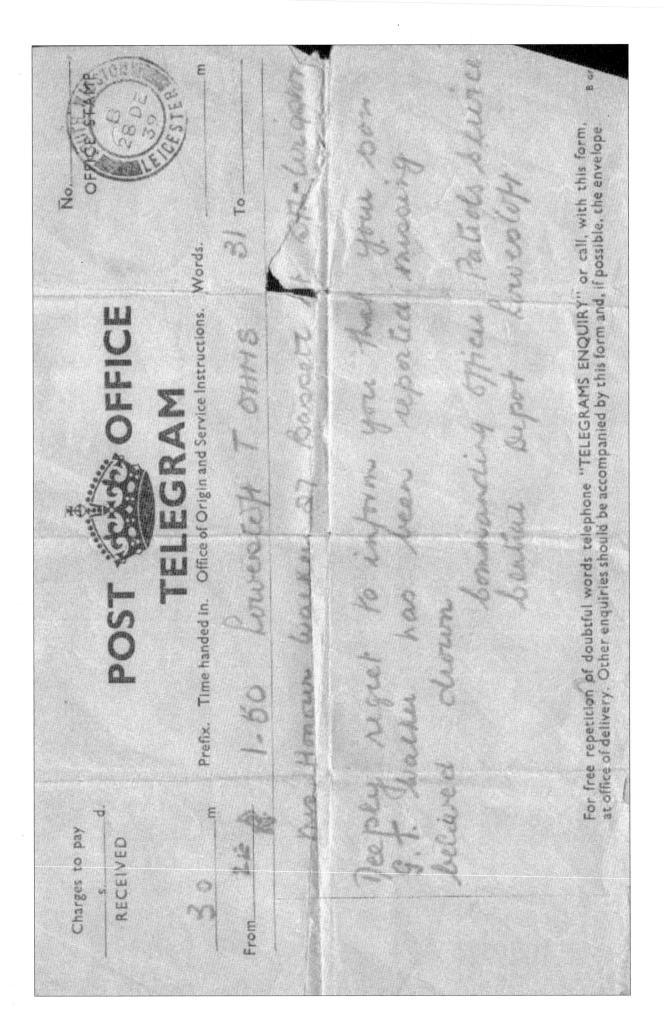

POST OFFICE TELEGRAM

Charges to pay

s. d.

RECEIVED

No.

OFFICE STAMP

LEICESTER

26 DE 39

Prefix. Time handed in. Office of Origin and Service Instructions. Words.

From 1.60 Lowestoft T OHHS 31 To

Mrs Harman Becher 27 Beaconsfield Aylwraam

Deeply regret to inform you that your son G.T. Harman has been reported missing believed drowned

Commanding Officer Patrols service Button Depot Lowestoft

BUCKINGHAM PALACE

The Queen and I offer you
our heartfelt sympathy in your
great sorrow.

We pray that your country's
gratitude for a life so nobly
given in its service may bring
you some measure of consolation.

George R.I.

Mrs. H. B. Walker.

ORDINARY SEAMAN
FREDERICK JAMES CLOSE

Frederick James Close was born on the 14th August 1920 in West Ham, London. He was the son of Henry Thomas Arnold and Winifred Selina Close. He was one of nine children having four brothers, Harry, Vince, Vic and Patrick and four sisters, Anna, Winnie, Doris and Teresa who died as a baby.

Frederick attended school at the Frederick Street School in Tidal Basin situated between CanningTown and Silver Town in London.

After leaving school Frederick worked at the Echo Battery Company in London before joining the Merchant Navy with his father in 1937. Frederick's father served in the Merchant Navy for forty two years. The family was a seafaring family with his two brothers, Vic and Vince in the Royal Navy, Vince serving twenty five years.

Frederick's family home in West Ham was destroyed by enemy bombing in 1940 forcing his family to take shelter in church halls in Chingford. After a short while they were moved again living in church rooms in Chigwell. Later the family was split as they were accommodated separately in private family homes in New Barnet. The youngest child Patrick spent three weeks in hospital suffering from pleurisy and pneumonia consequences of the poor living conditions.

Frederick James Close

Two of Frederick's sisters, Winnie and Anna and their families were then evacuated to South Wigston in Leicestershire where they settled into their new life on the Hooley Estate, now known as Lansdowne Grove. Winnie's husband James also serving in the Navy survived more than one torpedo attack.

The two sisters Anna and Winnie then found it possible to secure the house next door to them for their mother and other family members making it possible for them to leave London also. Patrick, the youngest brother attended the South Wigston Secondary Modern School for one year and was a keen member of the South Division of the Leicester Sea Cadets. In 1945 Patrick volunteered to join the Royal Navy following in the family tradition.

In 1941 Frederick was serving as an Ordinary Seaman aboard M.V. Zealandic, a 10,578 ton vessel of the Shaw Savill & Albion Company. The ship had sailed from Southampton and on Friday 17th January 1941 was south of the Westman Islands, Iceland, when she was torpedoed by U Boat 106 captained by Kpit. Jurgen Oesten. All seventy four lives were lost. Frederick was just twenty years old when he died.

Frederick James Close is commemorated on the Tower Hill Memorial which stands on the south side of Trinity Square Gardens close to the Tower of London. The memorial commemorates men of the Merchant Navy and fishing fleets of the First and Second World Wars.

Frederick James Close and Brother Victor

AIRCRAFTMAN EDWARD CHARLES (TED) HICKFORD

Edward Charles Hickford was born in 1915. He was the son of Owen Charles, a tanker driver and Ethel B Hickford. He lived at 59 Glen Gate, South Wigston, Leicestershire with his parents, brothers Frank and Harold and sister Gertrude. His paternal grandparents were Charles Owen and Susan Hickford. Charles Owen was employed as a butler to the brother of Lord Burghley, Henry Cecil, at Stocken Hall near Oakham in Rutland. He later owned a general store on the corner of Timber Street and Canal Street in South Wigston. Edward's maternal grandparents were named Clarke and were farmers at Countesthorpe in Leicestershire.

Edward Charles was known by his family as Ted and with his brothers attended Bassett Street School. Sadly, his sister Gertie was unable to attend for all of her short life she was ill. Gertie died when she was ten years old with heart problems.

As a young man Ted was employed as a draughtsman and worked for a company in Rugby in Warwickshire. He travelled to work every day on his motor cycle. He liked to play cricket and was a member of a local team.

Ted joined the Royal Air Force and served with 504 Squadron, Royal Air Force Volunteer Reserve, his rank being 2nd Class Aircraftman. He married Phyllis Green, a local girl and was only married a short time when at twenty six years old; on Saturday 5th April 1941, German bombs hit Exeter Airport. Ted was killed in the blast. His remains are buried in Countesthorpe Cemetery, Leicestershire.

Edward Charles Hickford (Ted)

Above: Cricket Team
Ted Hickford - Back Row - 4th Left

Left: Ted's Sister Gertie

Above: Ted's Grandparents
Sue and Charles Owen Hickford

Right: Ted's Niece, Nephew and Dog Tony

ABLE SEAMAN LEONARD ROY JARVIS

Leonard Roy Jarvis was born on the 18th May 1922. He was the son of Ernest Charles and Ada Hannah Jarvis. He was one of five children. His brothers were Walter, Desmond and Ernest and his sister was named Florence. The family lived in a house on 'The Bank' at Wigston Magna in Leicestershire close to Willett's Farm before moving to 49 Clifford Street in South Wigston. The older children attended Long Street School in Wigston Magna but when the family moved Desmond and Roy transferred to Bassett Street School in South Wigston. Later the family moved to Enderby in Leicestershire.

Roy, as he was known, always wanted to join the Navy and did so in 1938 when he was sixteen years old. Walter, his elder brother joined the Army and became a Major but Roy achieved his ambition beginning his naval career as a Devonport Rating. His training was taken at the Naval Barracks, HMS Wildfire.

Roy's first ship was a destroyer, HMS Janus but he was later transferred to the battle cruiser, HMS Hood.

Roy was nineteen years old when on Saturday 24th May 1941 HMS Hood was sunk in the Atlantic by the heavily armoured German battleship, Bismarck.

Able Seaman Leonard Roy Jarvis, is commemorated on the Portsmouth Naval Memorial, Hampshire, The memorial stands on Southsea Common overlooking the Promenade.

Roy's name is also inscribed on his mother's gravestone in Wigston Cemetery, Leicestershire.

HMS HOOD

PRIVATE WILLIAM HENRY HOPKINS

William Henry Hopkins was born in December 1918 five months after his father died of his wounds which he sustained in the Great War. His father also William Hopkins served with the King's Own (Royal Lancaster Regiment). He was forty two years old when he died on Friday 12 July 1918 and his grave is in Wigston Cemetery. Before his death he had lived with his wife Nellie and children at 15 North Street, Wigston Magna in Leicestershire but his family had originated from Mowsley End, Spa Lane, Wigston Magna.

William Henry lived with his mother, brother and sister Ethel and was known as Bill. He joined the Army and eventually served with the 1st Battalion, Leicestershire Regiment. He was twenty three years old when he was killed in action on Wednesday 10th December 1941. One can imagine the family's grief at the loss of the father in the First World War and the loss of the son in the Second.

William is commemorated on the Singapore Memorial, Kranji War Cemetery, Singapore. The cemetery is on the North side of Singapore Island overlooking the Straits of Johore.

William Henry Hopkins

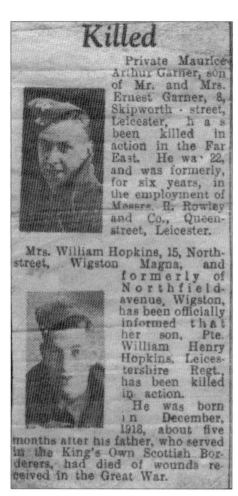

Killed

Private Maurice Arthur Garner, son of Mr. and Mrs. Ernest Garner, 8, Skipworth - street, Leicester, h a s been killed in action in the Far East. He wa; 22, and was formerly, for six years, in the employment of Messrs. R. Rowley and Co., Queen-street, Leicester.

Mrs. William Hopkins, 15, North-street, Wigston Magna, and formerly of Northfield-avenue, Wigston, has been officially informed t h a t her son, Pte. William Henry Hopkins, Leicestershire Regt. has been killed in action.

He was born i n December, 1918, about five months after his father, who served in the King's Own Scottish Borderers, had died of wounds received in the Great War.

Left;
Top Picture Maurice Arthur Garner
Below Picture William Henry Hopkins

Below;
Memorial Garden Singapore

ERNEST ROBERT GEORGE LEWIS

Ernest Robert George Lewis was born in 1918 and was the son of Walter Charles and Constance Lewis of Central Avenue, Wigston Magna. He had one brother named Walter Butlin Lewis.

Ernest attended Long Street School in Wigston Magna later progressing to Alderman Newton School in Leicester.

After leaving school Ernest was employed by the Post Office as an engineer which involved the erection of telegraph poles and wires.

By 1941 he was serving his country as a Sergeant Wireless Operator/Air Gunner, 70 Squadron with the Royal Air Force Volunteer Reserve. His marriage to Marjorie Hill lasted only one week before he was reported missing. Ernest, one of the crew of ten men; was flying in a Wellington Aircraft which was shot down at Martuba in Lybia on Saturday 13 December 1941. He was twenty three years old.

Ernest Robert George Lewis

Ernest is commemorated at Knightsbridge War Cemetery, Acroma, Lybia. Knightsbridge War Cemetery is situated west of Tobruk.

Ernest's brother, Walter Butlin, also served with the Royal Air Force as a Flight Sergeant. He was injured when a grenade was thrown into his face causing a brain injury. Walter spent several months in hospital in Edinburgh paralysed from head to foot and with gangrene setting in. Miraculously he did recover but the injury ended his war service as he became registered disabled.

His disability also ended his pre-war ambition to play football professionally when he had passed a trial with Leicester City Football Club. Walter was employed by Thorn Lighting of Leicester until he suffered a stroke and a heart attack. He died in 1961.

Ernest and Walter's mother Constance lost her son Ernest Robert in the Second World War and her brother Ernest Robert Butlin in 1917 in the First World War.

SERGEANT WALLACE HAROLD MACE WATTS

Wallace Harold Mace Watts was born on the 6th January 1922.   He was the son of Walter, a postman and Gladys Edith Watts of Leicester Road, Wigston Fields, Leicestershire.   He had one brother, Derek Charles, six years his junior who became a Petty Officer in the Royal Navy stationed at the RNAS Station in Singapore. He served on the Aircraft Carrier, HMS Unicorn.

Before joining the Royal Air Force, Wallace served in the Home Guard as a member of Number 7 Platoon, 'B' Company, 2nd (South) Leicester Battalion.

Serving with 220 Squadron Sergeant Watts was detailed for low flying attacks and was a Wireless Operator/Air Gunner.   His letters home to his parents give a vivid insight into the early days of his training.

Wallace married Mary Phipps of Wigston.   They had one son. Victor Wallace who was born only two weeks prior to his father's death. Home on compassionate leave, Wallace saw his son before returning to duty the following week.

Wallace was twenty years old when on Sunday 1st February 1942 the tail of his aircraft struck a tree and crashed in Ireland.   There were no survivors.

Wallace Harold Mace Watts, Sergeant W.Op. /Air Gnr. 220 Squadron Royal Air Force Volunteer Reserve is commemorated at Wigston Cemetery, Leicestershire.

Right; Wallace Harold Mace Watts

Top Left; Wallace Harold Mace Watts
Top Right; Wallace Harold Mace Watts with Friend Thomas Bull
Below; Wallace Harold Mace Watts and Wife Mary

Wallace Harold Mace Watts

1.

Dear Mam, Dad, and Derek,

Thanks for your letter received Friday morning. Well I've had one or two more flights since Monday. On Tuesday I went up in a "D. Havilland", I was over Leicester at 2-25 p.m. and we went on to Rutland afterwards, over Oakham, our pilot saw a Wellington bomber below us and we dived 5,000 feet to get level with him and then played at "follow the leader" for about half an hour. I did my last D/F exercise on the way back. On Wednesday I went up in a "Proctor", it's a small plane just big enough for pilot and wireless-operator and something like a "Spitfire". I did my first operational exercise in that and got good for it.

Page 145

On Thursday and Friday the weather was too bad for flying and it didn't clear up until this dinner-time (Saturday). I went up this afternoon in a "Proctor" again and I had the same pilot as before. When I'd finished my exercise he asked me if I wanted some tricks. First of all he dived to within twenty feet of the ground and chased some sheep across a field. Then he started rolling and banking over Lincoln. In fact he did everything with that plane but crawl down a manhole. I've got my photo's back but I don't think much to them myself, anyway I've enclosed two of them but if I get any better I'll send you one. We're flying again tomorrow morning (Sunday) at 8-0am. (no lay in).

Cheerio
Love
Wallace.

XXXXXXXXX
XXXXXXXX
XXXXXXXX

1209099, Sgt. W. Watts A.6,
c/o. Sergeants Mess,
R.A.F. Station, Silloth,
Cumberland, Sun. 6-9-41.

Dear Mam, Dad, and Derek,
                                    I'm sorry I
had to rush away so quickly
yesterday but I hadn't got much time.
I only had six hours in Leicester
and I was travelling for 16 hours.
I caught the 12-15 pm train at dinner
and got into Carlisle at 7-15 p.m.
Tell Derek I was sorry I didn't see him
again but I'll see him next time
I come. I've no idea when that
will be as we are short of
crews up here and the big?-pots
seem to think we don't need any
leave at all. We are starting on
"Lockheed Hudson's" tomorrow and also
starting night flying, tell Derek I'll
send him a photo of one if he
wants one. We should have been

flying today but it was cancelled and we had exams instead, morse 22 w.p.m. sending and receiving, Aldis lamp 8 w.p.m., and Wireless theory. Thanks for your letter and the tobbacco, that was welcome, I can't get it up here. Well it's time for bed now so I'll sign off now.

xxxxxxxxx   Cheerio,
                            Love,
                                Wallace.

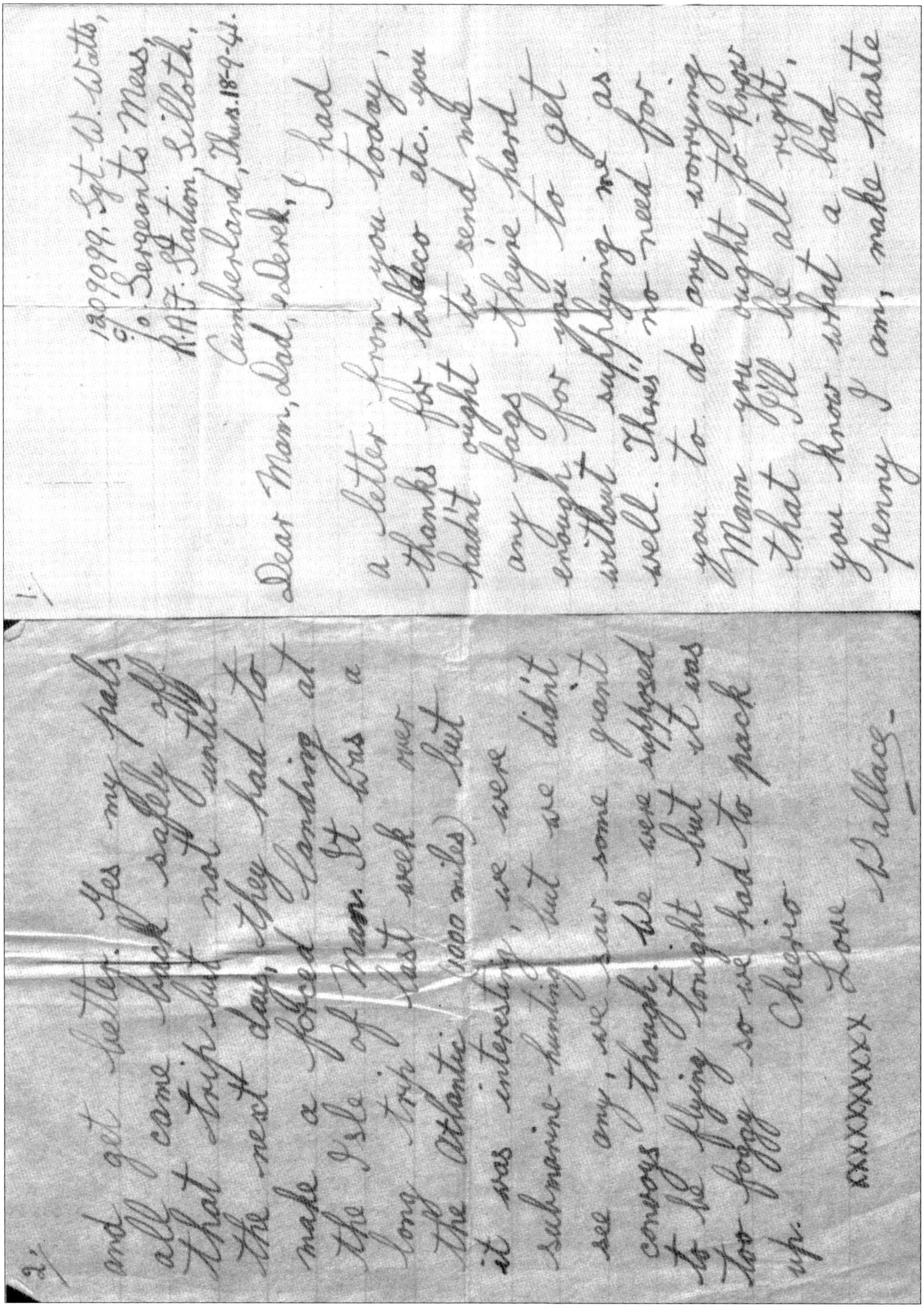

1.

1809099, Sgt. W. Watts,
c/o Sergeants Mess,
R.A.F. Station, Silloth,
Cumberland, Thurs. 18-9-41.

Dear Mom, dad, +Derek, I had
a letter from you today,
thanks for tobacco etc. you
hadn't ought to send me
any fags they're hard
enough for you to get
without suffering me as
well. There no need for
you to do any worrying
Mom you ought to know
that I'll be all right,
you know what a bad
penny I am, make haste

2.

and get better. Yes my pals
all come back safely off
that trip but not until
the next day, they had to
make a forced landing at
the Isle of Man. It was a
long trip last week over
the Atlantic (1000 miles) but
it was interesting, we were
submarine-hunting but we didn't
see any, we saw some giant
convoys though. We were supposed
to be flying tonight but it was
too foggy so we had to pack
up. Cheerio
Love Wallace -

xxxxxxxxx

GVI RI

This scroll commemorates

Sergeant W. H. M. Watts
Royal Air Force

held in honour as one who
served King and Country in
the world war of 1939-1945
and gave his life to save
mankind from tyranny. May
his sacrifice help to bring
the peace and freedom for
which he died.

SERGEANT ROBERT ALFRED BELL

Robert Alfred Bell was born on the 12th May 1910 at Notting Hill in London. He was the son of Robert Calder Bell born in Manchester and Christina Bell born in Chelsea

Robert was living in Horsewell Lane, Wigston Magna, Leicestershire as a young man and worked in the yarn room for W H Holmes and Son, a hosiery factory in Newton Lane, Wigston Magna.. He was an active social events organizer for the firm and also arranged dances to raise money for charitable causes.

Robert married Lena Jones in February 1930 and they had two daughters, Christina and Margaret.

At the outset of the war in 1939 Robert volunteered to join the Royal Air Force. He was stationed at the Royal Air Force Headquarters at Cranwell in Lincolnshire and became a Sergeant and Wireless Operator/Air Gunner. His duties took him to Lossiemouth, Pempray, Blackpool and Prestwich in Scotland. His family were able to spend a few weeks with him in Scotland.

Robert aged thirty one years was reported missing during operations on Friday 13 March 1942. His name is commemorated on the Runnymede Memorial, Surrey. The memorial overlooks the River Thames on Coopers Hill between Windsor and Egham and commemorates over twenty thousand airmen.

Sergeant Bell's autograph book survives poignantly signed by his comrades.

Robert Alfred Bell

Above: Lena Bell and daughters Christina and Margaret
Bottom Left: Robert Alfred Bell
Bottom Right: Robert Alfred Bell, Wife Lena
and Daughter Christina

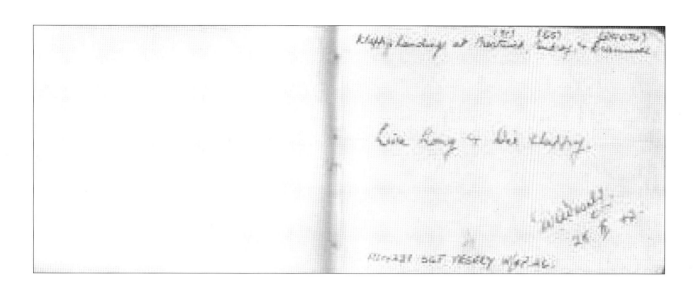

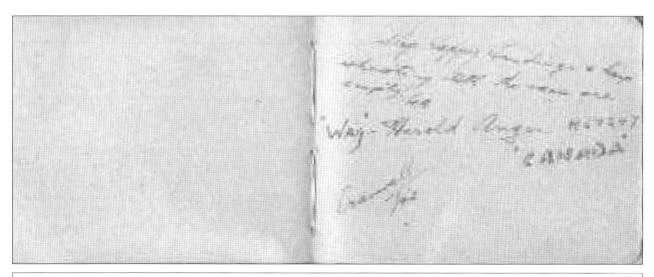

Pages from Bob Bell's autograph book (1942)

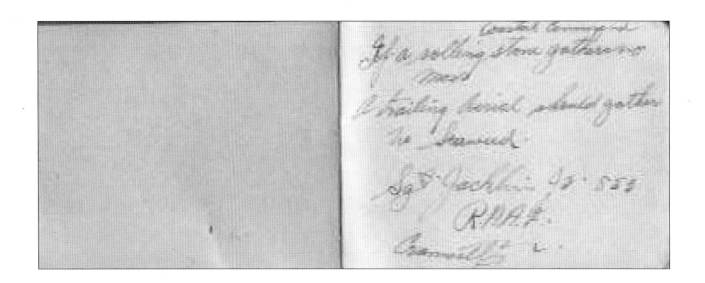

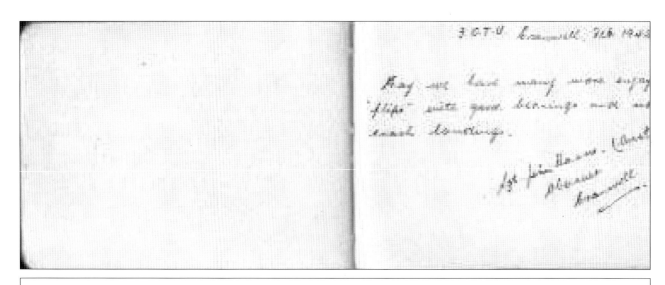

Pages from Bob Bell's autograph book (1942)

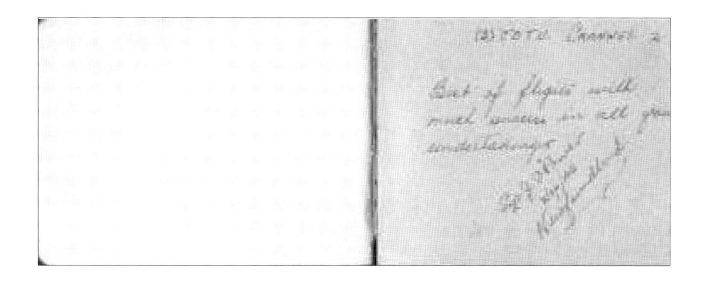

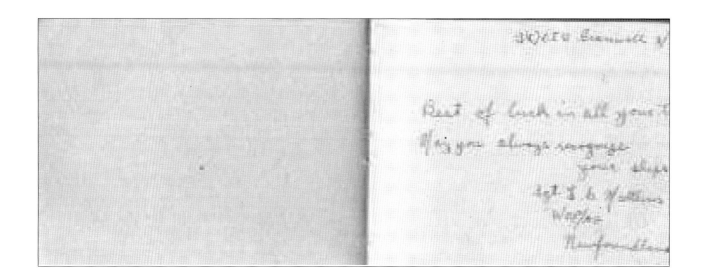

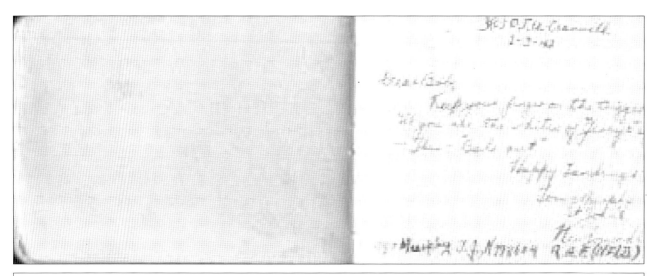

Pages from Bob Bell's autograph book (1942)

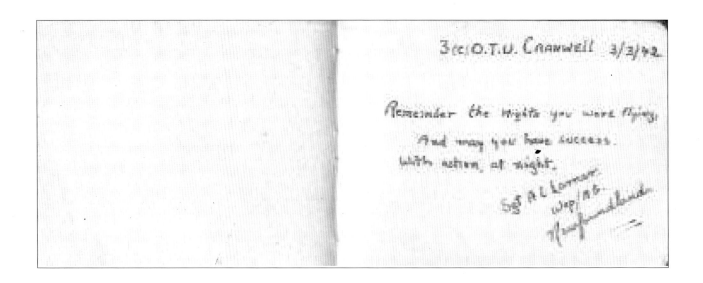

3cc O.T.U. Cranwell 3/3/42

Remember the nights you were flying,
And may you have success.
With action, at night.

Sgt A L Lorman
Wop/Ag
Newfoundland

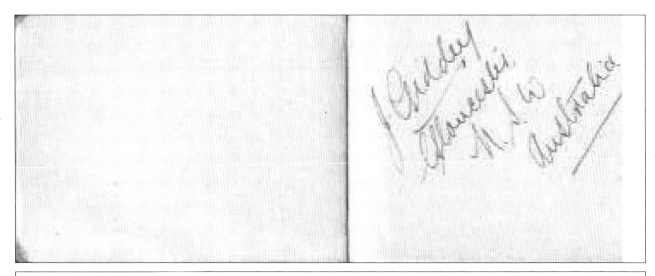

Pages from Bob Bell's autograph book (1942)

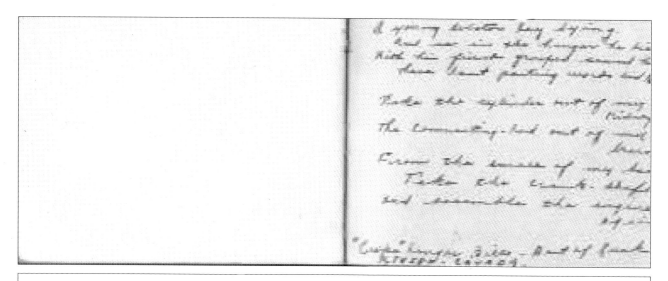

Pages from Bob Bell's autograph book (1942)

SERGEANT ALFRED JOHN LEAVER

Alfred John Leaver was born in 1922, the son of Frederick Clifford and Blanche Muriel Leaver. John and his brother Don lived with their parents in Cooks Lane, Wigston Magna. It is thought that Alfred Leaver originated from Portsmouth and met his future wife Blanche in London. Blanche had been sent by the Wigston firm of Two Steeples to work in their London office. On their return to Leicestershire Alfred worked as a clerk for the auctioneers, John Shakespeare.

As a young man John Leaver belonged to the Mallamews Drama Society which was connected to All Saints Church in Wigston Magna and the last show he performed in was in the part of a policeman.

During the war John was serving in the Royal Air Force Volunteer Reserve and was based at Lossiemouth on the north east coast of Scotland. He was a sergeant with 217 Squadron. He is well remembered in his uniform and as a lovely young man. The last time he was seen by family members he had come to say goodbye before returning to base. Shortly afterwards on Sunday 15th March 1942 John and the whole crew died when their aeroplane crashed into the sea eight miles south of the Isle of May. The accident happened on their return from a mission over Germany. John was twenty years old. His grave is in Wigston Cemetery.

On the anniversary of John's death each year, his mother was visited by her niece Ruth Horlock, nee Sibson, an occasion which was never overlooked and one which was very important to Blanche.

Sergeant Alfred John Leaver

ABLE SEAMAN THOMAS EDWARD WRIGHT

Thomas Edward Wright was born on 6 June 1910 in Morpeth, Northumberland. He was the son of William James and Sarah Wright. Thomas was one of five children having a brother George, sisters Nancy and Minnie and step sister Maud.

Thomas moved to Leicester as a young man to look for work. He was a skilled plasterer by trade and at one time worked on the 'Royal Oak' public house at Wigston Fields. Whilst living in lodgings, the landlady being Mrs Wood, in Humberstone Lane in Leicester; he met his future wife, Doris. Doris lived with her mother in Gipsy Road at that time. Doris originated from Empingham in Rutland and had been employed in service in a manorial house in Bourne in Lincolnshire. She had also worked for Miles Timber Merchants.

After Thomas and Doris's marriage at the Leicester Registry Office in Pocklington's Walk they had three sons. They were named Ronald, Anthony and Brian.

In 1937 the family moved from Leicester to South Wigston living at 7 Florence Avenue on the Hooley Estate, {now Lansdowne Grove}. They were only the second family to occupy a house there. Two years later in 1939 war was declared and as the war intensified empty houses on the estate were allocated for people being evacuated from London. Doris and Mrs Rene Norton were employed to clean the houses before the evacuees moved in. The two ladies also worked for many years at the Secondary Modern School on Blaby Lane (now the High School on St. Thomas Road} in South Wigston.

Being associated with building, Thomas's trade as a plasterer had been declared a reserved occupation so Thomas unable to enlist for war service in his own region volunteered in another town to join the Royal Navy. He went in on the 23rd July 1940. In order to raise his pay he completed a training course in gunnery and when guns were fitted to merchant ships Thomas was posted to merchant shipping as well. He served as an Ordinary Seaman, an Able Seaman and Acting Leading Seamen. His service is recorded as –

HMS VICTORY 1	-	23 July 1940 – 31 August 1940
HMS FLYING FOX	-	1 September 1940 – 27 September 1940
HMS CORACERO	-	28 September 1940 – 27 January 1941
SAN CIRILO	-	28 January 1941 – 23 June 1941
TORDENE	-	24 June 1941 – 30 March 1942
Defensively Equipped Merchant Ships – Avonmouth –		
	-	31March 1942 – 27 April 1942
SS EMPIRE MICA	-	28 April 1942 – 29 June 1942

Tommy as he was known by his family came home to South Wigston on his last leave in 1942 and spent all his money on gifts. He bought a new coat for his wife who was delighted with it and presents for his three children before returning to duty on SS Empire Mica taking with him all the photographs of his wife and children which he attached to the inside lid of his suitcase. He wanted to see their faces each time he opened it. Brian, the youngest child was found crying on South Wigston Park after his father's departure. His brand new football had burst.

Six weeks later on Monday 29 June 1942 at the age of thirty two years Thomas was killed in action on the tanker SS Empire Mica. On the return trip of her maiden voyage, twenty one miles from Appalachicola; she was hit by two torpedoes from a German U-boat. There was a very small number of survivors which included the captain.

Thomas is commemorated on Portsmouth Naval Memorial on Southsea Common.

SS Empire Mica, coral encrusted, lies in one hundred feet of water at Pensacola, North West Florida.

PRIVATE OLIVER RAYMOND FROST

Oliver Raymond Frost was born in Nottingham on the 3rd October 1917.   He was the son of Thomas Ernest Edwards Frost and Sarah Elizabeth Frost. He was the third child of seven and lived with his parents, brother, Frederick Ernest, and sisters, Vera Irene, Gladys, Doris, Ivy Doreen. and Madeline. His father was a builder in Nottingham and the older children attended school there. Later the family moved to South Wigston in Leicestershire and lived in the large four bedroomed house next to the park on Blaby Road.

Raymond's father worked as a general foreman in South Wigston for the firm Ernest Hooley; the builders of the Lansdowne Grove houses known as the Hooley estate.   The younger children attended the South Wigston schools.

Oliver Raymond, known as Ray, worked with his father as a builder for Ernest Hooley too.   He was at one period working on the library at the Saffron Road Crossroads known locally as the Pork Pie Library due to it's unusual shape.

Two months after the outbreak of war Ray married Ivy Irene Medhurst, a South Wigston girl. The wedding took place on the 11th November 1939 at St. Thomas the Apostle Church in South Wigston. They had one son, Michael.

Ray joined the Army and as Christmas 1942 approached he desperately wanted to see his baby son's face on his first Christmas morning.   His leave began on Christmas Eve and Ray made the journey home. Later on Christmas Day, Ray having no transport due to the holiday period walked back to his unit.   He never saw his son again.

On Thursday the 8th April 1943 while serving with the 1/4th Battalion, Hampshire Regiment Ray was killed.   His grave is at Enfidaville War Cemetery, Tunisia.

The cemetery marks the end of the Eighth Army's advance across North Africa and men from the final battles are buried there.

Oliver Raymond Frost's Wedding to Ivy Medhurst

GUNNER DAYKIN MOORE

Daykin Moore

Daykin Moore was born in 1913 and was one of three children having a brother, Jack and a sister Kathleen. The children attended Bell Street, Long Street and the National School in Long Street. Their father Bertram Moore originated from Aylestone in Leicestershire but their mother died in the 1940s.

Before the war Daykin was a knitter with a hosiery firm in Wigston Magna. His wedding to Margaret, an Aylestone girl, took place at Aylestone Church. Daykin's father and sister lived at Bull Head Street, Wigston Magna, Leicestershire.

Daykin served with the 148 (Bedfordshire Yeomanry) Field Regiment, Royal Artillery. On Saturday 11th September 1943 at the age of thirty years he died in a Japanese prisoner of war camp. He was first buried in the jungle but later his body was moved to Kanchanaburi War Cemetery, Thailand.

Daykin Moore is also commemorated on the memorial in the Oadby and Wigston Council Chamber. Leicestershire.

Left: Daykin and Margaret
at Aylestone Church
Right: Daykin Moore and
David Smith (Luton)

SQUADRON LEADER
ALEXANDER FREDERICK CHISHOLM DFC

Alexander Frederick Chisholm was born in 1912. His father, Alexander Samuel Chisholm was the station master at the little country railway station at Welton situated north of Daventry in Northamptonshire. His father was originally from Bletchley in Buckinghamshire.

Alexander spent his childhood in Welton with his family. He had one brother, Donald and a sister Helen who later made her home on Saffron Road in South Wigston, Leicestershire.   Alexander attended the Warren Road School in Rugby in Warwickshire.

Before joining the Royal Air Force in 1937 Alexander was employed in the motor industry in Coventry.   His two sons, Alexander and Ian were born in 1937 and 1938 respectively.

Alexander Frederick Chrisholm

Alexander was serving with the Royal Air Force, Air Bomber 83 Squadron when he was killed on Tuesday 23rd November 1943 at the age of thirty one years.

Alexander is commemorated at Berlin 1939-1945 War Cemetery, Brandenburg, Germany. Approximately 80% of the total number of men buried at this cemetery are airmen who lost their lives in raids over Berlin and towns in Eastern Germany. The remainder are men who died in prisoner of war camps in the regions and of some who were forcibly marched into Germany from camps in Poland in front of the advancing Russians. There was fierce fighting in the cemetery area between the Germans and Russians during the Battle for Berlin.

AIRCRAFTMAN 2nd CLASS
HARRY KENNETH MUNDIN

Harry Kenneth Mundin was born in 1921 the son of Ernest George and Mary Jane Mundin. He was one of six children. His brothers and sisters were, Horace, Ronald, Clifford, Beatrice and Phyllis. The family lived at 69 Glen Gate, South Wigston, Leicestershire and the children attended the South Wigston schools some of them progressing to the grammar schools in the city. The boys were very keen motor cyclists.

Harry joined the Royal Air Force Volunteer Reserve. He was twenty two years old when he died on Monday 29 November 1943. Harry's name is commemorated on the Singapore Memorial, Singapore. The memorial commemorates the names of over twenty four thousand soldiers and airmen of the Commonwealth and Empire who have no known graves. The airmen died during operations over the whole of southern and eastern Asia.

Harry Kenneth Mundin

CAPTAIN WILFRED AUSTIN BRAY

Wilfred Austin Bray was born on the 9th October 1916 at 47 Canal Street, South Wigston, Leicestershire. He was the son of Ernest and Emily Bray who named him after his two uncles, Company Sergeant Major Austin Bray and Wilfred Brown.

Wilfred lived with his parents and was educated at the Bassett Street Schools. In 1938 the family moved from Canal Street to 43 Marstown Avenue in the village.

Widely read in current affairs Wilfred was also an accomplished pianist and interested in philately.

Before joining the armed forces Wilfred was employed as a traveller with the firm David Sandeman & Co (Leicester) Ltd of Welford Road, Leicester.

On joining the Army Wilfred was originally posted to the Welsh Fusiliers achieving the rank of corporal before being selected for officer training. On being commissioned he elected to join the 2/5 Battalion, Leicestershire Regiment because of his family connections with that regiment.

Whilst serving with the 2/5th Battalion Leicestershire Regiment in Italy he stepped upon a mine. Wilfred was taken to hospital where he died on Saturday 4th December 1943. He was twenty seven years old.

Wilfred is buried in Minturno War Cemetery, Italy. Minturno is situated north of Naples and the cemetery lies close to the western end of the German 1943/1944 winter line known as the Gustav Line. In 1944 heavy casualties were incurred when crossing the Garigliano River on their advance towards Rome.

Left: Mr and Mrs Bray Mother and Father. Right: Wilfred Austin Bray

Page 168

LANCE CORPORAL FREDERICK WILLIAM WESSON

Frederick William Wesson was born on the 12 October 1917. He was the son of Frederick William and Ellen Wesson of 76 Clifford Street, South Wigston, Leicestershire. Frederick's sisters were Edna, Freda and Alma. The children first attended Bassett Street School and Frederick who moved across the road to the boys school later left in 1931 at the age of fourteen years.

Fred, as he was known to his family, had his first job with the well known grocery shop, Worthington's at Oadby. Changing his employment later he worked for Will's Grocers at Evington.

Frederick's war service was with the Royal Army Service Corps taking him to India, Palestine, Syria and Madagascar. He was also involved in the evacuation of Dunkirk. Frederick had served for four years.

In Italy, on Wednesday 29th December 1943, whilst collecting mail with another soldier; the truck they were travelling in was blown up. The other soldier lost his legs but Frederick was killed. He was twenty six years old. His body was first buried in a garden and later moved to the Sangro River War Cemetery, Italy.

The cemetery contains many men who lost their lives in fierce fighting on the Adriatic front, men from three Indian Divisions, New Zealand Divisions and British escaped prisoners of war who died from exposure trying to reach the British lines.

Frederick William Wesson

Frederick William Wesson

S/Sergeant L/Cpl WESSON F.W.
Comp. PLATOON
17th INF BDE COY RASC
C.M.F.
Sun 28.11.43.

Dear Edie and all

Have just received your letter, (card) dated, (sorry there's no date on it) anyway I have just received it and can you imagine my surprise at hearing from you, it was certainly a shock but I must say very nice to hear from you, I thought you had forgotten all about me, and how is everyone at home all O.K. I hope, as this leaves me the same.

I was rather suprised to hear that Geo, was working at Nuneaton, whats he doing now? I am glad you liked the photos I sent Mam, as you say I am not looking too bad and I musn't grumble, but I shall certainly be glad to be back home again, as its getting to much of a joke now.

So you would like some Oranges

eh! I only wish I could send some, but there's not much hope, you say after all the travelling about I have done I wont want to settle at home again, well sometimes I wonder, I think I could manage it alright though.

And I'm all for the Dancing, but shall want a little tuition before going so you had better arrange it, theres one thing though, I have started to swim, if you want a few lessons.

I see you are getting in to bad habits as well, started smoking eh! what is it a craze at home now, I'm going to stop when I come home, cant afford to hand them round like that, as Geo, started as well? tell Brian to carry on saving the ends they might come in usefull one day.

You say you will have to come out here to have some decent weather well I shouldn't bother just at present

wait till summer comes, as its real winter here, and mighty cold as well, in fact I believe its worse, than Wigston Wake weather, still who cares we keep getting a little nearer home, the trouble is Jerry's lost is running pumps now, and having to walk back, which is not as quick as they might go.

Well I haven't much more to say just now, so write again soon and give my love to all
Yours as Ever
Fred

P.S. See you under the Missilto Bough at Xmas
Cherio and
Boon. Note

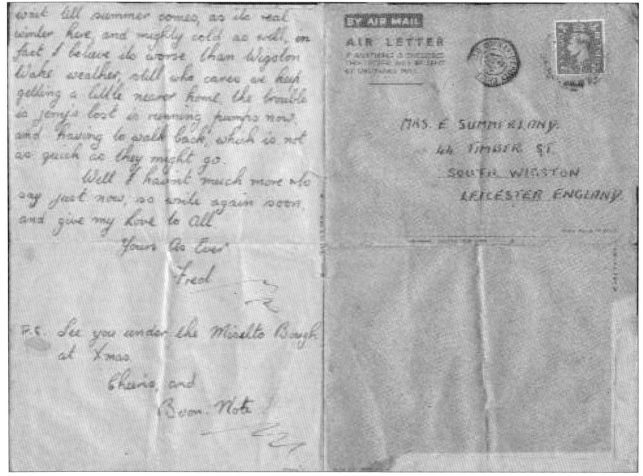

BY AIR MAIL
AIR LETTER

MRS. E. SUMMERLANY.
44 TIMBER ST.
SOUTH WIGSTON
LEICESTER ENGLAND.

2/14096. L/CPL. WESSON. F. W.
COMP. PLATOON.
IX th INF. BDE. COY. R.A.B.C.
C. M. F.

28.12.43.

Dear Edna, + all,

Many thanks for your kind letter, which I received yesterday, very pleased to hear you are well, as these few lines leave me the same.

Just bearing up after the Xmas attacks, and its been a struggle as well. I didn't have to had a time, what I remember of it, (not much) thats with drinking Vino, try it some time? it put me to sleep for nearly fourteen hours, and what a head when I did wake up, don't talk to me about it.

I must say it was a wonderful Xmas dinner, that was served up, but I didn't get hodged up as you call it, after all we only had Turkey. Roast Pork, tatees and mashed study, peas and pudding, finishing up with drink and sweets as you'd get jealous.

What sort had a time did you have? I hope it was as good as possible, has Cicon had his Piano that Elsie told me about?

I hope you didn't finish up with a thick head.

You ask if I have got over the shock of hearing from you, ha, and I hope you will carry on with this good work as it is nice to hear from you, I shall have to see what I can do as regards getting on the front rank next time there is any parade, takit, so keep working.

So you wouldn't leave the old home town, its surprising how you miss it when you are away for a time, it keeps calling me back, I would love to be there again, but it wont be long, so stand back.

I'm afraid, if you don't like more than five inches of water, its not much good me giving you time to attend, some of them quick, but may, we could try it in the bath, or maybe its because you a back full, that put you off?

I say! you a bit of an optimist, aren't you, trying to get fags out of Dad, what next, it sounds as if you are doing a steady line, I could send you some "Desert Players" if they would help, they might put you off though, there dicoly I am not going to give up the habit, or I can see it will cost me a small fortune.

I hope you are still sticking the berries on the Mistletoe, it wont be for long, but of course I could manage without it, after all, you know me? nice shy lad, (errr

did you say something), anyway its nice to know someone is proud of us.

Hope you got brest burrants on. O.K. its a good job we don't have to use them on Jerry, it would be a sad day it would be a case of people not, want not pick it up and it will him

Well the end of this page is in sight and I haven't very much more to say. So I don't suppose you will mind if I sign of now so its nice to hearing from you again soon

Lots of Love to All, and Good Luck
Yours as Ever
Fred

P.S. Tell Ca that "Buon Note" is Italian for "good-night", not what he was thinking? Brian should have quite a few fag-ends for my pipe now, you have started smoking thats if he is still saving them for me.
amore la tutte.
Fred

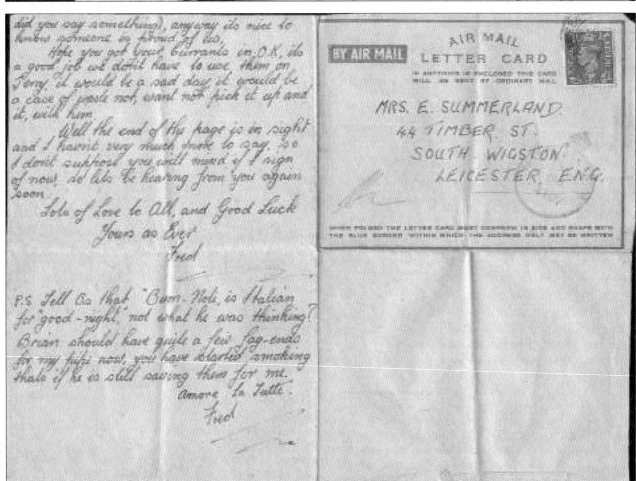

BY AIR MAIL   AIR MAIL LETTER CARD

MRS. E. SUMMERLAND
44 TIMBER ST.
SOUTH WIGSTON
LEICESTER. ENG.

Left: Frederick William Wesson Grave
Right: Holy Sepulchre Church

Page 174

SOUTH WIGSTON N.C.O. KILLED IN ITALY

MR. and MRS. FREDERICK WESSON, of Clifford-street, South Wigston, have been officially informed that their only son, L/Cpl. Frederick Wesson, RASC, has been killed in the fighting in Italy.

L/Cpl. Wesson, who had been in the Army for over four years, was in the evacuation from Dunkirk, and had also L/Cpl. Wesson served in India, Palestine, and Persia.

He was in the Madagascar, Irak, and Sicily campaigns. Aged 26, he was formerly employed by Wills, grocers, Evington-road, Leicester.

KILLED IN ACTION

Lance-Corpl. Frederick William Wesson, R.A.S.C., only son of Mr. and Mrs. Frederick Wesson, of Clifford-street, South Wigston, has been killed in action.

In the Army for over four years, Lance-Corporal Wesson was in the Dunkirk evacuation, and also served in India, Palestine, Syria, Madagascar, Persia and Sicily. He was 26.

Top Left; Mrs Wesson Frederick's Mother
Top Right and Middle Left; Newspaper Clippings of Frederick William Wesson
Below; Mr Wesson Frederick's Father

CORPORAL GEORGE CHARLES BIRKIN

George Charles Birkin was born in 1910. He was the son of Alfred Ernest and Sarah Jane Birkin of Wigston Magna, Leicestershire. George's father was a sailor for twenty years and originated from Burton on Trent. George was one of seven children having two sisters and four brothers. His brothers were Edwin, Percy, Wilfred and Ernest. Ernest was injured by a steam powered flour wagon outside the Star and Garter public house in Wigston Magna. He lost an arm and one leg in the accident.

George married Elsie May Martin and they lived in North Street in Wigston Magna with their daughter Peggy and three sons, John, Brian and Terrence. The family suffered great sadness when Peggy died at the age of seven years with diphtheria. Elsie's father had been killed in the First World War by a sniper and her brother was killed in the Second World War in Sicily.

Before George's war service began he worked as a long distance lorry driver for Walker's transport at Blaby in Leicestershire. Later his employer became Lady Hall.

George joined the Royal Army Ordnance Corps serving with 5 Base Ordnance Depot in Egypt. He was thirty four years old when he died in Egypt on Wednesday 7th June 1944 the day after D Day. He is commemorated at Tel El Kebir War Cemetery, Egypt.

Tel-El-Kabir lies north north east of Cairo and south of Port Said and the War Memorial Cemetery is east of the railway station at Ismailia (Sweet Water) Canal.

In 1939-1945 a great ordnance depot was established at Zagazig with many workshops for the repair of armoured cars and other weapons of war. A hospital centre was also included there.

(see Gunner Leonard Kemp, cousin)

George Charles Birkin

Top Left; Comrades in Egypt - Top Right; Burriel in Egypt
Bottom; Pictures of Egypt

Terry, John and Brian Birkin
Sons of George Birkin

CHIEF STOKER ATHOL EKINS BIGGENDEN

Athol Ekins Biggenden was born in 1895 in Easington, Hull. He was the son of John Miller Biggenden and Alice Maud Biggenden. His brother was Walden John Biggenden. The family worked on the Coastguard service and the lifeboats and Athol and Walden joined the Royal Navy as boy sailors. Both boys completed twenty two years service with the Royal Navy. At the outbreak of war in 1939 both boys were recalled for service.

Walden married to Olive was living in Hull when the news of his death reached the family. Walden John Biggenden, Chief Stoker HMS Hood, died at the age of fifty two years. On 24 May 1941 the German battleship, Bismarck, attacked and sunk HMS Hood in the Atlantic.

Walden John Biggenden is commemorated at Portsmouth Naval Memorial, Hampshire.

Athol Ekins Biggenden left Hull and moved to Wigston Magna, Leicestershire. After his twenty two years service with the Royal Navy, he was employed with the Post Office. He married Jessie Bishop and lived at 25 Victoria Street.

Like his brother, Athol was a Chief Stoker in the Royal Navy and on his recall to service joined the crew of a former British Rail cargo ship; the trawler serving as an auxiliary net layer, HMS Minster.

On Thursday 8th June 1944 at the age of forty nine years, as part of Operation Neptune, a phase of Overlord, the Normandy Invasion, Athol died when HMS Minster was reported lost after hitting a mine near the Cardonet Bank.

He is commemorated also at Portsmouth Naval Memorial, Hampshire. The memorial overlooks the promenade on Southsea Common. His name also appears on the memorial in the council chamber of Oadby and Wigston Borough Council as does his cousin's. (See Daykin Moore. 1943)

Athol Ekins Biggenden

Athol Ekins Biggenden and his Bride

Family wedding party

JOHN PATRICK MURRAY

John Patrick Murray was born in Park Road, South Wigston, Leicestershire in 1923. He was the eldest of eight sons of John Walter and Dorothy Emma Murray. John's five sisters completed the family of thirteen children. His seven brothers were Ralph, Peter, Charles, Kenneth, Donald, David and Michael. Sadly, Ralph died when he was six months old. His five sisters were named Winifred, Theodora Mary, Patricia, Kathleen and Margaret. Margaret died when she was just two weeks old.

As a child John attended Bassett Street Infants School in South Wigston following on to the Intermediate School, also in Bassett Street, until he was fifteen years old. By this time the family had moved to Station Street in the village. During his schooldays he was a keen all round sportsman. He gained his Central Schools Certificate of the East Midlands Educational Union in 1937 in general subjects which included, English, Arithmetic, Drawing of Plant Form, French, Geography and Mathematics. John was considered to be exceptionally bright but his family could not afford to let him continue his studies at University.

Life was hard for the family and two of John's sisters, Winifred and Pat, moved in with their Aunt Mag and Uncle Tom Twigger in Leopold Street. John remained at the family home until they eventually moved to Braunstone. John then moved in with his Aunt Nel and Uncle Mick in Irlam Street, South Wigston.

On leaving school John worked at a hosiery firm in Oxford Street in Leicester but in 1940 when he was seventeen, he joined the Royal Air Force Volunteer Reserve and was sent for his military training to Blackpool in the North of England.

On Sunday 11 June 1944 Sergeant W/Op (Air) John Patrick Murray, 460 (R.A.A.F.) Squadron was killed when his plane was shot down in France. John was twenty one years old and the only Englishman with an Australian crew. An attempt was made to force land the plane but in vain as the aircraft hit an electrical installation. John was reported missing for six months.

John was commemorated at Ellancourt in France before his remains were moved. He is permanently commemorated at Viroflay New Communal Cemetery, Yvelines, France. Viroflay is a small town close to Versailles.

Left: John's Father age 44
John Walker Murray
7 September 1940

Right: John with four of his
brothers and sister
Theodora Mary

St. Mary's Church Sunday School, South Wigston.

Top to bottom: John Paterick 2nd Row 4th left. - Winifred Standing 2nd Row 1st left.

Theodora Mary 2nd Row 3rd Right. - Charlie Sitting 1st Row 3rd Left Peter 1st Row Sitting 7th Left

Top Left; Comrades
Top Right; John Paterick Murray
Below; D Squadron - Blackpool
John Paterick Murray, 3rd on the right, 2nd Row down

EAST MIDLAND
EDUCATIONAL UNION

CENTRAL SCHOOLS' CERTIFICATE.

1937

THIS IS TO CERTIFY

that................ JOHN PATRICK MURRAY .... has passed

the Central Schools' Examination of the

East Midland Educational Union, in the

.... GENERAL .... Group, the subjects of examination being

English, Arithmetic, Drawing of Plant Form, French, Geography

and Mathematics.

H. Percival President.

L. Hitchman Secretary.

Above; Viroflay - France

Right; Ellancourt - France

PRIVATE LEONARD TAYLOR

Leonard Taylor was born in 1916 in Aylestone, Leicestershire. He was one of three children having a brother Sidney and a sister Rose. Sadly his mother died when Leonard was quite young and his sister died at a young age too.

Leonard moved to South Wigston in Leicestershire and married Kathleen Mary Lee. They had one daughter, Ann. It is believed that Leonard was employed in the boot and shoe industry.

Leonard was serving with 1/7 Battalion, The Queen's Royal Regiment, (West Surrey) when he died on Wednesday 14th June 1944. He was twenty eight years old.

Leonard is commemorated at the Bayeux Memorial. The memorial commemorates over eighteen hundred men who died in Normandy and have no known graves. Men of the land forces of the British Commonwealth and Empire who fought in Normandy, at the Normandy landings and in the advance to the River Seine.

Private Leonard Taylor

LANCE CORPORAL
KENNETH ARTHUR MEASURES

Kenneth Arthur Measures was born on the 28th April 1920. He was the son of Archibald Stanley Heard Measures and Minnie Measures of Wigston Fields, Leicestershire formerly of the Orchards in Wigston Magna. Kenneth's father was employed by Cook and Hurst of Wigston as a hosiery mechanic and worked well into his seventies. Grandparents Arthur and Julia Measures lived at 28 Long Street, Wigston Magna. The three little cottages which included number 28 have long since been demolished.

Kenneth was one of three children having two sisters, Iris and Dorothy. The children attended Long Street Junior School and Kenneth was a member of the school cricket team. He left his education at the age of fourteen years.

After leaving school Kenneth was employed by the building firm George Duxbury and served an apprenticeship for carpentry and joinery. Beginning in 1934, his day release each week would take him to the Leicester College of Art and Technology in the Newarkes. It was there that he successfully achieved his City and Guilds certification with a First Class grade. His mother collected his certificate as by the time it was issued in 1940 Kenneth had received his call up papers for war service.

On Tuesday 1st August 1944, whilst serving with the 7th Battalion, Leicestershire Regiment in Burma, Kenneth died of pneumonia. He was twenty four years old.

Kenneth is commemorated at Digboi War Cemetery, India. Digboi is in the north eastern state of Assam on the Burmese border and a military hospital was established there.

Top Left; Kenneth Arthur Measures
Bottom Left; Full Platoon Chindits

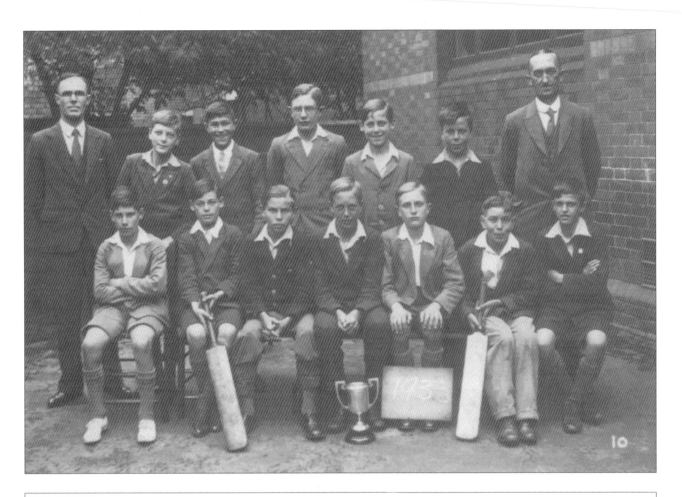

Above; Sportsmen of church of England junior school - Wigston
with Mr Harold and Mr Broughton (Kipper) Ken Measures top left.

Below; Ken Measures top right

PRIVATE ALBERT GEORGE JONES

Albert George Jones was born in 1923. His parents were Albert and Catherine Lilian Jones. Albert's father, a former London policeman, was employed as a manager at a cold storage depot in Clarkes Road in Wigston. The family lived at 3 Manor Street, Wigston Magna, Leicestershire.

Albert first attended Bell Street school in Wigston Magna later transferring to the school in Long Street. He left at the age of fourteen years and began his working life in engineering. His career was cut short when he received his call up papers for war service in 1941. He was just eighteen years old.

While serving with the 6th Battalion, Green Howards, (Yorkshire Regiment) Albert was killed on Wednesday 9th August 1944. He was twenty one years old. Albert is commemorated at the Banneville-La-Campagne War Cemetery, Calvados, France.

Banneville-La-Campagne is a village in Normandy and the cemetery is situated between Caen and Pont I'Eveque. It contains graves of men killed during the capture of Caen in July 1944 to August 1944 when the Falais Gap was closed and the allied forces were preparing to advance beyond the River Seine.

Albert George Jones
Aged 10 years in 1933, with Bob the dog
3 Manor Street, Wigston Magna

STAFF SERGEANT
THOMAS WILLIAM MAYS

Thomas William Mayes was born in 1920. He was the son of Arthur William and Eleanor May Mays of 20 Healey Street, South Wigston, Leicestershire.

It has not been possible to locate any members of Thomas's family but a report by the Leicester Mercury 17 October 1944 gives an insight to the facts of the day and fortunately provides a photograph of Thomas.

TRANSCRIPT

'Staff Sergeant Mayes, a glider pilot, of the Army Air Corps, is announced missing, believed a prisoner of war. His mother lives at 20 Healey Street, South Wigston. He has served over four years and was formerly with Cascelloid. Ltd.'

The records published by the Commonwealth War Graves Commission now show that on Monday 18 September 1944, Staff Sergeant, Thomas William Mays, 1st Wing, Glider Pilot Regiment, A.A.C. died at the age of twenty four years.

Thomas is commemorated at Arnhem Oosterbeek Cemetery, Netherlands.

On the 17 September 1944 the British 1st Airborne Division began landing west of Arnhem in order to capture and hold the bridges over the River Rhine as part of 'Operation Market Garden'.

Thomas William Mays
The Leicester Mercury
Tuesday 17th October 1944

LIEUTENANT
ERNEST JOHN MOWL

Ernest John Mowl was born on the 2nd April 1911 in Nottingham.   He was the eldest son of Frank Wilkinson Mowl and Ellen Mowl.   His brothers were Arthur Sidney and Joseph William and his sister was Annie, known by the family as Peggy.   Ernest was twelve years old when his father, a coachman, died in 1923.   His mother then took the decision to move the family to South Wigston in Leicestershire.   Their new home was established at 43 Fairfield Street.

Ellen Mowl soon became well known in South Wigston as the district nurse working for the local doctors and tending families in the village especially delivering the new born babies into the community. Many people today will remember Nurse Mowl.

Ernest and his brothers and sisters attended the local schools but Ernest soon wanted to join the Royal Navy. As a boy sailor his harbour training and seamanship began at Chatham. Records from 1926 to 1932 list, Education, Gunnery, Torpedo and Field Training as part of his tasks. Ships for training and duty included, Benbow, Repulse, Ganges, Canterbury, Pembroke, Royal Oak, Cycloss, Insbrook, Cleopatra, Ark Royal, and Renown.

Ernest was discharged from the Royal Navy at the age of twenty one years distinguishing himself as Able Seaman.

Back at home Ernest joined the Leicester City Police Force. He became an active member of police social activities too becoming keenly involved in the drama group, the cricket team and the football team, his position being that of goalkeeper. It wasn't long however before PC Mowl was proving to be a great asset to the force in his day to day role as a police constable. The Leicester Mercury reported on his enormous bravery on more than one occasion.

On Saturday 24th April 1937 PC Mowl was seen by a large crowd close to the Walnut Street canal

bridge to jump from his cycle, throw down his helmet, clear two iron paling fences and slither down a steep bank into the canal to save a boy who had been fishing from drowning. The rescue was carried out fully clothed in seconds. It was described later as one of the smartest rescues imaginable.

A month later PC Mowl was making the headlines again. Whilst on point duty in May at the junction of Hinckley Road at the height of busy traffic he was dragged fifty yards by a bolting horse attached to a dray, along Braunstone Gate. Witnesses saw PC Mowl jump at the reins to stop the runaway horse as it careered towards him and it was described later as a 'wonderful bit of gallantry'. As goalkeeper for the Leicester City Police X1 the newspaper reported that 'never has he made a finer save'. Some time afterwards at a meeting of the Watch Committee, Alderman W E Wilford presented PC Mowl with a bravery award. In addition, Ernest travelled to London where at Buckingham Palace he proudly received the Police Medal for Gallantry from King George V1.

Ernest completed six years service with the Leicester City Police Force before deciding to embark on a business career with the Prudential Assurance Company. He was not with the company long when he was called to serve his country at war. Because of Ernest's experience in police work in civilian life he was appointed to the Military Police Service.

On the 18 April 1940 Ernest married Iris Mary Danvers at Aylestone Parish Church. In 1942 their daughter Judith was born.

On Monday 9 October 1944 in thick fog in France, Ernest died in a motor accident. He was thirty three years old.

Lieutenant Ernest John Mowl, General List, is buried in Kortruk (St Jean) Communal Cemetery, Kortrijk, West Vlaanderen, Belgium.

Left; Ernest John Mowl
Below; Ernest's Gunnery Class Inspection

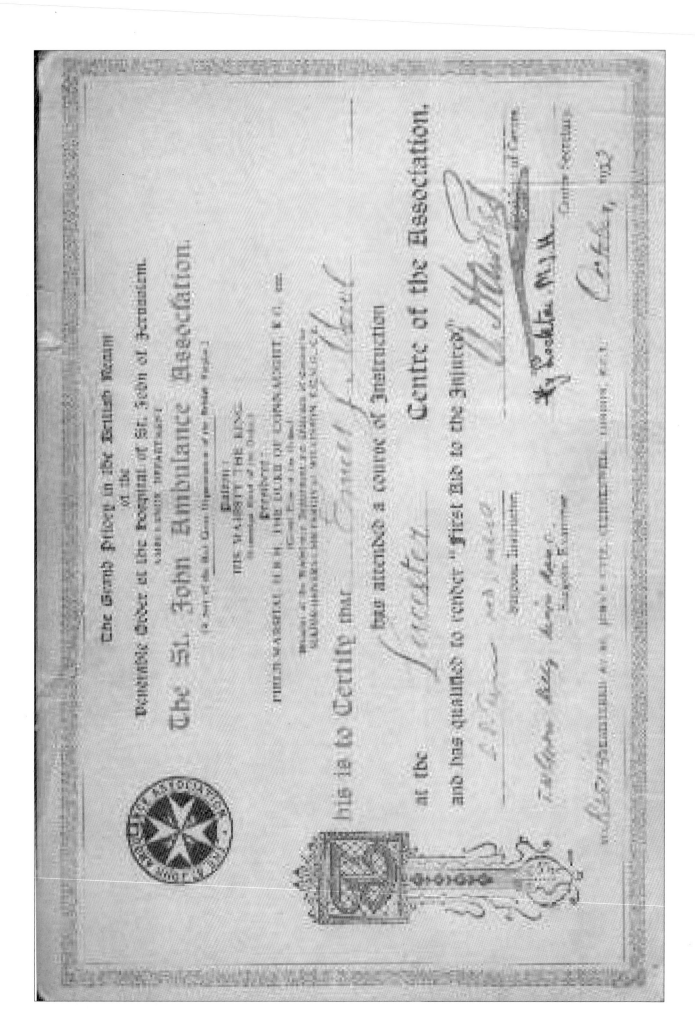

The Grand Priory in the British Realm
of the
Venerable Order of the Hospital of St. John of Jerusalem

The St. John Ambulance Association

(A branch of the Order Department of the Order Chapter)

Patron:
HIS MAJESTY THE KING
Sovereign Head of the Order

President:
FIELD MARSHAL H.R.H. THE DUKE OF CONNAUGHT, K.G., etc.
Grand Prior of the Order

This is to Certify that   Ernest J. Wood

has attended a course of instruction

at the   Leicester   Centre of the Association,

and has qualified to render "First Aid to the Injured"

Surgeon-Instructor

Surgeon-Examiner

President of Centre

Centre Secretary

October, 1932

Ernest John Mowl

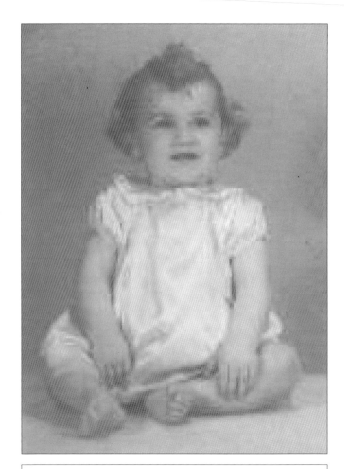

Judith Mowl - Ernest's Daughter

Parish Church - Aylestone
Ernest John Mowl marris Iris Mary Danvers
Extreme Right Ernest's Mother South Wigston's District Nurse Mowl

Above; Leicester City Police Team
Below; Ernest John Mowl - Fairy Queen at Police Concert - Leicester Isolation Hospital

Page 199

Top; Police Black and White Minstrel Show
Below; Leicester City Police Dramatic Society

THE LEICESTER MERCURY, SATURDAY, 24th APRIL, 1937

Don't be Vague—
ASK FOR
Haig
Obtainable also in small sizes

LARGEST NET READER SALE
EXTRA SPECIAL

Leicester Mercury

Your LOCAL Evening Newspaper · The Paper Everybody Reads

Estab. 1874 (Registered as a Newspaper)   SATURDAY, 24th APRIL, 1937   ONE PENNY

THE INSTITUTION FOR THE B
Assists the Sightless of all ag
and in all circumstances
"FROM THE CRADLE
TO THE GRAVE."
Over 800 Registered
Benefits Last Year over £16,0
SUBSCRIPTIONS, DONATIO
LEGACIES   Urgently Requir
50, GRANBY ST., LEICESTE

SMART CANAL RESCUE

Footballer-P.C. Dives To Save Boy

LAD BROUGHT OUT IN FEW SECONDS

Newcomer To Leicester Who Had Been Fishing

A LARGE crowd of people watched a dramatic rescue by a policeman of a ten-year-old boy struggling in the canal, close to the Walnut-street bridge, Leicester, this afternoon.

EYE-WITNESSES described it afterwards as one of the smartest rescues imaginable. Only a matter of seconds after he had jumped from his cycle, Police Constable F. L. Mowle, of 18, Mavis - avenue, off Heyworth-road, Narborough - road, was swimming with the exhausted boy to the side.

To reach the canal side and dive in, he had to clear two iron paling fences and slither down a steep bank.

He effected the rescue fully clothed, only bothering to throw down his helmet.

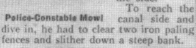
Police-Constable Mowl

Police-constable Mowl is the goalkeeper for the Leicester City Police football team which last week won the Leicestershire Thursday Cup.

(CONTINUED ON PAGE TWELVE)

KENNETH STRIPLING

'Plane Crashes On Railway

A single-seater R.A.F. aeroplane from North Weald aerodrome, piloted by Flying-Officer Frank White, crashed on to a railway line at Colchester to-day during a routine flight.

The pilot was unhurt. Railway traffic from Clacton and Bri...

Medal For Brave City Constable

Runaway Stopped At Great Risk

POLICE CONSTABLE EDWARD MOWLE, a member of Leicester City Force, received a bravery award at a meeting of the Watch Committee last night for stopping a runaway horse.

Alderman W. E. Wilford, chairman of the committee, made the presentation and Police-constable Mowle was commended for his bravery at the risk of his own life.

The incident occurred on Saturday, May 2, about 12.30 p.m., when the lunch time traffic was at its height. The horse, which was attached to a dray, bolted from the vicinity of Beasonsfield-road and dashed down Narborough-road towards the busy junction, where Police-constable Mowle was on point duty.

P.c Mowle

Gauging the distance, he flung himself at the reins, while people watched from doorways into which they had rushed for safety.

The constable was dragged for about 40 yards down Braunstone-gate, clinging to the animal before he was able to bring it to a standstill. He received slight injuries to the leg.

Police-constable Mowle is the City Police F.C. goalkeeper.

CITY POLICE TEAM.—Back row (left to right): Peplow, Eadie, Frost, Reed, Taylor. Seated: Mowle, Moore, Wright, Smith, Butcher, May.

LEICESTER P.C.'s HEROISM

THE bravery of P.c. Jack Mowl, of the Leicester city police force, was discussed at last night's meeting of Leicester Watch Committee.

Six weeks ago he rescued a child from

P.C. Mowl.

drowning in the canal and a fortnight ago, only a few days after returning to duty from sick leave, he stopped a runaway horse and dray in Western-boulevard after being dragged 50 yards by it.

It was felt that some special recognition should be made of the gallant police constable's efforts, and inquiries are to be made as to what can be done beyond the award of the customary bravery certificate.

CITY CONSTABLE'S GALLANTRY

Receives Police Medal From the King

MR. G. W. BRAKE, of Leicester, went to London on Wednesday to be invested by the King with the O.B.E. This he received in the New Year's Honours for his work as Divisional Inspector in the Ministry of Health.

P.C. Mowl

Police Constable E. J. Mowl, of the Leicester City Force, recipient of the King's police medal for gallantry, was invested at Buckingham Palace on Tuesday. Within a year he stopped two runaway horses in Leicester and rescued a boy from drowning.

Police-constable Mowl had breakfast at Scotland Yard, and was accompanied to the Palace by an officer from the Yard. Before he entered he saw Gracie Fields leave after receiving her honour.

The preliminaries and investiture took nearly an hour. Mr. Mowl, in full uniform, waited his turn, and on his name being called, a clasp was fixed to his coat and he was ushered into the room where the King was. The scene was one of great brilliance.

His Majesty placed the medal on the clasp on the constable's coat, shook hands with him, and said he was pleased to present the medal for such gallantry.

P.C. Dragged 50 Yards By Bolting Horse

AMAZING ESCAPE IN STOPPING ANIMAL: CROWD SEES DARING DEED

AT THE HEIGHT OF THE MID-DAY TRAFFIC IN BRAUNSTONE GATE, LEICESTER, TO-DAY, A POINT-DUTY POLICE CONSTABLE LEAPT AT THE REINS OF A RUNAWAY HORSE AS IT PASSED HIM, AND WAS DRAGGED 50 YARDS BEFORE HE MANAGED TO BRING THE ANIMAL TO A STANDSTILL.

THE horse, attached to a dray, bolted down Narborough-road. Police Constable Mowl was directing traffic at the junction of Hinckley-road when he saw the animal coming towards him.

An eye-witness stated afterwards that no one attempted to stop it, but scores of people shouted to the constable.

The constable appeared to prepare himself to jump, several seconds before it reached him, and then he made a dive for the reins.

His left hand caught the reins, and he was carried, clinging to the horse, fifty yards along Braunstone-gate before the frightened animal came to a standstill.

People Flee to Shops

"It is a miracle that the constable was not badly hurt," this eye-witness stated. "And certainly someone else would have been hurt or killed if he had not managed to stop it. It was a wonderful bit of gallantry."

There were crowds of people about at the time, the factories having just closed.

As the horse and dray tore along the road people scattered, some running into shops in case it should mount the pavement.

Motorists drew in hurriedly to the side of the road.

No damage was done to person or property, however, though the horse had approached one of the most congested parts of the city when it was brought to a stop. Its driver was nearly half a mile away, up Narborough-road.

P.C. Mowl is goal-keeper for the Leicester City Police XI. Never has he made a finer save! Quite a number of people went up to shake hands with him afterwards.

Page 204

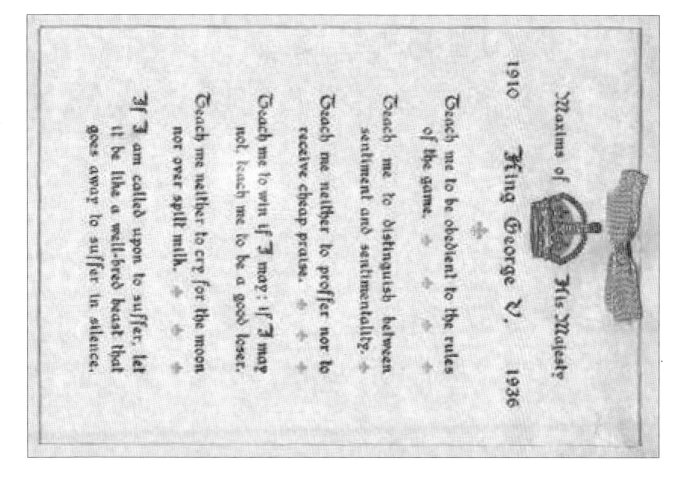

Maxims of His Majesty

1910   King George V.   1936

Teach me to be obedient to the rules of the game.

Teach me to distinguish between sentiment and sentimentality.

Teach me neither to proffer nor to receive cheap praise.

Teach me to win if I may; if I may not, teach me to be a good loser.

Teach me neither to cry for the moon nor over spilt milk.

If I am called upon to suffer, let it be like a well-bred beast that goes away to suffer in silence.

Local Men In The Casualty Lists

THE LEICES

KILLED.

Mr. and Mrs. G. A. Smith, of 101, Cossington-road, Sileby, have been notified that their son, L/Cpl. Dennis Smith, has been killed in action in N.W. Europe. He was employed at Messrs. Rowland Wilson, Seagrave-road, Sileby, before joining up.

Mrs. Iris Mowl, of 45, Fairfield-street, South Wigston, has received news that her husband, Lieut. Ernest John Mowl (C.M.P.), has died from injuries received in a motor accident while on duty in North West Europe. Previously to joining the Army five years ago, he was employed with the Prudential Assurance Co. in Leicester.

Mr. and Mrs. Pegg, of 57, Dunton - street, have been informed that their eldest son, Cpl. J. Pegg, who was with the 1st. Air borne Division, has been killed in action. He also served in India, Sicily and Italy. He was 22. His wife lives in Pontypool, South Wales.

L.A.C. Ronald F. McAllen (R.A.F.), 22, whose wife lives at 18, Dunbar - road, Leicester, and parents at 12, Westmeath-avenue, has been killed on active service. Before joining the R.A.F. three years ago, he was employed with his father at the Welded Shoe Co. Oliver road, Leicester.

Barwell. He was employed by G. Ward and Co., Barwell before joining the Forces two and a half years ago.

Mr. and Mrs. Hughes, of Brookslane, Whitwick, is reported killed in action in Italy. He had been serving for 4 years, and previously worked at Messrs. Whitwick Colliery, Coalville.

Mrs. R. Adcock, of 62, Aberdford, Coalville, has received news that her husband, Guardsman Reginald Adcock (30), was killed in action in Italy last February. He joined the Army seven years ago.

Pte. Leonard Massey (22, who lived with his grandmother at Ratby, been serving for four years. Before the war he was in business as a boy three years of age.

REPORTED DEAD

Pte. L. Birch (21), whose mother lives at 3, Ulmber-crescent, Braunstone, Leicester, was reported missing, North Central Mediterranean Forces. Now comes the report that he is dead.

MISSING

Pte. Charles Grogan, Army Air Corps, son of Mrs. and the late Mr. Grogan, of Victoria-road, North Leicester, is reported missing at Arnhem.

An old boy of Harrison - road School, he has been in the Army for two and a half years.

Mrs. James, 63, The Newry, Leicester, has been notified that her eldest son, Sergt. A. James

CORPORAL HAROLD WHAIT

Harold Whait was born in 1913 in Leicester. He was the second son of Jabez Henry and Mabel Whait. Harold's elder brother was named Exton and his younger brother was Alfred. Sadly, the children's father Jabez died when they were young boys. The family moved to South Wigston and lived at 20 Leopold Street.

Harold and his brothers all attended the South Wigston schools. On leaving school Harold at first was employed by the firm Bruce and Son. It was an Elastic Web Factory in Garden Street in the village. Ernest later joined his two brothers at the hosiery manufacturers of HGH Peck working on knitting machines.

The three boys were all keen members of the South Wigston Mutual Cricket Team and for many years Harold's brother Exton was the captain.

In July 1939 Harold married Margery Smith at the Congregational Chapel on Blaby Road in South Wigston and after their wedding the couple moved to Alderleigh Road in Glen Parva less than a mile away.

The marriage was interrupted by the war and Harold joined the Army. Serving with the 1st Battalion Leicestershire Regiment Harold died on Saturday 21st October 1944. He was thirty one years old.

Harold is commemorated at Geel War Cemetery, Geel, Antwerpen, Belgium.

In September 1944 in Geel British troops encountered some of the heaviest fighting since leaving Normandy.

Harold Whait

Top Left; Harold Whait
Top Right; Alfred Whait
Left; from Left to Right
Exton Whait,
Harold Whait
and Alfred Whait

Above; Harold Whait and Margery Wedding

Below; Harold (Second from left) with conrades

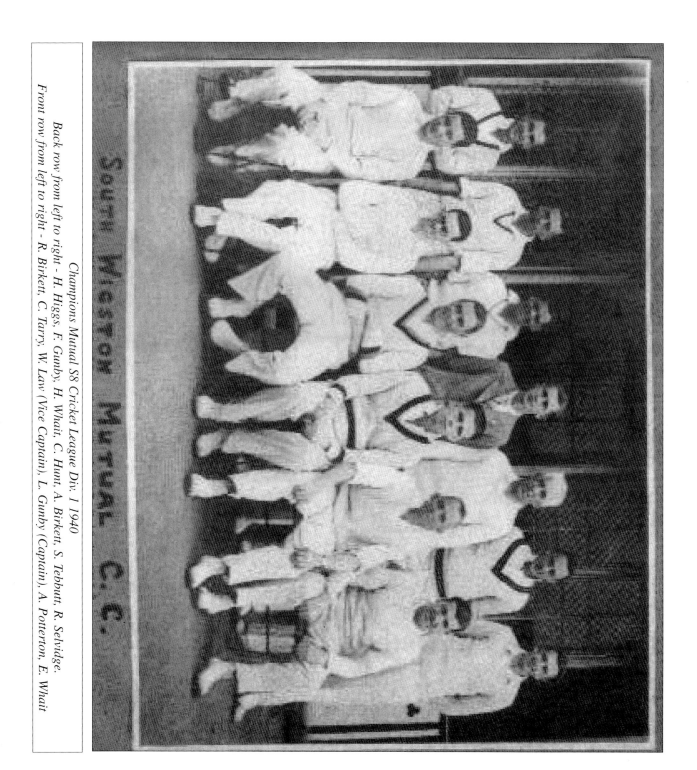

Champions Mutual S8 Cricket League Div. 1 1940

Back row from left to right - H. Higgs, F. Gunby, H. Whait, C. Hunt, A. Birkett, S. Tebbutt, R. Selvidge.

Front row from left to right - R. Birkett, C. Tarry, W. Law (Vice Captain), L. Gunby (Captain), A. Potterton, E. Whait

PRIVATE JOSEPH WILLIAM HALL

Joseph William Hall was born in 1925. He was the son of Mr and Mrs L Hall living at 54 Glen Gate, South Wigston, Leicestershire. Joseph's mother died from tuberculosis when Joe was a baby and he and his father known as Percy shared rooms with his Uncle George. Joe and his father lived in the front two rooms whilst George lived at the back until they moved next door to number 52.

Joe attended Bassett Street School in the village. His father used to take him and his school friend Clifford Elliott who also lived in Glen Gate out on many day trips to Wicksteed Park in Kettering, Northamptonshire. This would be a real treat as Wicksteed Park was a magical place for children with a boating lake and miniature railway.

On leaving school Joe was employed for a short period by the Co-operative Society in the butchers

shop in Dunton Street in South Wigston. He later worked for the hosiery manufacturer J Glover based in Canal Street in the village. His job was to operate a machine stitching fancy tops to boys three quarter socks. This was known as Top Heading.

Joe was inevitably called up for war service and was attached to the 1st Battalion, Royal Berkshire Regiment. He was taken prisoner of war by the Japanese in Burma where he worked on the notorious Burma Railroad. On Saturday 10 March 1945 Joe died. He is commemorated at Taukkyan War Cemetery, Myanmar. The war cemetery is outside Yangon, formerly Rangoon. Myanmar, (Burma) once part of British India was occupied by the Japanese from 1942 to 1945.

Joseph William Hall

Above; Joe Hall (left) and Clifford Elliott (right) at Wicksteed Park

61 SQUADRON R.A.F.
MARCH 1945

FLIGHT SERGEANT RALPH TAYLOR

Ralph Taylor was born in May possibly in 1913 in Wigston Magna, Leicestershire. His elder brother was named Frank. Their parents owned the fish and chip shop which was situated between a little row of cottages opposite the Horse and Trumpet on Bull Head Street.

Ralph attended the local school in Wigston Magna and won a scholarship to a grammar school. He was unable to take up his place as his parents were not able to afford the annual fee needed.

Ralph's marriage to Edith Marjorie Smith at Saint Thomas's Church in South Wigston was thought to have taken place in December 1937. Their three children were Graham, John and Patricia. Sadly, John died from pneumonia when he was only a few months old.

Living in Healey Street, South Wigston, Leicestershire, Ralph was a master plasterer and at one period worked his skilled art on the vast interior of the Grand Hotel in Granby Street, Leicester. In addition, he volunteered for the fire service and was accepted. The fire station was at that time situated in Bassett Street the premises extending on to Countesthorpe Road in South Wigston.

Because of a major building programme in the 1930s plastering was a reserved occupation in the 1940s. Ralph and some of his fellow volunteer fireman also volunteered to join the armed services and were readily accepted.

Ralph was serving with Air Bomber 61 Squadron, Royal Air Force Volunteer Reserve. He was killed on Wednesday 21st March 1945. He is commemorated at Durnbach War Cemetery, Bayern, near Munich, Germany.

LANCE BOMBARDIER
WILLIAM DOUGLAS BENNETT

William Douglas Bennett was born in 1917 in Frederick Street, Wigston Magna, Leicestershire. He was the son of John T Bennett and Nellie Bennett and he was known by his family as Doug. He had one sister named Kathleen.

Doug attended the Bell Street Infants School later moving to Long Street Junior and Senior School to complete his education.

On leaving school Doug was employed as a counter man at the firm of Wigston Hosiers in Bell Street.

On 23rd September 1939 Doug married Kathleen Joan Pepper of Queen Street, Oadby, Leicestershire and began his married life at Queen Street. They had one daughter named Janet Anne.

William Douglas Bennett

Doug joined the Royal Artillery in 1939 and saw action at Dunkirk. Doug was then posted to Burma and Ceylon.

Whilst serving with the 115 Field Regiment, Royal Artillery, Doug after being shot contracted malaria. He was twenty eight years old when he died on Friday 20th April 1945.

Douglas is commemorated at Maynamati War Cemetery, Bangladesh. Maynamati is situated between Dhaka and Chittagong.

William Douglas Bennett with Comrades Taffy and Ben

SERGEANT BERNARD PURKISS

Bernard Purkiss was born in 1897 in Aldershot where he spent his early life. He moved to Birmingham as a teenager enlisting in the Royal Warwickshire Regiment Territorial Army at the age of sixteen years just before the outbreak of World War One. His army career spanned thirty two years. Over twenty five of those years were served with the Leicestershire Regiment.

Whilst stationed in South Wigston his quarters were at Glen Parva Barracks on Saffron Road which he shared with his wife and son John until overcrowding due to increased recruitment forced his wife and son to move out. Their home was made on Blaby Lane (now Saint Thomas Road) just a short distance away.

Official record lists Bernard's service as follows.
Enlisted into the Royal Warwickshire Regiment Territorial Army where he was:

posted to the 6th Battalion on	21.11.1913
Embodied	05.08.1914
Discharged after re-enlisting into the Regular Army	02.02.1919
Re-enlisted into the Leicestershire Regiment Regular Army	03.02.1919
Posted to the Depot	03.02.1919
Posted to the 2nd Battalion	30.06.1919
Posted to the 3rd Battalion	09.07.1919
Posted to Depot	19.08.1919
Posted to 3rd Battalion	23.08.1919
Posted to 1st Battalion	24.08.1919
Discharged on reduction of Establishment	02.02.1923
Re-enlisted into the Leicestershire Regiment Regular Army	03.02.1923
Posted to the Depot	05.02.1923
Posted to the 2nd Battalion	01.04.1926
Posted to the 1st Battalion	03.09.1926
Posted to the 2nd Battalion	27.10.1927
Posted to Depot	02.12.1927
Posted to Battalion	01.06.1932
Posted to Depot	30.10.1935
Posted to No. 10 Infantry Base Depot	31.01.1941
Posted to 22nd Training Centre	14.08.1941
Posted to 2/5 Battalion	19.08.1941
Transferred to the Army Catering Corps	05.04.1941
Attached to the 2/5 Battalion Leicestershire Regiment	05.04.1941

Service with the Colours	05.08.1914 to 02.02.1919
	03.02.1919 to 02.02.1923
	03.02.1923 to 02.10.1945

Overseas Service:	France	22.03.1915 to 16.01.1917
	Egypt	03.09.1926 to 26.10.1927

Medals:	Long Service and Good Conduct Medal,	1914-15 Star
	British War Medal, British Victory Medal,	
	Defence Medal, War Medal	1939-45.
Promotions	Appointed Lance Corporal	24.03.1924
	Promoted Corporal	05.03.1926
	Appointed Lance Sergeant	01.05.1929
	Promoted Sergeant	06.07.1932

Whilst serving with the Leicestershire Regiment Army Catering Corps. Bernard died at home on Tuesday 2nd October 1945. He was forty eight years old and his son John was just eleven. Bernard is buried at Wigston Cemetery, Leicestershire.

Bernard Purkiss

GUNNER LEONARD KEMP

Leonard Kemp was born on 13 September 1907. He was the son of Frank and Margaret Kemp of 12 Kedleston Avenue, Birstall, Leicestershire. He had one sister named Margaret.

Leonard attended the schools in Leicester and by the time he reached his twenties was living in Fairfield Road in the city.

Before war was declared in 1939 Leonard was employed for sixteen years as a knitter by the hosiery manufacturers, A. W Swann and Co. The company was based in Brazil Street in Leicester.

On Boxing Day, 26 December 1934 Leonard married Constance Winifred Harrington at Melbourne Hall. Constance was a Sunday School teacher there and leader of the Life Boys and Leonard belonged to the older group, the Boys Brigade. On their wedding day, the boys formed a guard of honour holding high their bugles as the bride and groom walked out of the Hall after the official ceremony.

After their marriage the couple lived at 25 Kingston Avenue, Wigston Fields and their children, a daughter Pauline and a son Malcolm were born. Constance's uncle William Harrington lived at Gared House on Station Road, Wigston.

Leonard joined the Army in 1941 and served with 208 Field Regiment, Royal Artillery as a gunner for four years. He had been abroad for three and a half years and spent time in the jungle in Burma.

On Monday 12 November 1945 Leonard died at the age of thirty eight years. After surviving the horrors of war the aeroplane, a Stirling, bringing twenty seven men home to England crashed the day before off the coast of Castel Benito. It was said that the runway was not long enough for take off. Troops and crew on board died outright except Leonard who suffered extensive broken bones and died in hospital the next day.

A Wigston neighbour had seen Leonard at the Assembly point waiting to be transported home but the neighbour had been brought home on an earlier flight. Leonard's wife expecting him home had prepared a special meal for him to celebrate with her and his ten year old daughter and five year old son.

Leonard is commemorated in Tripoli War Cemetery, Libya. An important Axis base, Tripoli was taken in January 1943 by Montgomery's forces. It became a great hospital base and over a thousand war casualties are buried on this site.

(see Corporal George Charles Birkin, cousin)

Top Left; Leonard with his Mother   -   Top Right; Leonard Kemp - Boys Brigade
Below;Leonard with three other Boys Brigade Members

Holiday Photo
War Declared

Leonard's Wife Constance
and children
Pauline and Malcolm

Page 220

Brother-in-Law Berts Wedding.
Far Left Leonard Kemp

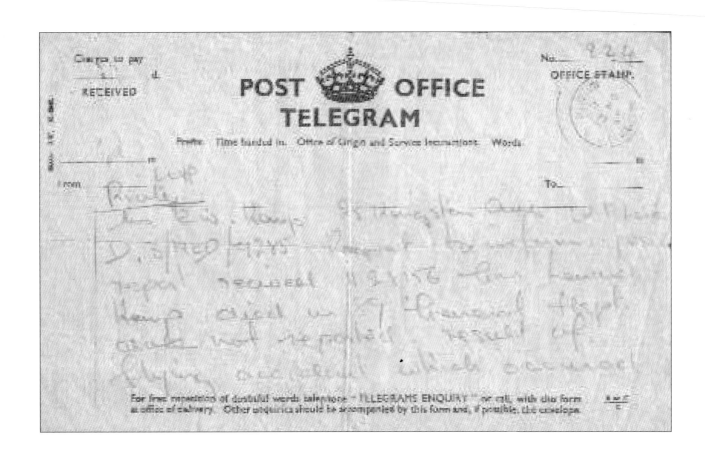

POST ✠ OFFICE
TELEGRAM

Charges to pay ___ d.

RECEIVED

No. 224

OFFICE STAMP.

Prefix. Time handed in. Office of Origin and Service Instructions. Words.

From ___

To ___

[handwritten, faded and largely illegible:]

Ruislip

... ... Air Office
D. ... regret to inform you
report received ... ... Air ...
... died on ... financial flight
... not reported ... result of
flying accident which occurred

For free repetition of doubtful words telephone "TELEGRAMS ENQUIRY" or call, with this form at office of delivery. Other enquiries should be accompanied by this form and, if possible, the envelope.

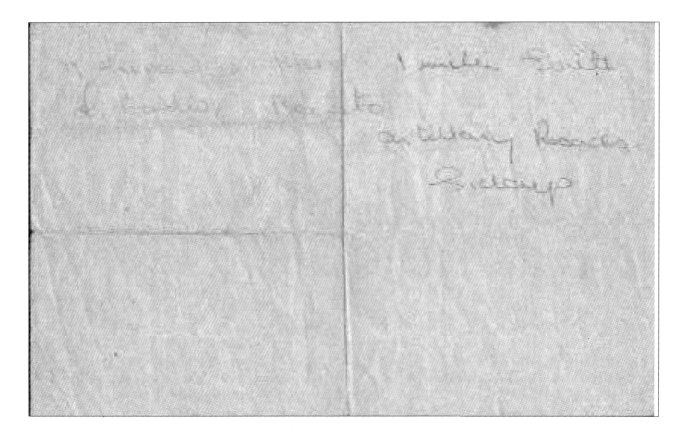

[handwritten, faded and largely illegible:]

... ... Smith
... Road
Sidcup

Leicester Man Killed In Tripoli Plane Crash

Leonard Kemp with Comrades

DRIVER LEONARD KEMP, R.A., of Wigston Fields, Leicester, was one of the 28 victims of the 'plane crash near Tripoli.

The machine, a Stirling, crashed when taking off from Castel-benito. It was bringing troops home to the United Kingdom.

He leaves a widow and two children, who live at 25, Kingston-avenue, Wigston Fields. He was the only son of Mr. and Mrs. Kemp, of 12, Rolleston-avenue, Birstall.

He had served for over four years in the Army, and had been abroad for three and a half years.

A Wigston man and a neighbour of his who saw Driver Kemp at the assembly point where troops leave for England, reached Leicester by an earlier plane, and he called upon Mrs. Kemp on Monday to tell her that her husband was flying home.

Mrs. Kemp thus expected her husband round about midnight and prepared a special supper for the reunion party.

He did not arrive and the next afternoon there came a message that he had been killed in the crash.

Driver Kemp was, prior to joining the Army, a hosiery knitter, and had been 16 years in the employ of A. W. Swann and Co., Ltd., Brazil-street.

CHAIRMEN OF COUNCIL

Driver KEMP.

APPENDIX A

TRANSCRIPT OF THE
SINKING OF BISMARCK

THE SINKING OF THE BISMARCK

TRANSCRIPT OF THE SINKING OF BISMARCK

The following account was hand written by Eric Farmer which relates events as he saw them of the sinking of the Bismarck. The Bismarck finally sank on the 27 May 1941. Mr Farmer left his record for safe keeping with Petty Officer (Stoker) Alfred William Winfield in the event that he never returned after the war had ended. A Telegraphist, Eric Farmer served on H.M.S Cossack in the Royal Navy. He did not return.

Petty Officer (Stoker) Winfield P/KX.104331 served for thirteen years in the Royal Navy from 31 December 1940 to the 4 June 1953. He kept Mr Farmer's account until his death on the 15 March 2001. It was subsequently passed to his son David Winfield for safe keeping.

Petty Officer {Stoker) Alfred William Winfield's record of service in the Royal Navy is as follows –

Trained at   HMS Victory 1, 11, 111
Served on   H.M.S Cormorant
                  H.M.S Lord Hothan
                  H.M.S Calliope
                  H.M.S Braganza
                  H.M.S Suvla
                  H.M.S Jupiter
                  H.M.S Finisterre (Excellent)

THE SINKING OF "BISMARCK"

The day was one of the typical Atlantic wintry days. A fairly strong wind, squally and on board any ship, not at all comfortable. Visibility was only a few miles, six of the most, and spray from the bows passing over the bridge obscuring everything.

The German battleship "Bismarck" and cruiser "Prince Eugene" had been reported as being at Bergen, Norway. This meant only two things. They had been sent there as reinforcement or were about to proceed to sea, make their way into the Atlantic, and begin a series of convoy raiding expeditions.

On 23 May, two of our cruisers, Norfolk and Suffolk, were on patrol in the Denmark Straits, (the strip of sea between Iceland and Greenland) when they suddenly saw two more dark forms ahead, emerging from the fog. As they became clearer it was seen that they were warships; and as there were none of our own big ones in the vicinity, enemy warships.

20.15/23. An enemy report was made that one battleship and one cruiser of enemy type were at large, and had been sighted. The chase was on. Our cruisers knew they were no match for the Germans so they at once took up shadowing positions. This was extremely difficult owing to the weather and at 22.15 contact was lost. About 22.30 contact was regained by RD/F with a range of eleven miles. Visibility eight miles approximately. From this time the cruisers kept contact until daylight gave up. Occasionally a PC and 3 of enemy.

By now our big ones had arrived on the scene, and at 05.56 HMS Hood sends a report of enemy in sight. Visibility had cleared by now, and the enemy were eighteen miles away. A bit of manoeuvring and the engagement was on, which resulted in Hood receiving a thousand to one hit in her magazine, and blowing up. At 06.23 a message was made to destroyers to proceed and pick up survivors of which there were only three. A Midshipman, a Signalman and one AB.

HMS Prince of Wales then took up the engagement, but the enemy turned away and broke off. Not before Prince of Wales had had "Y" turret put out of action, but only for the time being.

Norfolk and Suffolk took up the shadowing again for the day and kept contact. At dusk, a striking force was flown off from Victorious, which reported registering one hit. This however was only an eighteen inch torpedo and failed to reduce the speed of the enemy. They were still going at twenty-two knots.

The cruisers were able to shadow until about 03.00 on the 25th when at 03.06 a report was made that contact had been lost. This meant that the enemy had made a large turn, but it was not known in what direction. This made the situation rather awkward, because our main fleet was closing in and were expected to meet at 08.00 or thereabouts. The Fleet was then spread out in hope of regaining contact.

Aircraft were flown off from Victorious but of no avail. C in CHF in King George V made a signal. Her destroyer escort had run down to a small percentage of oil fuel. The fourth destroyer flotilla were forced to leave the convoy and proceed towards King George V as relief escort.

Visibility was still about eight miles and the sea rough, when at 10.54 a signal was received from Catalina aircraft of the RAF stating:-

Battleship in sight and giving the course and position. This was south of us and we turned right round and made towards the spot at 27 knots, increasing to 30 knots. By now aircraft of the Ark Royal had taken over and the Catalina proceeded on patrol. Just after noon a TB attack was made by Ark Royal A/C and one hit was observed. All A.C returned safely. Reports were made at short intervals throughout the day of PC and three of enemy. Approximately course 180 degrees, speed 22 knots, but she was leaving a trail of oil behind her. The fourth DF still carried on at 30 knots.

At about 11.30, the fourth DF sighted the enemy, who immediately opened fire with everything she had. The fire was too good to allow us to close range too much so we took up shadowing positions.

The big ones were by now heading full speed in our direction, and hoped to make a dusk attack, turning it into a night action. When dusk came however it was found that they were too far away for this, so it was summed up that if nothing drastic was done that night the enemy would be lost probably and by dawn, even in Brest.

The cruiser "Prince Eugene" was nowhere around, so we concentrated on "Bismarck".

A plan of attack was decided on by the destroyers. A torpedo attack was to be carried out when darkness fell in an attempt to stop, and may be if enough torpedoes struck home, to sink the enemy. One thing was certain though. The enemy had to be stopped, even if it meant the loss of the fourth DF.

At about 01.30 the attack started, but "Bismarck" was ready and waiting. She opened fire on us by RD/F and was so heavy and accurate, that we had to withdraw to a safer distance. The fourth was then split up and told to make the attack independently, and at the most favourable time.

It was pitch black, and the only thing to be seen were the starshells fired by the destroyers to keep in touch with "Bismarck". The sea had calmed down a bit, but visibility was still only about eight miles.

Approximately 02.00 Zulu reported having fired her fish, but no hits registered. "Bismarck" was firing at Zulu and Maori, concentrating more on the latter, and straddling every time. Now was our chance. Cossack, full speed ahead, went into the attack. We are spotted and "Bismarck" opens fire on us. The first salvo was 50 yards short. The next one burst over the bridge causing everyone to duck. The range was less than a mile now. A sharp turn, several swishes as the torpedoes are fired, a thick smoke screen and we are away into the night. A very loud explosion and large flash is observed in the after part of "Bismarck" as one of our fish hit. Almost at the same time, Maori reports having completed her run and getting one hit, which caused a large fire on the forecastle. A few minutes later Zulu reported:-

        Enemy on fire and stationary.

By now it was found out that one of our torpedoes had not left the tubes, so we went in again. The range closed rapidly as we sped in. Another sharp turn, another heavy smoke screen and we are away again. A few seconds after our second run a huge shot of flame was seen to come from "Bismarck". It is not known whether our second run had been a success, or whether the flash came from the 15 inch guns of the enemy. Anyway the fish had all gone and "Bismarck" had been stopped.

About an hour later she was on her way again. This time instead of 22 knots, the most she could muster was 8 knots. To add to her disablement, she was noticed to have a list of about 30 degrees. All we could do now was to shadow until the big ones gained contact. At 08.00 we lost contact, but regained it after a few minutes. She opened fire almost at once, but made no hits on any of us. At 08.55 there was a heavy explosion and after a few seconds a huge sheet of water rose alongside "Bismarck" The big ones had arrived and the final stage of the engagement was on. Rodney came into view firing 16 inch salvos which were getting home. Then came King George V. The "Bismarck" was fighting furiously to get away but she could not do more than 8 knots. It was a nasty sight to all; Germans racing along the deck to jump over the stern. They would sooner be in the open sea which was very rough than in "Bismarck" which by now was nothing more than a floating hell ship. The 16 inch and 14 inch salvos of Rodney and King George V were tearing into her continuously. Finally the big guns dropped down like dead flowers and ceased firing at our ships, who kept at it. There was no possible chance of her getting away now. She was on fire, and at last stopped amidst a cloud of steam.

Germans were seen jumping into the sea, and the fourth DF together with a cruiser, the Dorsetshire, were ordered to close in and pick up survivors – if any. During this errand of mercy, Maori had a torpedo fired under her from a U-boat so the fourth DF left without picking anyone up. Dorsetshire was able to pick up more than 100 survivors before she left, bringing them back to England as prisoners of war.

On our way back with the big ones, the German aircraft spotted as we expected
(two line are illegible here)

but we arrived back safely.

Before the final battle took place the Admiral commanding "Bismarck" must have known his end was near because he sent a message to Germany saying that he would fight to the last shell. As she rolled over we had to take our hats off to the Germans, and admit that they had fought a magnificent battle, and had died as all sailors wish to do. Engaging a superior enemy and with all guns blazing.

Thus, the sinking of our Battle Cruiser, HMS Hood was avenged in the way they would have wished had they been afloat.

"Cossack", "Zulu", "Maori", "Sikh", had a special mention for their part played; comprising fourth DF.

By Eric Farmer.

APPENDIX B

MEMORIES OF A LITTLE EVACUEE GIRL

MISS KEITH'S DANCING CLASS

SOUTH WIGSTON ARP

Memories Of A Little Evacuee Girl.

I was born on the 10th November 1934 at 195 Victoria Dock Road, Tidal Basin, West Ham, London.

Our house was a terraced house with a garden at the back. Across the road was a railway line and beyond that was the Victoria Docks. From the upstairs front window you could see the ships coming and going to load and unload their cargo.

When the war was declared in 1939, the authorities decided it would be safer for the women and children to be evacuated, as we would be very vulnerable living so near to the docks. My Mum, my sister aged thirteen years, my brother aged eight years, myself almost five years and my baby brother of six months, were all evacuated to Taunton in Somerset. We were given a small cottage to live in and we were well looked after by the Lord Mayor and his wife. We stayed there over the bitter cold winter of 39 and after six months nothing seemed to be happening regarding the war, so my Mum decided to take us back home to London to be with my Dad, my Grandma, and my three older brothers, two of which were now in the armed forces, with the younger of the three, Leslie, helping with the Home Guard.

It was not long after we returned to London that the bombing started in earnest. We were given an Anderson shelter in our back garden and seemed to spend a great deal of time down there, especially at night. I always felt very frightened as when the bombs dropped, the soil used to shake through and I remember well thinking we would be buried.

After a particularly bad night raid, we came out of the shelter to find the roof missing from our home, as a bomb had dropped at the end of the road, and the blast had taken the tops off all the houses.

We were all taken into two local schools. In the school opposite to us was our next door neighbour and they came across asking us to join them so that we could all be together, this we did. That night a bomb dropped on the school we had just left and over four hundred people were killed.

We were then taken by bus to a forest in Chingford, Essex and placed in a large wooden hut, where we had to sleep on the floor and we could still hear the bombing all around.

After a short time there, my sister, my brother and myself, were evacuated to Stoney Stratford where my sister and me were taken in by an elderly couple. My brother with three other boys went into a different house. We were there for some four months. At this point I do not know where my Mum and baby brother went.

Eventually my Mum and brother arrived in South Wigston where for a start they had to share a house, then Mum was given one on Lansdowne Grove and she then sent for us to join her. My Dad was not allowed to leave his job in London and therefore had to find lodgings, my eldest brother was already in the Army, the next brother in the Air Force and the youngest of the three eventually joined the Navy, but was not to return. He died at the age of nineteen years.

During my childhood in South Wigston I joined a dancing class which had been set up especially for evacuee children by a professional dancer named Miss Keith. Later other village children joined the troupe and we did put on concerts in the village. I also belonged to the Brownie Guides and attended the church, an annexe of Saint Thomas's, on Lansdowne Grove.

I began my education in South Wigston at the Bassett Street Infants School and later the Bassett Street Junior School where I passed the Eleven Plus Examination which resulted in my acceptance at Kibworth Grammar School.

Miss Keith's Dancing Class
Front Row; 1L Gladys Darkins - 2L Myra Gregory
2nd Row; 3L Jean Thompson - 4L Freda Knott - 5L Maureen Moore
3rd Row; 3L Thelma Barlow - 4L Ruth Harrison - 3R Irene Bird
Back Row; 1L June Moore - 5L Betty Moore - 6L Iris Reeve

South Wigston ARP, Taken in the Junior School Playground
Back Row Left to Right - 5th Mr Copson - 8th George Baker - 10th Tom Reeves
Front Row Left to Right - 1st Mrs Cranfield - 4th Mr O J Kind - 7th Ernie Hubbard - 8th Mrs Hendrick

APPENDIX C

WAR MEMORIAL
SOUTH WIGSTON

War Memorial
Blaby Road, South Wigston

TO THE GLORY OF GOD AND IN MEMORY OF THE MEN OF SOUTH
WIGSTON AND GLEN PARVA WHO GAVE THEIR LIVES IN THE WARS OF
1914 - 1918 AND 1935 - 1945

BATTLES OF THE GREAT WAR

1914 – 1918

Mons	August 1914
Tannenberg	August 1914
Heligoland	August 1914
Marne	September 1914
Aisne	September 1914
Albert	September 1914
Arras	October 1914
Ypres	October – November 1914
Neuve Chapelle	March 1915
Gallipoli Campaign	March 1915 – January 1916
Artois	May 1915
Isonzo	June 1915
Artois-Loos	September 1915
Verdun	February – December 1916
Jutland	May 1916
Somme	July – November 1916
Gorizia	August 1916
Flers-Courcelette	September 1916
Gaza	March – April 1917
Arras	April – May 1917
Aisne	April – May 1917
Messines	June 1917
Passchendaele	July – November 1917
Caporetto	October 1917
Cambrai	November 1917
Aisne	May 1918
Le Hamel	July 1918
Marne	July 1918
Amiens	August 1918
Albert	August 1918
St. Mihiel	September 1918
Meuse-Argonne	September 1918
Canal du Nord	September 1918
Vittorio Veneto	October 1918

WAR CASUALTY LISTS

The following names have been taken from the records of The Commonwealth War Graves Commission, The Great War CD Rom, Naval and Military Press Limited, The Royal British Legion and from epitaphs on the Wigston War Graves at Welford Road Cemetery, Wigston, Leicestershire. I would like to apologise here too for any names which may have been missed at Wigston Cemetery. Many other men are not actually buried there but their names are sometimes inscribed on family monuments.

All memorials and cemeteries are taken from the records of the Commonwealth War Graves Commission.

An asterisk * denotes some discrepancies between the official sources. Eg. The spelling of names, initials or differences in dates. Note also the spelling of 'sergeant' and 'serjeant'. Both have been used and both are correct.

It has not been possible to discover family details on a few of the service records.

Where places of birth are shown, some men had enlisted in other towns, resided in other towns or additional information has not been found. Many men have no known graves. Listed are the countries where they fell or where memorials have been erected in their memory.

MEN LOST IN 1914

NAME	RANK	DATE/MEMORIAL	PERSONAL DETAILS WHERE KNOWN
William Frederick Waldron *	Private 2nd Bn. Lancashire Fusiliers	Died Wednesday 26 August 1914 La Ferte-Sous-Jouarre Memorial Seine-et-Marne, France	
Thomas Paramore	Driver 113th Bty. Royal Field Artillery	Died Saturday 19 September 1914 Age 18 La Ferte-Sous-Jouarre Memorial Seine-et-Marne, France	Parents: Tom and Helen Paramore Bassett Street, South Wigston
Albert Edward Hannay Ball	Serjeant 2nd Bn. Leicestershire Regt.	Died Tuesday 20 October 1914 Mazargues War Cemetery, Marseilles, Bouches-du-Rhone, France	Born at Glen Parva
Robert J Taylor	Lance Sergeant 2nd Bn. Royal Scots Fusiliers	Died Friday 23 October 1914 France and Flanders	Born South Wigston
Arthur Gregory North	Private 1st Bn. Leicestershire Regt.	Died Sunday 25 October 1914 Age 29 Ploegsteert Memorial Comines-Warneton, Hainaut. Belgium	Parent Mrs A H North Garden Street, South Wigston
Thomas Henry Foster	Corporal 2nd Bn. South Staffordshire Regt.	Died Friday 6 November 1914 Ypres (Menin Gate) Memorial, Ieper West-Vlaanderen, Belgium	South Wigston
Patrick Albert Hubbard	Serjeant 'D' Coy. 2nd Bn. Leicestershire Regt.	Died Sunday 15 November 1914 Age 29 Le Touret Military Cemetery, Richebourg-L'Avoue, Pas de Calais, France	Parents Albert and Agnes Hubbard Park Road, South Wigston
David Henry Gale	Private 2nd Bn. Leicestershire Regt.	Died Monday 16 November 1914 Le Touret Military Cemetery Richebourg-L'Avoue, Pas de Calais, France	Wigston Magna

Name	Rank / Regiment	Died	Family
Henry O Chamberlain DCM	Private 2nd Bn. Leicestershire Regt.	Died Tuesday 8 December 1914 Age 22 Brighton Cemetery	Parent: Mrs Amy Chamberlain Freeman's Cottages, Welford
Edgar Bell	Driver 63rd Bty. Royal Field Artillery	Died Monday 14 December 1914 Age 25 Hollybrook Memorial Southampton	Parent: Mrs Annie M Bell Kirkdale Road, South Wigston
Harry White	Serjeant 2nd Bn. Leicestershire Regt.	Died Thursday 17 December 1914 Le Touret Military Cemetery Richebourg-L'Avoue. Pas de Calais, France	
James Edward Mason	Private 2nd Bn. Royal Warwickshire Regt.	Died Saturday 19 December 1914 France and Flanders	Wigston Magna
MEN LOST IN 1915			
Arthur Boothaway	Private 2nd Bn. Coldstream Guards	Died Saturday 2 January 1915 Age 23 Le Touret Military Cemetery Richebourg-L'Avoue, Pas de Calais, France	Parents: Alonzo and Maria Boothaway Central Avenue, Wigston Magna
Edward George Gale	Private 2nd Bn. Leicestershire Regt.	Died Thursday 4th February 1915 Le Touret Military Cemetery Richebourg-L'Avoue, Pas de Calais, France	Wigston Magna
Roland Reginald* Herbert	Lance Serjeant 2nd Bn. Coldstream Guards	Died Saturday 13 February 1915 Age 29 Le Touret Memorial, Pas de Calais, France	Born Wigston Parent: William C Herbert Wife: Daisy Elizabeth Herbert Swaffham
William Murphy	Second Lieutenant 2nd Bn Leicestershire Regt.	Died Thursday 11 March 1915 Age 36 Le Touret Military Cemetery Richebourg-L'Avoue, Pas de Calais, France	Wife: Sarah Murphy Kirkdale Road, South Wigston

Name	Rank / Regiment	Death	Parents / Born
Arthur Andrews	Private 1st Bn. King's Own Yorkshire Light Infantry	Died Saturday 13 March 1915 Age 27 Wulverghem-Lindenhoek Road Military Cemetery, Heuvelland, West Vlaanderen, Belgium	Born: Wigston Parents: Mr and Mrs M J Thacker Vernon Road, Leicester
Thomas Gilliam Baker	Lance Corporal 1st/4th Bn. Leicestershire Regt.	Died Thursday 29 April 1915 Packhorse Shrine Cemetery, Wulverghem Huvelland, West Vlaanderen, Belgium	South Wigston
Gordon Sutton	Private 'H' Coy. 1st/4th Bn. Leicestershire Regt.	Died Sunday 2 May 1915 Packhorse Farm Shrine Cemetery, Wulverghem, Heuvelland, West-Vlaanderen, Belgium	Parents: John and Emma Sutton Kirkdale Road, South Wigston
Oliver Beaumont Taylor	Private Princess Patricia's Canadian Light Infantry Eastern Ontario Regt. Served in the South African Campaign, Royal Humane Society's Medal for saving life in Modder River.	Died Saturday 8 May 1915 Age 34 Ypres (Menin Gate) Memorial Ieper, West-Vlaanderen, Belgium	Parents: Joseph Henry and Jane Taylor Aylestone Lane, Wigston
George Alexander Hayman	Private 2nd Bn. Northamptonshire Regt.	Died Sunday 9 May 1915 Ploegsteert Memorial, Comines-Warneton, Hainaut, Belgium	
Ernest Edwin Walker	Private 1st/4th Bn. Leicestershire Regt.	Died Sunday 9 May 1915 Age 23 Packhorse Farm Shrine Cemetery, Wulverghem, Heuvelland, West-Vlaanderen, Belgium	Parents: Arthur and Ada Walker, Orange Street, South Wigston
Ernest Edward Daniel Johnson	Private Leicestershire Yeomanry	Died Thursday 13 May 1915 Age 25 Ypres (Menin Gate) Memorial, Ieper, West-Vlaanderen, Belgium	Parents: Daniel and Ada Johnson Newgate End, Wigston Magna
J C Needham	Corporal Leicestershire Yeomanry	Died Thursday 13 May 1915 Bedford House Cemetery Zillebeke, Ieper, West-Vlaanderen, Belgium	

Name	Rank/Regiment	Death/Memorial	Family
Alfred James T* Tomlinson	Private Leicestershire Yeomanry	Died Thursday 13 May 1915 Ypres (Menin Gate) Memorial. Ieper, West-Vlaanderen, Belgium	
William Johnson	Second Lieutenant 2nd Bn. Leicestershire Regt.	Died Sunday 16 May 1915 Age 37 Le Touret Military Cemetery, Richebourg-L'Avoue, Pas de Calais, France. Served in the South Africa Campaign.	Wife: Daisy Johnson Clifford Street South Wigston
George H Sharpe	Private 2nd Bn. Leicestershire Regt.	Died Wednesday 19 May 1915 Ormskirk Cemetery, Lancashire.	
Thomas Harry Johnson	Private 1st Bn. Lincolnshire Regt.	Died Wednesday 16 June 1915 Age 20 Ypres (Menin Gate) Memorial, Ieper, West-Vlaanderen, Belgium	Parents; Mr G and Emma Johnson Manor Street, Wigston Magna
George Edward Boulter	Private 1st/4th Bn. Leicestershire Regt.	Died Tuesday 20 July 1915 Ypres (Menin Gate) Memorial, West-Vlaanderen, Belgium	South Wigston
George Tattershall	Private 2nd Bn. Leicestershire Regt.	Died Saturday 25 September 1915 Loos Memorial, Pas de Calais, France	Parents: George and Eliza Tattershall Orange Street, South Wigston
Thomas Norman	Lance Corporal 10th Bn. Gloucestershire Regt.	Died Saturday 25 September 1915 Loos Memorial, Pas de Calais, France	
Ernest Simpkin	Serjeant 2nd Bn. Leicestershire Regt.	Died Saturday 25 September 1915 Loos Memorial, Pas de Calais, France	
Francis Arthur Wignall *	Private 3rd Bn. Coldstream Guards	Died Friday 8 October 1915 Age 21 Loos Memorial, Pas de Calais, France	Parents: John George and Mary Jane Wignall Chestnut Cottages, Bull Head Street, Wigston Magna

Name	Rank / Regiment	Death	Family
Edgar Carr	Serjeant 1st/4th Bn. Leicestershire Regt.	Died Wednesday 13 October 1915 – (Brother Horace also fell.) Loos Memorial, Pas de Calais, France	Parents: Joseph and Henrietta Carr 51 Danvers Road, Leicester
Cyril Clare	Private 'C' Coy. 1st/4th Bn. Leicestershire Regt.	Died Wednesday 13 October 1915 Loos Memorial, Pas de Calais, France	Parents: Benjamin C and E A Clare Blaby Road, South Wigston
Albert Henry Cooke	Private 1st/4th Bn. Leicestershire Regt.	Died Wednesday 13 October 1915 Loos Memorial, Pas de Calais, France	South Wigston
Arthur Randle	Private 1st/4th Bn. Leicestershire Regt.	Died Wednesday 13 October 1915 Loos Memorial , Pas de Calais, France	Parents: Mr H and Mrs A Randle Glen Gate, South Wigston
Harold Sutton	Private* 1st/4th Bn. Leicestershire Regt.	Died Wednesday 13 October 1915 Age 18 Loos Memorial, Pas de Calais, France	Parent: John Sutton Kirkdale Road, South Wigston
Albert Charles Squires	Private 1st/4th Bn. Leicestershire Regt.	Died Wednesday, 13 October 1915 Age 22 Loos Memorial, Pas de Calais, France	Parents: Mr and Mrs A Squires Clifford Street, South Wigston
George Philip Walker	Private 1st/4th Bn. Leicestershire Regt.	Died Wednesday, 13 October 1915, Age 20 Loos Memorial, Pas de Calais, France	Parent: Mrs Mary Walker Park Road, South Wigston
Cecil Chapman	Lance Corporal 1st/4th Bn. Leicestershire Regt.	Died Wednesday 13 October 1915 Loos Memorial, Pas de Calais, France	Parents: John and Sarah Ann Chapman Long Street, Wigston Magna
William Heard	Private 1st/4th Bn. Leicestershire Regt.	Died Wednesday 13 October 1915 Age 21 Loos Memorial, Pas de Calais, France	Parents: Arthur and Harriet Heard Leicester Road, Wigston Magna
Frederic George Looms	Private 1st/4th Bn. Leicestershire Regt.	Died Wednesday 13 October 1915 Loos Memorial, Pas de Calais, France	
Francis Gerald Shipp	Private 1st/4th Bn. Leicestershire Regt.	Died Wednesday, 13 October 1915 Age 24 Loos Memorial, Pas de Calais, France	Brother: Albert G Shipp White House, Wigston

Name	Regiment	Death	Family
Ralph Edwin Spence	Private 1st/4th Bn. Leicestershire Regt.	Died Wednesday 13 October 1915 Age 21 Loos Memorial, Pas de Calais, France	Parent: Elizabeth J Spence Burgess Street, Wigston Magna
Richard Chandler	Private 1st/4th Bn. Leicestershire Regt.	Died Wednesday 13 October 1915 Loos Memorial, Pas de Calais, France	South Wigston
John Henry Hall	Private 1st/4th Bn. Leicestershire Regt.	Died Wednesday 13 October 1915 France and Flanders	South Wigston
Raymond Hardy Turner	Private 1st/4th Bn. Leicestershire Regt.	Died Wednesday 13 October 1915 Age 18 Loos Memorial, Pas de Calais, France	Parents: Samuel and Elizabeth Turner Fairfield Street, Leicester
Wallace Vane Hougham	Private 6th Bn. Leicestershire Regt.	Died Thursday 18 November 1915 Beauval Communal Cemetery, Somme – France	Parents: W and Rachel Hougham Healey Street, South Wigston
Walter Harrison	Private 4th Bn. Leicestershire Regt.	Died Sunday 19 December 1915 Age 28 Wigston Cemetery, Leicestershire	Parents: Mr and Mrs Harrison Wife: Annie Harrison Long Street, Wigston Magna
William Reginald Maddams	Private 1st Bn. Leicestershire Regt.	Died Tuesday 21 December 1915 White House Cemetery, St. Jean-Les-Ypres, Belgium	Parents: William and Sarah Maddams South Wigston Wife: Barrow Hill, Chesterfield

MEN LOST IN 1916

Name	Rank / Regiment	Died	Family
Percy Hougham	Corporal 2nd Bn. Leicestershire Regt.	Died Saturday 8 January 1916 Basra Memorial, Iraq	
Percy Reuben Foister DCM	Second Lieutenant 'B' Coy. 2nd Bn. Leicestershire Regt.	Died Thursday 13 January 1916 Age 29 Basra Memorial, Iraq	Parents: Charles Foister and H Moulden (formerly Foister) Sutherland Street, Leicester
William Pettit Maycock	Private 1st Bn. Leicestershire Regt.	Died Wednesday 19 January 1916 Age 37 Lussenthoek Military Cemetery, Poperinge, West-Vlaanderen, Belgium	Parent: William Maycock Newton Lane, Wigston Magna
Harold Percy Elliott	Driver 73rd Bde. Royal Field Artillery	Died 2 March 1916 Age 18 Le Treport Military Cemetery, Seine-Maritime, France	Parents: Arthur and Rebecca Elliott Wigston
George Randolph Noble	Corporal 5th Bn. Oxford and Bucks. Light Infantry	Died Sunday 5 March 1916 Age 21 Etaples Military Cemetery, Pas de Calais, France	Born: South Wigston Parents: Elijah and Harriet Noble Stockingford, Warwickshire
Albert William Knight	Private 2nd Bn. Leicestershire Regt.	Died Thursday 6 April 1916 Age 34 Basra Memorial, Iraq	Son: B J Knight Bull Head Street, Wigston Magna
Albert Arthur Abell *	Private 1st/4th Bn. Leicestershire Regt.	Died Friday 14 April 1916 Aubigny Communal Cemetery Extension Pas de Calais, France	Wigston Magna
William Frederick Franklin	Private 'C' Coy. 4th Bn. Leicestershire Regt.	Died Friday 21 April 1916 Age 18 Ecoivres Military Cemetery, France	Parents: William and Annie Franklin Midland Cottages, Wigston Magna
Herbert Basil Freeman	Sapper B. Coy. Royal Engineers	Died Monday 1 May 1916 – Fort Pitt Military Cemetery, Kent	Parents: Samuel and Sarah Freeman South Wigston

George Henry Dewick	Able Seaman HMS 'Shark' Royal Navy	Died Wednesday 31 May 1916 Age 27 – Portsmouth Naval Memorial	Parents: Edwin and Mary Dewick, Leicester. Wife: E B Silverwood (formerly Dewick), Moat Street, Wigston Magna
George Melville Proctor	Lance Corporal 2nd Bn. Leicestershire Regt.	Died Tuesday 6 June 1916 Age 22 Amara War Cemetery, Iraq	Parents: Arthur and Elizabeth Proctor Leicester Road, Wigston Magna
John Edward Mosse	Lieutenant Colonel Commanding Depot Leicestershire Regt.	Died Saturday 17 June 1916 Welford Road Cemetery, Leicester	
Arthur Ernest Wesson	Private 1st/5th Bn. Leicestershire Regt.	Died Saturday 1 July 1916 Thiepval Memorial, Somme, France	Born: South Wigston
William John Gurr	Colour Sergeant 'A' Coy. 2nd Bn. Leicestershire Regt.	Died Thursday 6 July 1916 Age 45 Wigston Cemetery, Leicestershire	Wife: M Cosgrove (formerly Gurr) South Wigston
Alexander Christie	Private 12th Bn. Royal Scots	Died Saturday 8 July 1916 Thiepval Memorial, Somme, France	Wife: Ada Hemmings Glen Gate, South Wigston
William Beattie	Private 11th Bn. Royal Scots	Died Friday 14 July 1916 Age 38 Thiepval Memorial, Somme, France	Parents: William Bell Beattie and Robina Beattie, Dunfriesshire. Wife: Mary Beattie, Bushloe End, Wigston Magna
Arthur Noel Deacon	Private 7th Bn. Leicestershire Regt.	Died Friday 14 July 1916 Thiepval Memorial, Somme, France	Brother: Mr Barzillai Deacon Lansdowne Road, Leicester
Ernest Mason	Lance Corporal 8th Bn. Leicestershire Regt.	Died Saturday 15 July 1916 France and Flanders	Born: Wigston Magna
Arthur Warren	Private 8th Bn. Leicestershire Regt.	Died Saturday 15 July 1916 Thiepval Memorial, Somme, France	
William Tite	Private 6th Bn. Leicestershire Regt.	Died Monday 17 July 1916 Age 35 London Cemetery and Extension, Longueval, Somme, France	Wife: Ada Lewin Tite Bull Head Street, Wigston Magna

Name	Rank / Regiment	Death	Additional Information
Stephen D Lewin	Lance Corporal 6th Bn. Leicestershire Regt.	Died Monday 17 July 1916 Thiepval Memorial, Somme, France	South Wigston
William Copson	Serjeant 'C' Coy, 9th Leicestershire Regt.	Died Friday 21 July 1916 Abbeville Communal Cemetery, Somme, France	Parents: Joseph and Harriet Copson Wigston Magna
Joseph Edmund Carter	Private 7th Bn. Leicestershire Regt	Died Saturday 22 July 1916 Age 20 Welford Road Cemetery, Leicester	Parents: Joseph and Zillah Carter Bell Street, Wigston Magna
Oliver Thomas Hipwell	Corporal 2nd Bn. Leicestershire Regt.	Died Sunday 23 July 1916 Amara War Cemetery, Iraq	Wigston Magna
Ernest Faulkner	Serjeant 1st Bn. Leicestershire Regt.	Died Friday 28 July 1916 Potijze Burial Ground Cemetery, Ieper, West-Vlaanderen, Belgium	Wife: F Goodman (formerly Faulkner) Irlam Street, South Wigston
Wilfred Cawthorne	Private 9th Bn. Leicestershire Regt.	Died Tuesday 1 August 1916 Age 27 Habarcq Communal Cemetery Extension Pas de Calais, France	Parents: John Moore Cawthorn and Sussanah Cawthorn, Burgess Street, Wigston Magna
James William Ross	Private 7th Bn. Leicestershire Regt.	Died Monday 14 August 1916 Age 20 Faubourg D'Amiens Cemetery, Arras, Pas de Calais, France	Parents James and Isabella Ross North Street, Wigston Magna
Cyril Herbert Vigars	Rifleman 7th Bn. King's Royal Rifle Corps	Died Friday 18 August 1916 Thiepval Memorial, Somme, France	Born: Wigston Parents Henry and Ann Vigars Park Road, Hinckley
Stanley Craxford Griffin	Private 2nd Bn. Leicestershire Regt.	Died Wednesday 6 September 1916 Age 20 Amara War Cemetery, Iraq	Parents Frederick and Mary Ellen Griffin
Joseph Ernest Deacon	Lance Corporal* 1st Bn. Leicestershire Regt.	Died Friday 15 September 1916 Thiepval Memorial, Somme, France	

Name	Regiment	Death	Family
Douglas H Sibson	Private 1st Canadian Mounted Rifles (Saskatchewan Regt).	Died 15 September 1916 Age 27 Vimy Memorial, Pas de Calais, France	Parents: John and Elizabeth Sibson Wigston Magna
Cyril Dobson	Private 'B' Coy. 11th Bn. Leicestershire Regt.	Died Monday 18 September 1916 Age 18 Guillemont Road Cemetery, Somme, France Inscription in Wigston Cemetery "He fell for a cause which to die is gain."	Parents: Joseph Leonard and Maria Dobson Timber Street, South Wigston
Albert Edward Wood	Private 11th Bn. Leicestershire Regt.	Died Monday 18 September 1916 Age 19 Thiepval Memorial, Somme, France	Parent: Mrs Helen Wood Kirkdale Road, South Wigston
Ernest William Seaton	Private 6th Bn. Leicestershire Regt.	Died Saturday 23 September 1916 Age 24 Wigston Cemetery, Leicestershire	Parents: Samuel and Ann Alice Seaton Leicester Road, Wigston Magna
Ernest James Waldron	Private 8th Bn. Leicestershire Regt.	Died Monday 25 September 1916 Thiepval Memorial, Somme, France	
Joseph Brewin	Private 2nd Bn. Durham Light Infantry	Died Monday 25 September 1916 Age 24 Thiepval Memorial, Somme, France	Parents: Mr and Mrs John Brewin Moat Street, Wigston Magna
Graham Powell	Private 9th Bn. Leicestershire Regt.	Died Monday 25 September 1916 Thiepval Memorial, Somme, France	Wigston Magna
Ernest William Webster	Private 9th Bn. Leicestershire Regt.	Died Monday 25 September 1916 Age 24 Thiepval Memorial, Somme, France	Parents: William and Alice Webster Maynard Road, Leicester. Wife: Agnes Minnie Webster Hart Road, Leicester
Edward Mayfield	Private 6th Bn. Leicestershire Regt.	Died Monday 25 September 1916 * Thiepval Memorial, Somme, France	Born: South Wigston

Name	Rank / Regiment	Death	Additional Information
Arthur Frederick Simms	Private 'B' Coy. 8th Bn. Leicestershire Regt.	Died Monday 25 September 1916 Age 20 Thiepval Memorial, Somme, France	Parents: Thomas and Amy Simms Smisby Road, Ashby-de-la-Zouch, Leicestershire
Tom Knight	Private 8th Bn. Leicestershire Regt.	Died Monday 25 September 1916 Age 26 Thiepval Memorial, Somme, France	Parents: F G Knight and Louisa Knight, Charlton Kings, Cheltenham, Gloucestershire
Frank Perry	Private 1st Bn. Leicestershire Regt.	Died Tuesday 26 September 1916 Thiepval Memorial, Somme, France	South Wigston
Wilfred Boulter	Lance Corporal 6th Bn. Leicestershire Regt.	Died Friday 29 September 1916 Thiepval Memorial, Somme, France	
Harry Victor Boulter	Rifleman 2nd Bn. King's Royal Rifle Corps	Died Sunday 1 October 1916 Dernancourt Communal Cemetery Extension, Somme, France	Born: Glen Parva
Oswald Henry Perry	Private 8th Bn. Leicestershire Regt.	Died Wednesday 4 October 1916 St. Sever Cemetery, Rouen, Seine-Maritime, France	South Wigston
Thomas Brindley	Private 1st Bn. Leicestershire Regt.	Died Friday 6 October 1916 France and Flanders	Wigston Magna Parent: Mrs N Brindley, Club Yard, Oadby
Alfred William Tyers	Private 6th Bn. Leicestershire Regt.	Died Saturday 14 October 1916 Age 25 Vermelles British Cemetery, Pas de Calais, France	Wife: May Tyers, Aylestone Lane, Wigston Magna
Thomas William Ford	Private 2nd Bn. Sherwood Foresters, Notts. and Derby. Regt.	Died Tuesday 17 October 1916 Age 23 Grove Town Cemetery, Heaulte, Somme, France	Parents: Thomas and Jane Ford Wife: Florence Ford, Moat Street, Wigston Magna
Albert W Knight	Private 1st Bn. Leicestershire Regt.	Died Wednesday 18 October 1916 Thiepval Memorial, Somme, France	South Wigston

Sidney Hart	Private 19th Bn. Manchester Regt.	Died Thursday 19 October 1916 Thiepval Memorial, Somme, France	South Wigston
William Thomas Chapman	Private 3rd Bn. Dorsetshire Regt. 7th Bn. Royal Munster Fusiliers	Died Monday 23 October 1916 Age 29 Mikra British Cemetery, Kalamaria, Greece	Parents: John and Sarah Chapman Kilby Bridge, Wigston
John Albert Crooks	Stoker 1st Class. HMS Flirt, Royal Navy	Died Thursday 26 October 1916 Age 22 Portsmouth Naval Memorial	Parents: Sherbrook and Catherine Crooks, Railway Street, South Wigston
Arthur Smith	Gunner 191st Siege Bty. Royal Garrison Artillery	Died Wednesday 20 December 1916 Delville Wood Cemetery, Longueval, Somme, France	Born Wigston
John William Carter		Died 26 December 1916 Age 32 Wigston Cemetery, Leicestershire	Parents: Ben and Sarah Carter Wife: Edith Carter, Wigston
John Henry Sturgess	Lance Corporal 4th Bn. Coldstream Guards	Died Friday 29 December 1916 Age 24 Guards Cemetery, Combles, Somme, France	Parents: Mr and Mrs W H Sturgess Gentry Avenue, Lawrence Hill, Bristol. (Native of Clifford Street, South Wigston.)
Walter William Hall	Private 2nd Bn. Durham Light Infantry	Died Saturday 30 December 1916 Age 24 Cambrin Churchyard Extension, Pas de Calais, France	Parents Henry and Elizabeth Hall Welford Road, Wigston Magna.

Howard Howe	Private 2nd Bn. Leicestershire Regt.	Died 9 January 1917 Mesopotamia	Wigston Magna
A Garner	Private 1st/5th Bn. Leicestershire Regt.	Died Wednesday 10 January 1917 Age 29 Bienvillers Military Cemetery, Pas de Calais, France	Parents: Mr and Mrs J Garner, Kilby Road, Fleckney, Leicestershire
Thomas Frederick Peberdy	Private 4th Bn. Worcestershire Regt.	Died Tuesday 23 January 1917 Age 28 Grove Town Cemetery, Meaulte, Somme, France	Parents: Thomas and Sarah Peberdy. Wife: Harriet Emily Peberdy Weford Road, Wigston Magna
Arthur Edward Chapman	Private 1st Bn. Leicestershire Regt.	Died Friday 2nd February 1917 Vermelles British Cemetery, Pas de Calais, France	Parents: John and Sarah Chapman Kilby Bridge, Wigston Wife: Mary Ellen Chapman Healey Street, South Wigston
Edward H Norman	Private 15th Bn. Highland Light Infantry	Died Saturday 3 February 1917 Serre Road Cemetery, No. 1 Pas de Calais, France	
George E Williamson	Corporal 1st/8th Bn. Royal Warwickshire Regt.	Died Sunday 4 February 1917 Assevillers New Bitish Cemetery, Somme, France	
Robert Edward Brewin	Private 2nd Bn. Sherwood Foresters (Notts and Derby Regt.)	Died Friday 9 February 1917 Age 28 Vermelles British Cemetery, Pas de Calais, France	Parents: John and Sarah Ann Brewin Moat Street, Wigston Magna
Isaac Wheat	Private 1st Bn. King's Own (Royal Lancaster Regt.)	Died Monday 12 February 1917 Age 40 Fins New British Cemetery, Sorel-le-Grand, Somme, France	Parents: William and Emma Wheat Wigston Magna Wife: Hellender Elizabeth Starmer (formerly Wheat) Queen Street, Kettering, Northants.

Name	Rank/Regiment	Died	Family/Other
Ernest Boothaway	Private 2nd Bn. South Staffordshire Regt.	Died Saturday 17 February 1917 Thiepval Memorial, Somme, France	Wigston Magna
William Harding	Private 4th Bn. South Staffordshire Regt. *	Died Saturday 17 February 1917 Age 37 Adanac Military Cemetery, Miraumont, Somme, France	Parents: William and Mary Ann Harding, Moat Street, Wigston Magna
William Thomas Arthur Gudgeon	Private 1st Bn. Sherwood Foresters (Notts and Derby Regt.)	Died Sunday 4 March 1917 Age 33 Thiepval Memorial, Somme, France	Parents: George and Mary Gudgeon Wife: Ethel Gudgeon Glen Gate, South Wigston
William Sidney Roberts *	Private 1st/4th Bn. Leicestershire Regt.	Died Tuesday 13 March 1917 France and Flanders	Born: Wigston Magna
Walter George Kenney	Private 'B' Coy. 6th Bn. Leicestershire Regt.	Died Thursday 22 March 1917 Age 20 Vermelles British Cemetery, Pas de Calais, France	Parents: John Garratt Kenney and Emily Jane Kenney Fairfield Street, South Wigston
Arthur King	Gunner Royal Garrison Artillery	Died Wednesday 4 April 1917 France and Flanders	Wigston
Edgar Carter	Private 13th Field Amb. Royal Army Medical Corps	Died Monday 9 April 1917 Age 31 * Arras Memorial, Pas de Calais, France	Parents: Benjamin and Sarah Ann Carter, Moat Street, Wigston Magna. (Helping wounded comrades at Vimy Ridge, France). Wigston Cemetery.
George Thomas Tilley	Private 2nd/4th Bn. Leicestershire Regt.	Died Thursday 12 April 1917 Roisel Communal Cemetery Extension, Somme, France	
Ernest Robert Butlin	Private 2nd/4th Bn. Leicestershire Regt.	Died Friday 13 April 1917 Age 22. Roisel Communal Cemetery Extension, Somme, France.	Parents: Robert George and Sarah Ann Butlin Central Avenue, Wigston Magna
Benjamin Wignall	Private 4th Reserve Bn. Leicestershire Regt.	Died Saturday 14 April 1917 Age 34 Welford Road Cemetery, Leicester	Wife: Harriet Ellen Wignall, Cecil Road, Leicester

George T Hiom	Private 1st/4th Bn. Leicestershire Regt.	Died Saturday 21 April 1917 Mazingarbe Communal Cemetery Extension, Pas de Calais, France	
Horace Carr	Private 1st/4th Bn. Leicestershire Regt.	Died Sunday 22 April 1917 Arras Memorial, Pas de Calais, France	Parents: Joseph and Henrietta Carr, Danvers Road, Leicester
John Augustus Warner	Private 1st/5th Bn. Durham Light Infantry	Died Monday 23 April 1917 Arras Memorial, Pas de Calais, France	
Albert Hurst	Private 9th Bn. Northumberland Fusiliers	Died Monday 23 April 1917 Arras Memorial, Pas de Calais, France	
Thomas Walker	Private 11th Bn. King's Own (Royal Lancaster Regt.)	Died Wednesday 25 April 1917 Age 22 Fifteen Ravine British Cemetery, Villers-Plouich, Nord, France	Parents: William H and Sarah Walker Doncaster Road, Melton Turn, Leicester. (Born in South Wigston)
George Billington	Acting Bombardier 84th Bty. 11th Bde. Royal Field Artillery	Died 30 April 1917 Age 31 Cabaret-Rouge British Cemetery, Souchez, Pas de Calais, France	Wife: E Davenport (formerly Billington) Church Nook, Wigston
George Barnes	Private 8th Bn. Leicestershire Regt.	Died Thursday 3 May 1917 Age 22 Arras Memorial, Pas de Calais, France	Parents: William and Mary Barnes Cherry Street, Wigston Magna
Cecil Albert Harding	Private 9th Bn. Leicestershire Regt.	Died Thursday 3 May 1917 Arras Memorial, Pas de Calais, France	
Sydney Charles Robinson	Corporal 'A' Coy. 2nd Bn. South Staffordshire Regt.	Died Thursday 3 May 1917 Age 27 Orchard Dump Cemetery, Arleux-En-Gohelle, Pas de Calais, France	Parent: Mrs Alice Robinson, Belgrave, Leicester
Thomas Markham	Private 'C' Coy. 13th Bn. The King's (Liverpool) Regt.	Died Sunday 6 May 1917 Age 29 Duisans British Cemetery, Etrun, Pas de Calais, France	Born: Wigston Wife: Jane Markham, Vandyke Street, Liverpool
Leonard Smith	Private 1st Bn. Leicestershire Regt.	Died Tuesday 8 May 1917 Age 21 St Mary's ADS Cemetery, Haisnes, Pas de Calais, France	Parents: William Edwin and Alice Gertrude Smith Orange Street, South Wigston

R Robinson	Trooper Household Bn.	Died Friday 11 May 1917 Roeux British Cemetery, Pas de Calais, France	
Shirley Robinson	Private 1st Bn. South Staffordshire Regt.	Died Saturday 12 May 1917 Arras Memorial, Pas de Calais, France	South Wigston
T Chapman	Lance Corporal 136th Army Troops Coy. Royal Engineers	Died Wednesday 6 June 1917 Bailleul Communal Cemetery Extension, Nord, France	
Alcar Hill	Gunner 'D' Bty. 175th Bde. Royal Field Artillery	Died Thursday 7 June 1917 Age 21 Strand Military Cemetery, Comines-Warneton, Hainaut, Belgium	Born: Wigston Magna Parents: Albert and Lydia Hill East Street, Leicester
Shirley Lewin	Lance Serjeant 1st/4th Bn. Leicestershire Regt.	Died Friday 8 June 1917 Age 22 Arras Memorial, Pas de Calais, France	Parents: Matilda and James Lewin Healey Street, South Wigston
Frederick T Searle	Private 1st/4th Bn. Leicestershire Regt.	Died Friday 8 June 1917 Age 23 Loos British Cemetery, Pas de Calais, France	Parents: Lewis Arthur and Emma Searle Central Avenue, Wigston Magna
Walter Noble *	Private 1st/4th Bn. Lincolnshire Regt.	Died Friday 8 June 1917 Age 32 Arras Memorial, Pas de Calais, France	Parents: Henry and Eliza Noble Welford Road, Wigston
Alfred James Spencer	Private 6th Bn. Leicestershire Regt.	Died Monday 11 June 1917 Age 28 Croisilles British Cemetery, Pas de Calais, France	Wife: Louisa Spencer Station Street, South Wigston
Alfred William Rourke	Private 1st/5th Bn. Leicestershire Regt.	Died Thursday 21 June 1917 Age 30 Noeux-Les-Mines Communal Cemetery, Pas de Calais, France	Parents: Alfred Michael and Annie Maria Rourke Wife: Gertrude Rourke Newton Lane, Wigston

R W Turner	Private 2nd/2nd (Northumbrian) Field Amb. Royal Army Medical Corps	Died Wednesday 27 June 1917 Achiet-le-Grand Communal Cemetery Extension, Pas de Calais, France	
Horace Lee	Private 1st/4th Bn. Leicestershire Regt.	Died Thursday 28 June 1917 Age 23 – France	Parents: Mr and Mrs Robert Lee Clifford Street, South Wigston
Joseph Warren Brightwell	Private 1st/4th Bn. Leicestershire Regt.	Died Friday 29 June 1917 Age 19 Arras Memorial, Pas de Calais, France	Parents: John Thomas and Florence Eleanor Brightwell Glen Gate, South Wigston
Harold Ernest Baxter	Private 2nd/6th Bn. Sherwood Foresters (Notts and Derby Regt)	Died Friday 29 June 1917 Age 23 Metz-En-Couture Communal Cemetery British Extension, Pas de Calais, France	Parents: Abraham and Sarah Ann Baxter Midland Cottages, Wigston Magna
James Ross Wesley	Private 67th Field Amb. Royal Army Medical Corps.	Died Thursday 5 July 1917 Age 20 Mikra British Cemetery, Kalamaria, Greece	Parents: Frederick Ernest and Mary Elizabeth Wesley Station Road, Wigston Magna
William Edwin Walden	Gunner 160th Siege Bty. Royal Garrison Artillery	Died Sunday 22 July 1917 Age 27 Lussenthoek Military Cemetery, Poperinge, West-Vlaanderen, Belgium	Parent: William Henry Walden Wigston Magna Wife: Elsie Corbett, formerly Walden Gray Street, Leicester
David Sidney Webb	Private 7th Bn. Leicestershire Regt.	Died 28 July 1917 Age 22 Croisilles British Cemetery, Pas de Calais, France	Parents: John E and Sarah Ann Webb Welford Road, Wigston Magna
W F Brindley	Corporal 246th Coy. Machine Gun Corps (Inf)	Died Friday 3 August 1917 Age 27 Voormezeele Enclosure No. 3, Ieper, West-Vlaanderen, Belgium	Parents: Thomas and Bessie Brindley Wife: Ada Derry (formerly Brindley) Shakespeare Street, Aylestone Park
Thomas Henry Russell	Gunner 192nd Siege Bty. Royal Garrison Artillery	Died Thursday 16 August 1917 Dozinghem Military Cemetery, Poperinge, West-Vlaanderen, Belgium	Wife: Agnes Pallett Russell Harcourt Road, Wigston Magna

Name	Rank / Regiment	Died	Family
Albert Billings	Gunner 25th Heavy Bty. Royal Garrison Artillery	Died Sunday 26 August 1917 Age 28 Canada Farm Cemetery, Elverdinghe, Ieper, West-Vlaanderen, Belgium	Parents: Frances Mason (formerly Billings) and Albert Billings Countesthorpe Road, South Wigston
Harold Knight	Private 5th/6th Bn. Royal Scots (Lothian Regt.)	Died Sunday 26 August 1917 France and Flanders	Wigston
James Ival Baker	Private 21st (Tyneside Scottish) Bn. Northumberland Fusiliers	Died Sunday 9 September 1917 Age 28 Thiepval Memorial, Somme, France	Parents: Henry Fortune Baker and Eliza Baker, Glen Gate, South Wigston
Cecil J Freeston	Second Lieutenant 7th Bn. Yorkshire Regt.	Died Tuesday 18 September 1917 Age 28 Sunken Road Cemetery, Fampoux, Pas de Calais, France	Parent: E J Freeston Wife: E B Freeston Cooks Lane, Wigston
Leonard Gamble	Gunner 65th Howitzer Bty. Royal Field Artillery	Died Tuesday 18 September 1917 Age 23 Locre Hospice Cemetery, Heuvelland, West-Vlaanderen, Belgium	Parents: Alfred and Elizabeth Gamble Sileby, Loughborough, Leics.
John William Cawthorne	Private transf. to (110473) 185th Coy. Labour Corps	Died Tuesday 18 September 1917 Voormezeele Enclosures No. 1 and No. 2 Ieper, West-Vlaanderen, Belgium,	Wigston Magna
Frederick Moore	Private 28th Field Amb. Royal Army Medical Corps	Died Friday 21 September 1917 Age 19 Lussenthoek Military Cemetery, Poperinge, West-Vlaanderen. Belgium	Parents: John and Mary Elizabeth Moore Leicester Road, Wigston Magna
Charles Frederick Measom *	Private 1st/4th Bn. Leicestershire Regt.	Died Saturday 22 September 1917 Age 22 Philosophe British Cemetery, Mazingarbe, Pas de Calais, France	Parents: Harry and Eliza Measom Moat Street, Wigston Magna
John Hancock	Lance Sergeant 2nd Bn. Coldstream Guards	Died Monday 24 September 1917 Age 26 Dozinghem Military Cemetery, Poperinge, West-Vlaanderen, Belgium	Wife: Mary E Hancock Paddock Street, Wigston Magna
Thomas Chapman	Private 2nd/5th Bn. Leicestershire Regt.	Died Wednesday 26 September 1917 Tyne Cot Memorial, Zonnebeke, West Vlaanderen, Belgium	

Name	Rank / Regiment	Death	Family / Notes
T Silverwood	Private 2nd/5th Bn. Sherwood Foresters (Notts. and Derby Regt.)	Died 26 September 1917 France and Flanders	Wigston Magna
James Kenney	Private 'C' Coy Middlesex Regt.	Died Thursday 4 October 1917 Age 31 Dozinghem Military Cemetery, Westvleteren, Poperinge, West Vlaanderen, Belgium	Wife: Grace H Kenney Bassett Street, South Wigston
Walter Carter	Private 15th Durham Light Infantry	Died Thursday 4 October 1917 Age 34 – Ypres	Parents: Thomas and Ann Carter (Sixth Son). Wigston Magna. Inscription in Wigston Cemetery reads, "He sleeps besides his comrades in a distant grave unknown but his name is written in letters of love in the hearts he left at home."
William Peabody	Private 7th Bn. Leicestershire Regt.	Died Saturday 6 October 1917 Tyne Cot Memorial, Zonnebeke, West-Vlaanderen, Belgium	Wigston Magna
Edgar Hubbard	Private 2nd Bn. Royal Fusiliers	Died 11 October 1917 Age 19 Mendinghem Military Cemetery Poperinge, West-Vlaanderen, Belgium	Born South Wigston Parents: William Urban Hubbard and Jemima Hubbard Sileby, Loughborough, Leics.
James Spencer Potter	Trooper Household Bn.	Died Friday, 12 October 1917 Age 33 Tyne Cot Memorial, Zoonebeke, West-Vlaanderen, Belgium	Brother: Edward Potter Albion Street, South Wigston
William Thomas Clarke	Private 1st Bn. Leicestershire Regt.	Died Saturday 13 October 1917 Age 22 Loos British Cemetery, Pas de Calais, France	Parents: John Edward and Mary Ann Clarke Glen Gate, South Wigston
Douglas Quirrie Turner	Corporal 6th Bn. Attd. 110th TM Bty. Leicestershire Regt	Died Sunday 14 October 1917 Age 23 Kortrijk (St Jean) Communal Cemetery, Kortrijk, West-Vlaanderen, Belgium	Parents: Charles and Margaret Turner, Bassett Street, South Wigston Wife: Edith Mary Naylor (formerly Turner), Welby Lane, Melton Mowbray, Leics.

Frederick Arthur Mynard *	Rifleman 7th Bn Rifle Brigade	Died Monday 15 October 1917 Age 34 Tyne Cot Memorial, Zonnebeke, West-Vlaanderen, Belgium	Parents: Mr and Mrs Mynard Irlam Street, South Wigston
George Spence	Lance Corporal 9th Bn. Leicestershire Regt.	Died Wednesday 17 October 1917 Age 23 Etaples Military Cemetery, Pas de Calais, France	Parents: Mr and Mrs H A Spence Paddock Street, Wigston Magna
Alfonso Roberrs* Pawley	Lance Corporal 'B' Coy. 11th Bn. Leicestershire Regt.	Died Monday 22 October 1917 Age 26 Ypres Reservoir Cemetery, Ieper, West-Vlaanderen, Belgium	Parents: W and R M Pawley, Whetstone Wife: Ruby Pawley, Blaby Road, South Wigston
Frederick Charles Garner Mould	Private 7th Bn. Leicestershire Regt.	Died Sunday 28 October 1917 Age 34 Lijssenthoek Military Cemetery, Poperinge, West-Vlaanderen, Belgium	Born Wigston Magna Parents: Arthur and Lizzie Mould East Street, Oadby
Percy Cheater	Sergeant 11th Bn. Leicestershire Regt.	Died Monday 29 October 1917 Age 27 Ypres Reservoir Cemetery, Ieper, West Vlaanderen, Belgium	Parents: John and Ann Cheater South Wigston Wife: Florence Ellen Kimbury (formerly Cheater) Willoughby Waterleys
Allen Marshall *	Private 9th Bn. Leicestershire Regt.	Died Tuesday 30 October 1917 Lussenthoek Military Cemetery, Poperinge, West-Vlaanderen, Belgium	South Wigston
Harry Daniel Knight	Private 12th Bn. Royal Scots	Died Tuesday 30 October 1917 Age 27 Etaples Military Cemetery, Pas de Calais, France	Parents: Harry and Mary Hannah Knight, Adderley Road, Leicester
George Percy Linford Cox	Private 'C' Coy. 1st/28th Bn. London Regt. (Artists' Rifles)	Died Tuesday 30 October 1917 Age 30 Tyne Cot Memorial, Zonnebeke, West-Vlaanderen, Belgium	Parents: Mr and Mrs W S Cox Central Avenue, Wigston Magna Wife: Edith Ellen Cox Fosse Road South, Leicester

Name	Regiment/Rank	Death	Family
George Warren	Private 9th Bn. Leicestershire Regt.	Died Sunday 11 November 1917 Age 24 Tyne Cot Memorial, Zonnebeke, West-Vlaanderen, Belgium	Wife: Minnie Warren Lansdowne Road, Aylestone Park
Frank Veasey	Private 2nd/6th Bn. South Staffordshire Regt.	Died Tuesday 4 December 1917 Age 20 Etaples Military Cemetery, Pas de Calais, France	Parents: Fred and Ada Veasey Countesthorpe
William Holmes	Private 1st Bn. Grenadier Guards	Died Friday 7 December 1917 Rocquigny-Equancourt Road British Cemetery, Manancourt, Somme, France	Parents: William and Sarah Holmes Newton Lane, Wigston Magna

MEN LOST IN 1918

Thomas Burden	Corporal 180th Coy. Machine Gun Corps. (Inf)	Died Friday 18 January 1918 Age 24 Alexandria (Hadra) War Memorial Cemetery, Egypt	Parents: George and Susanne Eliza Burden Shakespeare Street, Knighton Fields
T J Silverwood	Private 1st/5th Bn. King's Own Yorkshire Light Infantry	Died Friday 25 January 1918 Nine Elms British Cemetery, Poperinghe, West-Vlaanderen, Belgium	
William H Roberts	Able Seaman Drake Bn. RN Div. Royal Naval Volunteer Reserve	Died Saturday 16 March 1918 St Sever Cemetery Extension, Rouen Seine-Maritime, France	
Harry Howard Howe	Private 6th Bn Leicestershire Regt.	Died Thursday 21 March 1918 Age 25 Hem Farm Military Cemetery, Hem-Monacu, Somme, France	Parent: Frederick Howe Bedale Road, Wellingborough
Robert Rolfe* Jeffrey	Private 2nd/4th Bn. Royal Berkshire Regt.	Died Thursday 21 March 1918 Age 19 Pozieres Memorial, Somme, France	Parent: Mrs Georgina Jeffrey Healey Street, South Wigston
George Riley	Lance Corporal 8th Bn. Leicestershire Regt.	Died Thursday 21 March 1918 Pozieres Memorial, Somme, France	

Arthur William Overton	Private 25th Coy. Machine Gun Corps (Inf)	Died Thursday 21 March 1918 Age 20 * Arras Memorial, Pas de Calais, France	Born South Wigston
Albert Randle	2nd/7th Bn. Manchester Regt.	Died Thursday 21 March 1918 Pozieres Memorial, Somme, France	Wigston
William James Cheater	Private 9th Bn. Cameronians (Scottish Rifles)	Died Friday 22 March 1918 Pozieres Memorial, Somme, France	South Wigston
T Rudkin	Private 1st Bn. Leicestershire Regt.	Died Friday 22 March 1918 Denain Communal Cemetery, Nord, France	
Percy Herbert	Private 2nd/4th Bn. Leicestershire Regt.	Died Friday 22 March 1918 Arras Memorial, Pas de Calais, France	Wigston Magna
Arthur Walsh	Private 13th Bn. Royal Sussex Regt.	Died Saturday 23 March 1918 Pozieres Memorial, Somme, France	
George Selvidge	Private 1st/8th Bn. Durham Light Infantry	Died Saturday 23 March 1918 Age 27 Heath Cemetery, Harbonnieres, Somme, France	Parents: Tom and Amy Selvidge Countesthorpe Road, South Wigston
William Rowley	Private 1st Bn. Leicestershire Regt.	Died Sunday 24 March 1918 Age 26 Lagnicourt Hedge Cemetery, Pas de Calais, France	Wife: Gertrude Rowley Bull Head Street, Wigston Magna
E A * Huckerby	Private 2nd/6th Bn. Lancashire Fusiliers	Died 24 March 1918 Age 20 Honnechy British Cemetery, Nord, France	Parents: John and Harriet Huckerby Bull Head Street, Wigston Magna
Joseph Amos Kenny	Private Durham Light Infantry	Died Monday 25 March 1918 France and Flanders	Born South Wigston
Jack Curtis Bruce	Second Lieutenant 2nd/5th Bn. Leicestershire Regt.	Died Monday 25 March 1918 Age 21 Arras Memorial, Pas de Calais, France	Parent: Mr A W Bruce Fernleigh, Glen Parva
William Henry Pentrey	Private 5th/6th Bn. Royal Scots (Lothian Regt.) Formerly Linc. Regt. *	Died Wednesday 27 March 1918 France and Flanders	South Wigston

Walter Samuel Willis	Private 2nd/6th Bn. Lancashire Fusiliers	Died Saturday 30 March 1918 Age 19 Pozieres Memorial, Somme, France	Parents: Walter S and Mary Ann Willis Kirkdale Terrace, South Wigston
Joseph Harold* Gee	Driver 'D' Bty. 291st Bde. Royal Field Artillery	Died Tuesday 2 April 1918 Age 25 Pozieres Memorial, Pas de Calais, Somme, France	Parents: Joseph and Eliza Ann Gee Bull Head Street, Wigston Magna
George Whyatt	Sapper 231st Field Coy. Royal Engineers	Died Tuesday 9 April 1918 Age 41 Ploegsteert Memorial, Comines-Warneton, Hainaut, Belgium	Wife: Mary Ann Whyatt Blaby Road, South Wigston
Charles William Johnson	Private 11th Bn. Lancashire Fusiliers	Died Tuesday 9 April 1918 Ploegsteert Memorial, Comines-Warneton, Hainaut, Belgium	Parent: Charles W Johnson Wife: Elizabeth Johnson Knighton Lane, Aylestone Park
Harry Veasey	Private 1st/5th Bn. Northumberland Fusiliers	Died Wednesday 10 April 1918 Age 18 Trois Arbres Cemetery, Steenwerck, Nord, France	Parents: Fred and Ada Veasey Glen Gate, South Wigston
Bernard Corbett	Private 4th Bn. South Staffordshire Regt.	Died Wednesday 10 April 1918 Ploegsteert Memorial, Comines-Warneton, Hainaut, Belgium	
Alec Walter Richardson	Private 6th Bn. Leicestershire Regt.	Died Monday 29 April 1918 Age 26 Esquelbecq Military Cemetery, Nord , France	Parents: Thomas and Mary Ann Richardson Wife: Annie Elizabeth Richardson Broughton Road, Cosby
Archibald Robinson	Sapper 4th Field Survey Corps, Royal Engineers	Died Wednesday 8 May 1918 Age 27 Borre British Cemetery, Nord, France	Wife: Beatrice E Robinson Leopold Street, South Wigston
Alonzo Broughton	Private 238th Coy. Machine Gun Corps (Inf)	Died Tuesday 21 May 1918 Age 25 Baghdad (North Gate) War Cemetery, Iraq	Parent: Mrs Harriet Broughton Wife: Agnes Broughton Paddock Street, Wigston Magna

Name	Rank/Regiment	Death	Family
John Daykin Broughton	Private 1028th MT Coy. Army Service Corps	Died Sunday 26 May 1918 Age 19 Baghdad North Gate War Cemetery, Iraq	Parent: Mr E Broughton Bull Head Street, Wigston Magna
William George Charles Root	Private 2nd Bn. Essex Regt.	Died Sunday 16 June 1918 Age 18 Mont-Bernanchon British Cemetery, Gonnehem, Pas de Calais, France	Born South Wigston Parents: Reuben and Julia Root Curzon Street, Leicester
John Joseph Hubbard	Private 1st/6th Bn. The King's (Liverpool Regt.)	Died Thursday 20 June 1918 Age 18 Etaples Military Cemetery, Pas de Calais, France	Born Ladysmith, South Africa Parents: Mr and Mrs James Hubbard Glen Parva
Wilfred Muggleton	Private 5th Bn. Machine Gun Corps (Inf)	Died Saturday 29 June 1918 Age 20 Merville Communal Cemetery Extension, Nord, France	Parents: Thomas and Emily Muggleton Moat Street, Wigston Magna
William Hopkins	Private King's Own (Royal Lancaster Regt)	Died Friday 12 July 1918 Age 42 Wigston Cemetery, Leicestershire	Wife: Nellie Hopkins North Street, Wigston Magna (William's son was killed in action in 1941 and is commemorated at Singapore.)
Sidney Charles Hipwell	Private 1st Bn. Leicestershire Regt.	Died Sunday 21 July 1918 Age 30 Kemmel No. 1 French Cemetery, Heuvelland, West-Vlaanderen, Belgium	Parents: George Arthur and Emma Hipwell Wife: Lillian Hipwell, Welford Road, Wigston Magna
William Arthur Whitehead	Private 2nd/5th Bn. Duke of Wellington's (West Riding Regt.)	Died Monday 22 July 1918 Soissons Memorial, Aisne, France	
Thomas Rudkin	Bandsman 1st Bn. Leicestershire Regt.	Died Wednesday 24 July 1918 France and Flanders	Born Wigston Magna
George Thomas Smith	Gunner Royal Field Artillery	Died Friday 2 August 1918 Age 26 Ste. Marie Cemetery, Le Havre, Seine-Maritime, France	Parents: Mr and Mrs Charles Smith Kibworth Beauchamp, Leicestershire

Thomas William Bale		Second Lieutenant 13th Bn. Tank Corps	Died Saturday 10 August 1918 Vis-En-Artois Memorial, Pas de Calais, France	
Harold Henry Vardy		Second Lieutenant 96th Light Railway Operating Corps. Royal Engineers	Died Thursday 22 August 1918 Age 42 Alexandria (Hadra) War Memorial Cemetery, Egypt	Parents: John and Sarah Ann Vardy Aston, Birmingham Wife: Hetty E Vardy Countesthorpe Road, South Wigston
John Loftus Freer		Corporal 6th Bn. Leicestershire Regt.	Died Wednesday 28 August 1918 Age 28 Abbeville Communal Cemetery Extension, Somme, France	Parent: Mr J Freer, Blaby Wife: Betsy Freer, Junction Road, Wigston Magna
Percy James Bailey		Private 1st/14th London Regt. Gordon Highlanders	Died Saturday 31 August 1918 France and Flanders	Born Wigston
Robert Bell Robson		Private 2nd Bn. Gloucestershire Regt.	Died Monday 2 September 1918 Karasouli Military Cemetery, Greece	
Joseph William Hall		Private 6th Bn. Leicestershire Regt.	Died Wednesday 18 September 1918 Age 25. Vis-En-Artois Memorial, Pas de Calais, France	Born South Wigston
William Russell		Private 1st Bn. Leicestershire Regt.	Died Thursday 19 September 1918 Age 28 Trefcon British Cemetery, Caulaincourt, Aisne, France	Parent: Charles Hall Glen Gate, South Wigston Wife: Clara Marion Rachel Measey (formerly Hall), Manor Cottages, Leicester Road, Oadby
Thomas Arthur* Faulkner		Private* 1st Bn. Leicestershire Regt.	Died Thursday 19 September 1918 Chapelle British Cemetery, Holnon Aisne, France	Parents: William and Elisabeth Russell, Blaby. Wife: Annie Sabina Russell Cherry Street, Wigston Magna
Leonard Gamble		Private 10th Bn. Lancashire Fusiliers	Died Monday 23 September 1918 * Abbeville Communal Cemetery Extension, Somme, France	South Wigston
				Parents: George and Emma Gamble Wigston Magna

Name	Rank/Regiment	Death	Family
Amos Barrett	Lance Corporal 1st/5th Bn. South Staffordshire Regt.	Died Saturday 28 September 1918 Age 21 Vis-En-Artois Memorial, Pas de Calais, France	Parents: Amos and Kesia Barrett Victoria Street, Wigston Magna
Arthur Varney MM	Serjeant 11th Bn Sherwood Foresters (Notts. and Derby Regt.)	Died Friday 4 October 1918 Age 20 Prospect Hill Cemetery, Gouy, Aisne, France	Born South Wigston Parents: Arthur and Zipporah Varney Belper, Derbyshire
William H Medhurst	Gunner 126th Heavy Bty. Royal Garrison Artillery	Died Monday 7 October 1918 Age 42 Hermies Hill British Cemetery, Pas de Calais, France	Parent: James Medhurst Wife: Minnie Medhurst Manor Street, Wigston Magna
Ernest Rourke	Private 1st Bn. Northumberland Fusiliers	Died Tuesday 8 October 1918 Masnieres British Cemetery, Marcoing, Nord, France	
Harry C Clowes	Private 7th Bn. South Staffordshire Regt.	Died Tuesday 8 October 1918 Flesquieres Hill British Cemetery, Nord, France	Parent: Mr T H Clowes Bushloe End, Wigston Magna
Arthur Agar	Lance Sergeant 6th Bn. Leicestershire Regt.	Died Tuesday 8 October 1918 Age 20 Prospect Hill Cemetery, Gouy, Aisne, France	Wife: Lucy Florence Agar Leicester Road, Wigston Magna
Ernest Thomas Powell	Rifleman 1st/7th Bn Prince of Wales Own (West Yorkshire Regt)	Died Friday 11 October 1918 Quievrain Communal Cemetery, Quievrain, Hainaut, Belgium	Parents: Joseph and Annie Powell Bull Head Street, Wigston Magna
Robert Carr	Gunner 33rd TM Bty. Royal Field Artillery	Died Monday 14 October 1918 Age 33 Roisel Communal Cemetery Extension, Somme, France	Wife: Lilian Carr Leicester Road, Wigston
George Kent	Private 1st/3rd (East Lancs.) Field Amb. Royal Army Medical Corps	Died Monday 21 October 1918 Age 39 Awoingt British Cemetery, Nord, France	Wife: A J Pentney (formerly Kent) Countesthorpe Road, South Wigston

Edgar Thomas Smith	Private B Coy. 1st/4th Bn. Leicestershire Regt.	Died Tuesday 22 October 1918 Age 24 Boisguillaume Communal Cemetery Extension, Seine-Maritime, France	Parents: Thomas and Louisa Lydia Smith South Wigston
Tom Lewin	Private 6th Bn. Leicestershire Regt.	Died Wednesday 30 October 1918 Age 29 Hamburg Cemetery, Germany	Parents: Alick and Maud Lewin Wife: Florence Emma Lewin Frederick Street, Wigston Magna
Edgar Lecois Boat *	Bombardier 'U' Bty. 16th Bde. Royal Horse Artillery	Died Tuesday 5 November 1918 Premont British Cemetery, Aisne, France	Born Wigston
Victor F Coleman	Lance Corporal 18th Bn. York and Lancaster Regt.	Died Tuesday 5 November 1918 Age 19 Dottignies Communal Cemetery, Mouscron, Hainaut, Belgium	Parents: Charles W and Ellen E Coleman, Woodford Haise, Byfield, Northamptonshire
Arthur Grace	Private 8th Bn. Leicestershire Regt.	Died Thursday 14 November 1918 Age 19 Hautrage Military Cemetery, Saint-Ghislain, Hainaut, Belgium	Parents: George and Mary Ann Grace Long Street, Wigston Magna
George Walter Goodman	Company Serjeant Major 53rd Bn. Northumberland Fusiliers	Died Wednesday 20 November 1918 Age 34 Wigston Cemetery, Leicestershire	Wife: Grace E Goodman Clifford Street, South Wigston
Edwin Noble	Gunner Royal Garrison Artillery	Died 22 November 1918 Age 37 Wigston Cemetery, Leicestershire	Parents: Harry and Eliza Noble Wife: Rachel Ellen Noble Central Avenue, Wigston Magna
G E Preston	Corporal Durham Light Infantry	Died Tuesday 17 December 1918 Wigston Cemetery, Leicestershire	

Name	Rank / Unit	Death	Family
Samuel Foster Gamble MC	Regimental Serjeant Major Leicestershire Regt.	Died Friday 7 February 1919 Age 35 Wigston Cemetery, Leicestershire	Wife: E H Getliff (formerly Gamble) Kirkdale Road, South Wigston
George Marshall	Corporal Northumberland Fusiliers	Died Wednesday 31 March 1920 Wigston Cemetery, Leicestershire	
A E Cooper	Private Leicestershire Regt.	Died Friday 16 April 1920 Wigston Cemetery, Leicestershire	
B Barratt	Private 12th Bn. Leicestershire Regt.	Died Saturday 15 May 1920 Age 29 Wigston Cemetery, Leicestershire	Parents: Amos and Kezia Barratt Victoria Street, Wigston Magna
Reginald Rowbotham	Private Royal Marine Light Infantry	Died 19 February 1922 Age 29 Memorial Wigston Cemetery, Leicestershire 'Lost at Sea'	

MEN LOST IN 1939

Raymond Charles Kane	Marine HMS Royal Oak, Royal Marines	Died Saturday 14 October 1939 Age 18 Portsmouth Naval Memorial	Parents: Charles John and Elsie Kane Station Street, South Wigston
Cyril Edward Bettoney	Assistant Steward HMS Rawalpindi Naval Auxiliary Personnel (MN)	Died Thursday 23 November 1939 Age 31 Liverpool Naval Memorial	Parents: Harry and Sarah Bettoney Countesthorpe Road, South Wigston
Brynmor Richards	Able Seaman HMS Exeter, Royal Navy	Died Wednesday 13 December 1939 Age 21 Plymouth Naval Memorial	Parents: Stanley and Margaret Richards South Wigston
George Thomas Edwin Walker	Ordinary Signalman HM Trawler Loch Doon. Royal Navy	Died Monday 25 December 1939 Age 18 Chatham Naval Memorial	Parents: Ernest Edwin and Lottie Hannah Beatrix Walker Bassett Street, South Wigston

MEN LOST IN 1940

Name	Rank/Unit	Death	Parents/Wife
Joseph William Bell	Private 6th (HD) Bn. Leicestershire Regt.	Died 30 January 1940 Wigston Cemetery, Leicestershire	Parents: Thomas N Bell and Catherine Bell. Wife: Lillian Sarah Charlotte Bell, Buckinghamshire
Frederick James Copson	Private 1st/5th Bn. Leicestershire Regt.	Died Tuesday 23 April 1940 Age 21 Lillehammer Northern Civil Cemetery, Norway	Parents: Fred and Rosetta Sarah Copson Wigston Magna
Charles Laurie Hughes	Second Lieutenant 2nd/5th Bn. Leicestershire Regt.	Died Sunday 26 May 1940 Age 32 Carvin Communal Cemetery, Pas de Calais, France	Parents: Charles William and Ellen Elizabeth Hughes. Wife: Molly Hughes, Blaby
Walter Charles Henney	Engineer Officer SS Aboukir (London) Merchant Navy	Died Tuesday 28 May 1940 Age 44 Tower Hill Memorial, London	Parents: Charles Harry and Elesabeth Mary Henney
William Frederick Lewis	Pilot Officer 59 Sqdn. Royal Air Force Volunteer Reserve	Died Saturday 2 November 1940 Halinghen Communal Cemetery, Pas de Calais, France	Parents: William Henry and Florence Maud Lewis Leicester

MEN LOST IN 1941

Name	Rank/Unit	Death	Parents/Wife
Frederick Michael Norton	Private 6th (HD) Bn. Leicestershire Regt.	Died Saturday 11 January 1941 Age 55 Wigston Cemetery, Leicestershire	Parents: Thomas and Mary Ann Norton Wife: Florence Norton Lansdowne Grove, South Wigston
Frederick James Close	Ordinary Seaman MV Zealandic (Southampton), Merchant Navy	Died Friday 17 January 1941 Age 20 Tower Hill Memorial, London	Parents Henry Thomas Arnold and Winifred Selina Close South Wigston
Horace Faulkner	Private 14th Ordnance Store Coy. Royal Army Ordnance Corps	Died Tuesday 25 March 1941 Age 25 Cairo War Memorial Cemetery, Egypt	Parents: Albert and Elsie Faulkner South Wigston
Edward Charles Hickford	Aircraftman 2nd Class 504 Squadron Royal Air Force Volunteer Reserve	Died Saturday 5 April 1941 Countesthorpe Cemetery, Leicestershire	Parents: Owen and Ethel B Hickford Glen Gate, South Wigston

Name	Rank / Unit	Death	Family
Louis Albert Smith	Private 5th Bn. Northamptonshire Regt.	Died Wednesday 23 April 1941 Age 21 Saffron Hill Cemetery, Leicester	Parents: Charles William and Ivy Lilian Smith. Wife: Elizabeth Smith
Walden John Biggenden	Chief Stoker HMS Hood, Royal Navy	Died Saturday 24 May 1941 Age 52 Portsmouth Naval Memorial	Parents: John Miller Biggenden and Alice Maud Biggenden Wife: Olive Biggenden, Hull Walden's brother died in 1944
Stewart Robert Joseph Rendell	Able Seaman HMS Hood, Royal Navy	Died Saturday 24 May 1941 Age 19 Portsmouth Naval Memorial	Parents: Robert Bertie and Gladys Rendell South Wigston
Leonard Roy Jarvis	Able Seaman HMS Hood	Died Saturday 24 May 1941 Age 19 Portsmouth Naval Memorial	Parents: Ernest Charles and Ada Hannah Jarvis. Clifford Street, South Wigston
Arthur Ernest Simpkin	Sergeant 104 Squadron Royal Air Force Volunteer Reserve	Died Sunday 3 August 1941 Age 21 Kiel War Cemetery, Germany	Parents: Ernest John and Kezia Simpkin Wigston Fields, Leicester
Wilfred George Dent	Bombardier 154 (The Leicestershire Yeomanry), Field Regt. Royal Artillery	Died Monday 29 September 1941 Age 28 Wigston Cemetery, Leicestershire	Parents: George and Alice Dent, Wigston Wife: Ada Dent, Leicester
Thomas William Bull	Sergeant W/Op. Air/Gnr. 115 Sqdn. Royal Air Force Volunteer Reserve	Died Monday 29 September 1941 Age 19 Wedge (Blijham) Protestant Churchyard, Groningen, Netherlands	Parents: Harry Byard Bull and Elsie Bull Wigston, Leicestershire
William Henry Hopkins	Private 1st Bn. Leicestershire Regt.	Died Wednesday 10 December 1941 Age 23 Singapore Memorial, Singapore	Parents: William and Nellie Hopkins North Street, Wigston Magna (William's father died in WWI 1918)
Ernest Robert George Lewis	Sergeant W.Op/Air Gnr. 70 Squadron Royal Air Force Volunteer Reserve	Died Saturday 13 December 1941 Age 23 Knightsbridge War Cemetery, Acroma, Libya	Parents: Walter F C Lewis and Constance M A Lewis. Central Avenue, Wigston Magna. Wife: Marjorie Lewis

MEN LOST IN 1942

Ralph Vann	Gunner 189 Bty. 14 AA 'Z' Regt. Royal Artillery	Died Saturday 24 January 1942 Age 35 Wigston Cemetery, Leicestershire	Parents: William John and Amy Elizabeth Vann. Wife: Doris Vann, Wigston
George Marsh Robinson	Sergeant 214 Squadron Royal Air Force Volunteer Reserve	Died Wednesday 28 January 1942 Age 20 Runnymede Memorial, Surrey	Parents: Thomas William and Annie Elizabeth Robinson, Wigston, Leics.
Wallace Harold Mace Watts	Sergeant W.Op/Air Gnr. 220 Squadron Royal Air Force Volunteer Reserve	Died Sunday 1 February 1942 Age 20 Wigston Cemetery, Leicestershire	Parents: Walter and Gladys Edith Watts Wife: Mary Watts, Wigston Magna
Edward John Frederick Valle	Sergeant Royal Army Service Corps	Died Friday 13 February 1942 Age 23 Singapore Memorial, Singapore	Parents: Edward and Emily Marion Valle Wigston, Leicestershire
Robert Alfred Bell	Sergeant Royal Air Force Volunteer Reserve	Died Friday 13 March 1942 Age 31 Runnymede Memorial, Surrey	Parents Robert Calder Bell and Christina Bell. Wife: Lena Bell, Melton Mowbray
Alfred John Leaver	Sergeant 217 Squadron Royal Air Force Volunteer Reserve	Died Sunday 15 March 1942 Age 20 Wigston Cemetery, Leicestershire	Parents: Frederick Clifford and Blanche Muriel Leaver, Wigston
Peter Gordon Arthur Malin	Sergeant 156 Squadron Royal Air Force Volunteer Reserve	Died Sunday 31 May 1942 Age 23 Vorden General Cemetery, Gelderland, Netherlands	Parents: Arthur and Martha Lilian Malin Wife: Betty Malin, Wigston, Leics.
Gordon Wilford	Private Leicestershire Regt.	Died Tuesday 9 June 1942 Age 25 Wigston Cemetery (Tamworth Comrades of Warwick)	Parents: Arthur and Lucy Wilford, Wigston
John Patrick Barrett	Sergeant 122 Squadron Royal Air Force Volunteer Reserve	Died Friday 19 June 1942 Age 21 Brookwood Military Cemetery, Surrey	Parents: John Gordon and Angela Mary Barrett. Countesthorpe
Thomas Edward Wright	Able Seaman HMS President 111 (lost in SS Empire Mica) Royal Navy	Died Sunday 29 June 1942 Age 30 Portsmouth Naval Memorial	Parents: William James and Sarah Wright Wife: Doris Emma Wright Florence Avenue, South Wigston
Arthur Henry Coleman	Aircraftman 2nd Class Royal Air Force Volunteer Reserve	Died Saturday 4 July 1942 Age 21 Khartoum War Cemetery, Sudan	Parents: Geoffrey Fred and Florence Louisa Coleman. South Wigston

Name	Rank / Unit	Death	Family
John George Colver	Private 2 Line Repair Workshop Royal Army Ordnance Corps	Died Wednesday 26 August 1942 Age 24 Ismailia War Memorial Cemetery, Egypt	Parents: Harry and Jessie Colver Wigston, Leicestershire
Horace Edgar Deacon	Private Royal Army Ordnance Corps	Died Saturday 7 November 1942 Age 31 Wigston Cemetery Leicestershire	Parents: Robert Percy and Harriet Deacon Wife: Rhoda Deacon, South Wigston
Thomas B Smith	Gunner 11th (Honourable Artillery Coy) Regt Royal Horse Artillery	Died Saturday 14 November 1942 Age 22 Alamein Memorial, Egypt	
Kenneth Gamble	Sergeant 39 Squadron Royal Air Force Volunteer Reserve	Died Monday 30 November 1942 Age 22 Malta Memorial, Malta	Parents: Edwin and Lily Elizabeth Gamble Wigston, Leicestershire
Arthur Andrew Heard	Third Radio Officer SS Empire Wagtail (London) Merchant Navy	Died Monday 28 December 1942 Age 15 Tower Hill Memorial	Parents: Andrew and Ada, Hockley, Birmingham

MEN LOST IN 1943

Name	Rank / Unit	Death	Family
Kenneth Arthur King	Driver 18 Bomb Disposal Coy. Royal Engineers	Died Friday 19 February 1943 Age 27 Benghazi War Cemetery, Libya	Parents: Arthur and Daisy Irene King Wigston Magna, Leicestershire Wife: Lilian Mary King, Bruntingthorpe, Leicestershire
John Thomas Woods	Lance Corporal 2nd/5th Bn. Leicestershire Regt.	Died Monday 22 February 1943 Age 25 Enfidaville War Cemetery, Tunisia	Parents: John George and Mary Elizabeth Woods, Wigston
Jack Mason	Private 5th Bn. Northamptonshire Regt	Died 26 February 1943 Age 19 Medjez-El-Bab War Cemetery, Tunisia	Parents: Joseph and Evelyn Mason, Wigston Magna
Leonard George Clare	Sergeant 2nd/5th Bn Leicestershire Regt.	Died Sunday 7 March 1943 Age 24 Medjez-El-Bab War Cemetery, Tunisia	Parents: Dyson Neville Clare and Jane E Clare. Wife: Violet Clare Galashiels, Selkirkshire
John Douglas Hitchman	Private Royal Army Medical Corps	Died Wednesday 7 April 1943 Age 24 Chittagong War Cemetery, Bangladesh	Parents: William and Edith Hitchman Wife: Joyce Edith Hitchman, Leicester
Oliver Raymond Frost	Private 1st/4th Bn. Royal Hampshire Regt.	Died Thursday 8 April 1943 Age 26 Enfidaville War Cemetery, Tunisia	Parents: Thomas Ernest Edwards Frost and Sarah Elizabeth Frost Wife: Ivy Irene Frost, Coventry

Joseph Patrick Doyle	Private 1st/5th Bn Leicestershire Regt.	Died Monday 26 April 1943 Age 24 Wigston Cemetery, Leicestershire	Parents: John and Annie Doyle Wife: Irene Winifred Elsie Doyle, Wigston Magna
Gerald Arthur Church* DFC	Flight Lieutenant 228 Squadron Royal Air Force Volunteer Reserve	Died Saturday 15 May 1943 Age 22 Runnymede Memorial, Surrey	Parents: Thomas William and Florence May Church, Blaby.
William Pretty	Driver Royal Army Service Corps	Died Saturday 26 June 1943 Age 35 Khayat Beach War Cemetery, Israel	Parents: Thomas and Annie Pretty Wife: Annie Pretty Timber Street, South Wigston
Peter Gervaise Caddick Brain	Ordinary Seaman HMS Towel Royal Naval Patrol Service	Died Friday 9 July 1943 Age 22 Wigston Cemetery, Leicestershire	Parents: Edward and Mary Eleanor Brain South Wigston
John Derek Woodward		Died Sunday 29 August 1943 Age 16 Wigston Cemetery, Leicestershire	Parents Edgar Wilfred and Hilda Woodward, Wigston
Daykin Moore	Gunner 148 (The Bedfordshire Yeomanry), Field Regt. Royal Artillery	Died Saturday 11 September 1943 Age 30 Kanchanaburi War Cemetery, Thailand	Parent: Bertram Moore Wife: Margaret Moore, Aylestone
Carter Edward W		Died Saturday 16 October 1943 Age 29 North Africa	Wigston Cemetery
Alexander Frederick Chisholm DFC	Squadron Leader Air Bomber 83 Squardron Royal Air Force	Died Tuesday 23 November 1943 Age 31 Berlin 1939-1945 War Cemetery, Brandenburg, Germany	Parent: Alexander Samuel Chisholm
Fred Allen Read	Corporal Royal Air Force Volunteer Reserve	Died Saturday 27 November 1943 Age 38 Wigston Cemetery, Leicestershire	Parents: Robert Kitson Read and Annie Elizabeth Read. Wife: Ethel Mildred Read, Wigston, Leicestershire
Harry Kenneth Mundin	Aircraftman 2nd Class Royal Air Force Volunteer Reserve	Died Monday 29 November 1943 Age 22 Singapore Memorial, Singapore	Parents: Ernest George and Mary Jane Mundin. Glen Gate, South Wigston
Wilfred Austin Bray	Captain 2nd/5th Bn. Leicestershire Regt.	Died Saturday 4 December 1943 Age 27 Minturno War Cemetery, Italy	Parents: Ernest and Emily Bray Canal Street, South Wigston

Name	Rank / Unit	Death details	Family
John Trevor Elliott	Leading Airman. HMS Owl, Royal Navy	Died Tuesday 14 December 1943 Age 20 Lee on Solent Memorial, Hampshire	Parents: William and Elsie Elliott Glen Gate, South Wigston
William Dickens	Lance Corporal 296 Army Field Coy. Royal Engineers	Died Thursday 16 December 1943 Age 29 Cassino Memorial, Italy	Parents: Edward and Naomi Dickens Wife: F M Dickens, South Wigston
George Arthur Draycott	Sergeant 625 Squadron Royal Air Force Volunteer Reserve	Died Thursday 16 December 1943 Age 26 Wigston Cemetery, Leicestershire	Parents: Maggie Draycott, Stepfather Harry Ellis
Frederick William Wesson	Lance Corporal Royal Army Service Corps	Died Wednesday 29 December 1943 Age 26 Sangro River War Cemetery, Italy	Parents: Frederick William and Ellen Wesson. Clifford Street, South Wigston
		MEN LOST IN 1944	
Ernest William Upton	Private Royal Pioneer Corps	Died Thursday 20 January 1944 Wigston Cemetery, Leicestershire (Epitaph from Officers and Comrades No. 74 POW Camp)	
James Henry Smith	Lieutenant Sherwood Foresters (Notts. and Derby Regt.)	Died Thursday 2 March 1944 Age 35 Taukkyan War Cemetery, Myanmar (formerly Burma)	Parents: George Henry and Elizabeth Catherine Smith Wife: Lilian Smith, South Wigston
Leslie Edward Knott	Ordinary Seaman HMS Wuchang. Royal Navy	Died Thursday 27 April 1944 Age 19 Trincomalee War Cemetery, Sri Lanka	Parents: James and Florence Caroline Knott. Lansdowne Grove, South Wigston
George Charles Birkin	Corporal 5 Base Ordnance Depot Royal Army Ordnance Corps	Died Wednesday 7 June 1944 Age 34 Tel El Kebir War Memorial Cemetery, Egypt	Parents: Alfred Ernest and Sarah Jane Birkin. Wife: Elsie May Birkin. North Street, Wigston Magna
Athol Ekins Biggenden	Chief Stoker HMS Minster, Royal Navy	Died Thursday 8 June 1944 Age 49 Portsmouth Naval Memorial	Wife: Jessie Biggenden Victoria Street, Wigston Magna (Athol's brother died on The Hood in 1941)
Frederick William Eastoe	Sapper 79 Assault Squadron Royal Engineers	Died Saturday 10 June 1944 Age 27 Hermanville War Cemetery, Calvados, France	Wife: Minnie Eastoe Glen Hills, Blaby

William Sperry	Corporal 1st Bn. Leicestershire Regt.	Died Wednesday 23 August 1944 Age 31 St. Desir War Cemetery, Calvados, France	Parents: William John and Annie Sperry Wife: Edith Ann Sperry, Oadby, Leicestershire
William Ford Norman	Gunner 148 (The Bedfordshire Yeomanry) Field Regt., Royal Artillery	Died Tuesday 12 September 1944 Age 25 Singapore Memorial, Singapore	Parents: Alfred and Matilda Norman Wife: Margaret E Norman, Thurmaston, Leicestershire
Thomas William Mayes	Staff Serjeant 1st Wing, Glider Pilot Regt. AAC	Died Monday 18 September 1944 Age 24 Arnhem Oosterbeek War Cemetery, Netherlands	Parents: Arthur William and Eleanor May Mayes Healey Street, South Wigston
Ernest William Barlow	Lance Corporal 4 Bomb Disposal Coy. Royal Engineers	Died Wednesday 20 September 1944 Age 36 Wigston Cemetery, Leicestershire	Parents: Charles and Eliza Ann Barlow Wife Connie Barlow, Wigston
Clifford Stewart Haylett	Captain 20 Lt. AA Regt. Royal Artillery	Died Thursday 21 September 1944 Age 29 Adegem Canadian War Cemetery, Maldegem, Oost-Vlaanderen, Belgium	Parents Percy and Elizabeth Ruth Haylett Wife: Enid Mary Haylett, Wigston, Leicestershire
Ernest John Mowl	Lieutenant General List Corps of Royal Military Police	Died Monday 9 October 1944 Age 33 Kortrijk (St. Jean) Communal Cemetery, Kortrijk, West Vlaanderen, Belgium	Parents Frank Wilkinson Mowl and Ellen Mowl. Wife: Iris Mary Mowl, Kirkdale Road, South Wigston
John Patrick Murray	Sergeant WOp. (Air) 460 (RAAF) Sqn. Royal Air Force Volunteer Reserve	Died Sunday 11 June 1944 Age 21 Viroflay New Communal Cemetery, Yvelines, France	Parents: John Walter and Dorothy Emma Murray Braunstone, Leicester
Leonard Taylor	Private 1/7th Bn. The Queen's Royal Regiment (West Surrey)	Died Wednesday 14 June 1944 Age 28 Bayeux Memorial	Wife: Kathleen Mary Taylor South Wigston
Jack Saddington Gibson	Pilot Officer 12 Sqdn. Royal Air Force Volunteer Reserve	Died Thursday 6th July 1944 Age 27 Wigston Cemetery, Leicestershire	Parents: Henry and Fanny Mary Gibson Wife: Gwendolen Margaret Gibson Retford, Nottinghamshire
Leonard Francis Wells	Corporal 4th Bn. Royal Welch Fusiliers	Died Sunday 16 July 1944 Age 24 Banneville-La-Campagne War Cemetery, Calvados, France	Parents: Leonard Loach Wells and Frances Jane Wells, South Wigston

Name	Rank / Regiment	Death	Parents / Wife
Kenneth Arthur Measures	Lance Corporal 7th Bn. Leicestershire Regt.	Died Tuesday 1 August 1944 Age 24 Digboi War Cemetery, India	Parents: Archibald Stanley Heard Measures and Minnie Measures, Wigston Fields
Albert George Jones	Private 6th Bn. Green Howards (Yorkshire Regt.)	Died Wednesday 9 August 1944 Age 21 Banneville-La-Campagne War Cemetery, Calvados, France	Parents: Albert and Catherine Lilian Jones Manor Street, Wigston Magna
Lawrence Geoffrey Hall	Driver Royal Army Service Corps Attd. Indian Army Corps of Clerks	Died Wednesday 16 August 1944 Age 25 Becklingen War Cemetery, Germany	Parents: Walter James and Florence Hall
Harold Whait	Corporal 1st Bn. Leicestershire Regt.	Died Saturday 21 October 1944 Age 31 Geel War Cemetery, Geel, Antwerpen, Belgium	Parents: Jabez Henry and Mabel Whait Wife: Marjorie Whait, Blaby
Raymond John Grenter	Leading Aircraftman Royal Air Force Volunteer Reserve	Died Wednesday 25 October 1944 Age 24 Singapore Memorial, Singapore	Parents: Henry Arthur and Sarah Ann Grenter, South Wigston.
William Joseph Whawell	Pilot Officer Royal Air Force Volunteer Reserve	Died Wednesday 7 November 1944 Age 26 Wigston Cemetery, Leicestershire	Parents: Charles Edward and Bessie Whawell Wife: Kathleen Jane Whawell, Wigston

MEN LOST IN 1945

Name	Rank / Regiment	Death	Parents / Wife
William Henry Kerwood	Serjeant Royal Electrical and Mechanical Engineers	Died Wednesday 7 February 1945 Wigston Cemetery, Leicestershire	Parents: William Henry and Mary Ann Kerwood. Wife: Lucy Maud Kerwood, South Wigston
Joseph William Hall	Private 1st Bn. Royal Berkshire Regt.	Died Saturday 10 March 1945 Age 20 Taukkyan War Cemetery, Myanmar (formerly Burma)	Parents: Mr and Mrs L Hall Glen Gate, South Wigston
Ralph Taylor	Flight Sergeant Air Bomber 61 Squadron Royal Air Force Volunteer Reserve	Died Wednesday 21 March 1945 Age 32 Durnbach War Cemetery, Bayern, Germany	Parents: Mr and Mrs Taylor Bull Head Street, Wigston Magna Wife: Edith Marjorie Taylor Healey Street, South Wigston

Name	Rank / Regiment	Death	Family
Clement James Wood	Lance Corporal Royal Corps of Signals	Died Saturday 24 March 1945 Age 21 Reichswald Forest War Cemetery, Germany	Parents: Clement and Jessie Mildred Wood, Blaby
William Douglas Bennett	Lance Bombardier 115 Field Regt. Royal Artillery	Died Friday 20 April 1945 Age 28 Maynamati War Cemetery, Bangladesh	Parents: John T and Nellie Bennett, Frederick Street, Wigston Magna. Wife: Kathleen J Bennett Queen Street, Oadby
Bernard Purkiss	Serjeant Army Catering Corps Leicestershire Regiment	Died Tuesday 2 October 1945 Age 48 Wigston Cemetery, Leicestershire	Wife: Margaret Purkiss Blaby Lane (now St Thomas's Road) South Wigston.
Leonard Kemp	Gunner 208 Field Regt. Royal Artillery	Died Monday 12 November 1945 Age 38 Tripoli War Cemetery, Libya	Parents: Frank and Margeret Kemp Wife: Constance Winifred Kemp Kingston Avenue, Wigston Fields
		DEATH IN 1946 – 1947 – 1951	
Joseph William Bent	Private 1st Bn. South Staffordshire Regt.	Died Sunday 2 June 1946 Age 32 Wigston Cemetery, Leicestershire	Wife: Lilian Bent, South Wigston
Charles Arthur Richard Miles	Leading Aircraftman Royal Air Force Volunteer Reserve	Died Monday 29 July 1946 Age 41 Wigston Cemetery, Leicestershire	Parents: Charles and Kate Miles Wife: Nellie Winifred Miles, Wigston
Joseph William Ainsworth	Corporal Royal Corps of Signals	Died Tuesday 10 December 1946 Age 24 Ramleh War Cemetery, Israel	Parents: William Edward and Winifred Ainsworth, Wigston
Thomas William Ephraim Harrold	Aircraftman 2nd Class Royal Air Force Volunteer Reserve	Died Tuesday 31 December 1946 Age 40 Wigston Cemetery, Leicestershire	Parents Edward Ephraim Harrold and Annie Harrold. Wife: Beatrice Ellen Harrold, South Wigston
Arthur Edward Hicks	Serjeant 2nd Bn. Grenadier Guards	Died Tuesday 7 October 1947 Age 26 Saffron Hill Cemetery, Leicestershire	Parents: Tom and Victoria Maud Hicks Wife: Lorna Kathleen Hicks Brighton, Sussex
Joseph Rourke	Lance Corporal 11th Bn. Leicestershire Regt.	Died Friday 8 June 1951 Enderby Dissenters' Cemetery	Wife: Emily Rourke Seine Lane, Enderby, Leicestershire

MEN LOST IN THE FIRST AND SECOND WAR
LIMITED INFORMATION

Name	Rank	Details Where Known
Douglas Arnett Job Barnett	Private Sherwood Foresters	
E Bell	Gunner	
D Bennett	HMS Towel	
Hector Bennett	Private Canada	First World War
Walter Bennett	Canada	
Bettoney	Lance Corporal King's Own Yorkshire Light Infantry	
J Bibby	Driver	
J Blanchard	Sapper Royal Engineers	
H Blanchard		
H Blanchon		
B Brown		
H H Broughton		First World War
Douglas G Caswell	Private Leicestershire Regiment	First World War
Horace Cave	CSM Tank Corps	
E Crane		First World War
C Clarke	Private	
H Clarke	P/O Royal Air Force	
D Copson		
C Davis		
J H Driver	Gunner	
L Edwards		
Falkener	Private Royal Army Ordnance Corps	
T Foister	Sergeant Royal Warwickshire Regiment	
Harry Green	Sapper Royal Engineers	
Walter Hennet		First World War
W G Henney	Private	
C Herbert	Quartermaster	

J Hilman		
S Hutchinson	Canada	
William D Kinchin	Private Worcestershire Regiment	First World War
W Lawrence	Gunner	
R Lee	Private Leicestershire Regiment	
L Lewin		
Albert Marshall	Private Leicestershire Regiment	
Charles Mills	Private Leicestershire Regiment	First World War
J K Murray		
Edward H Norman		
W E Norman	Gunner Royal Artillery	
John W S Phipps		First World War
Arthur Randall	Private Leicestershire Regiment	
George Randall		First World War
W Ridsdale		
R Robson	Able Seaman	
D Roper		
Frank M Ross	Private Leicestershire Regiment	First World War
John Samuel Rudkin	Lance Corporal Yorkshire Regiment	
J Seaton		
E Simpson	Sergeant	
George T Smith		First World War
James William Smith	Private Gordon Highlanders	
L Smith	Lance Corporal Royal Leicestershire Regiment	
Malcolm Turner	Private Royal Army Medical Corps	
J Vann		
S Walsh		First World War
George Whaite	Lance Corporal	First World War
C Walker	Canada	
J Walker	Canada	
O Waller		
Harry Woolman	Private South Staffordshire Regiment	

APPENDIX D

BLABY

BLABY WAR MEMORIAL

**The War Memorial is situated on Blaby Park, Leicester Road, Blaby, Leicestershire.
The inscriptions reads:- In memory of those who lost their lives in the 1939-1945 War.**

NAME	RANK	DATE/DIED	PERSONAL DETAILS WHERE KNOWN
Harry Burton	Sergeant WOp/Air Gunner 22 Squadron Royal Air Force Volunteer Reserve	Died Thursday 24 April 1941 Age 20	Parents: Henry and Lois Annette Burton
Harold Raymond Thomas Greasley	Assistant Cook (S) HMS Galatea, Royal Navy	Died Monday 15 December 1941 Age 24	Parents: John and Emma Greasley Wife: Doris Mary Greasley
Richard George Jeffs	Private 1st Bn. Leicestershire Regiment	Died Thursday 22 January 1942 Age 23	Parent: Sarah Jane Jeffs
William Lines	Gunner 171 Field Regiment Royal Artillery	Died Saturday 12 August 1944 Age 35	Parents: John Henry and Mary Lines Wife: Elsie Lilian Lines
Thomas William Meredith	No information.		
Arthur Ernest Russell	Driver Royal Army Service Corps	Died Thursday 5 February 1942 Age 21	Parents: Mr and Mrs W J Russell Wife: Dorothy May Russell of Enderby
John Edwin Charles Smith	Ordinary Seaman HMS Fidelity Royal Navy	Died Friday 1 January 1943 Age 19	Parents: John S M L and Beatrice M Smith
Robert Harold Taylor	Sergeant 83 Squadron Royal Air Force Volunteer Reserve	Died Sunday 22 February 1942 Age 20	Parents: William Harold and Marjorie Dorothy Taylor
Walter Sidney Toon	Private 1st Bn. Leicestershire Regiment	Died Thursday 1 January 1942 Age 28	Parents: Thomas and Florence Mabel Toon
Leslie John Wood	Lance Corporal 1st Bn Gordon Highlanders	Died Tuesday 14 November 1944 Age 25	Parents: John and Edith Ann Wood
Walter Charles Webster Vann (Not on War Memorial)	Private 'C' Coy 11th Bn. Leicestershire Regiment	Died Friday 22 March 1918 Age 20	Parents: Charles and Ada Vann of Sycamore Street, Blaby

APPENDIX E

COSBY

COSBY WAR MEMORIAL

The war memorial is situated within Saint Michael and All Angels Church on Main Street, Cosby, Leicestershire. A board erected in memory of the men of Cosby reads:-

FIRST WORLD WAR 1914-1918		SECOND WORLD WAR 1939-1945
Lt. W Stanley Eames	Pvt. Alfred Holland	Captain John Neal
CSM John Bull	Pvt. Harry Hawkins	Ofr. Cdt. Brian Gimson
Cpl. Albert Kenney	Pvt. Joseph Jones	Sgt. Robert O'Neil
Cpl. John Oliver	Pvt. Ernest Kenney	Cpl. Alfred Day
LCpl. Len Ayriss	Pvt. James Kenney	O/S Thomas Harrop
Pvt. Richard Chandler	Pvt. Joseph Kenney	Marine Howard Kenney
Pvt. Herbert Hains	Pvt. Josiah Langton	Driver Ivan Pougher
Pvt. Ernest Charlton	Pvt. William Mallett	A/C Arthur Lewitt
Pvt. Tom Furborough	Pvt. Thomas Merry	Pvt. Kenneth Harrop
Pvt. Robert West	Pvt. Frank Nicholson	Pvt. Stan Wells
Pvt. Bert Ayriss	Gnr. Edgar Pawley	Pvt. Henry Hurst
Pvt. Fred Bacon	Pvt. John Pougher	Pvt. Stanley Hopper
Pvt. Walter Bodicot	Pvt. James Pratt	Pvt. Thomas Green
Pvt. Tom Chamberlain	Pvt. William Smith	Pvt. Max Palmer
Pvt. George Curtis	Pvt. Harry Southam	Pvt. Len Wilson
Pvt. William Dexter	Pvt. Samuel Starmer	Pvt. Bert Brown
Pvt. Alfred Fenton	Pvt. Herbert Stretton	Pvt. Joseph Boyle
Pvt. Victor Furborough	Pvt. Edgar Tibbles	
Pvt. Horace Furborough	Pvt. Walter White	

APPENDIX F

COUNTESTHORPE

Countesthorpe War Memorial is situated within Saint Andrew's churchyard. The church in the centre of the village stands on the corner of Main Street.

COUNTESTHORPE WAR MEMORIAL

TO THE GLORY OF GOD AND IN MEMORY OF THE MEN OF COUNTESTHORPE WHO FELL IN THE GREAT WAR 1914-1918.

GREATER LOVE HATH NO MAN THAN THIS THAT A MAN LAY DOWN HIS LIFE FOR HIS FRIENDS.

(ERECTED BY THE EX-SERVICEMEN OF COUNTESTHORPE. UNVEILED BY HRH THE DUKE OF YORK, 24 NOVEMBER 1921.)

1914-1918	1914-1918	1939-1945
W Buckingham VC *	H W E Jarratt	J P Barrett
R Boat	A A Johnson	H E Creasey
J A Chapman	W Johnson	C K Hughes
J S Coleman	T L Lord	L Norton
B Cox	E Mason	R S Brothwell
J W Cox	E R Olive	L Cutler
H E Findley	A Oldershaw	L Lucas
R F Gamble	H Oldershaw	J Parsons
W A Gamble	W C Peat	D H Chapman
T Garratt	W Simms	T L Fielding
S Gillam	J C S Soars	H Mason
J H Gilliam	A W Stafford	H Riddington
G A Glass	H Swann	J K Chapman
N C J Harrison	F Thornton	T Hill
D Heathcote	J H Tilley	D Moore
W J A Herbert	F Veasey	N A Smith
W E Herbert	Hubert Veasey	
W Hebbert	E C Wallis	
J Hubbard	H S Wallis	
J H Hubbard	A Wells	
W H Hubbard	S Weston	
C Immins	A E York	
E Immins	F York	

* Willliam Buckingham VC
See 'A TIGER AND A FUSILIER' By Derek Seaton.

APPENDIX G

CROFT

PRIVATE
ROBERT GLYN
HAMILTON HANDS

Robert Glyn Hamilton Hands was born in 1923. He was one of three sons born to William and Ann Hands. Robert known affectionately as Robin and his brother Ernest were born in North Wales close to the Blanau Festiniog Railway. His parents and elder brother George had moved there from Midlothian, Scotland in 1924. The family moved from Wales to Croft in Leicestershire in 1930.

The children attended the school in Croft where Mr Looker was one of the schoolmasters. Robin became a choir boy and a bell ringer at Croft Church.

On leaving school Robin secured an apprenticeship with Vickers Armstrongs Ltd, Rugby Road, Hinckley. It was an Auto company. It is believed that after war was declared in 1939 the firm became involved in the production of munitions.

Robin joined the Army and was serving with the 5th Battalion King's Own Scottish Borderers. Whilst on active duty his battalion was ordered to siege Weese in Germany which was successfully carried forcing the enemy to retreat to the small village of Voltlage. Fierce fighting and heavy loss of life on both sides occurred before Voltlage was taken but Robin was killed in the battle. It was Sunday 8th April 1945. He was twenty two years old.

Robin is commemorated at Sage War Cemetery, Germany. There are over nine hundred and fifty casualties buried on the site.

Remembering Robin at Croft, a photograph of him was placed in the bell tower of Saint Michael's Church. There is also a photograph of his friend and fellow bell ringer, Reginald Collis who was killed in the Far East.

Robin Hands

No. CAS/KOSB/21.
(If replying, please quote above No.)

Army Form B. 104—82.

Infantry .... Record Office,

PERTH.

18th April, ... 194 5.

Dear Madam,

It is my painful duty to inform you that a report has been received from the War Office notifying the death of :—

(No.) 14791601 .... (Rank) .... Private

(Name) .... Robert Glyn Hamilton Henderson HANDS

(Regiment) .... KING'S OWN SCOTTISH BORDERERS

which occurred .... in Western Europe

on the .... 8th April, 1945.

The report is to the effect that he .... was Killed in Action.

I am to express the sympathy and regret of the Army Council.

I am to add that any information that may be received as to the soldier's burial will be communicated to you in due course, by the Directorate of Graves Registration and Enquiries, War Office (A.G.13), 32 Grosvenor Gardens, S.W.1, to whom all enquiries with regard to graves or places of burial should be addressed.

I am,
Madam,

Mrs. Ann Hands,
29, Kendall Avenue,
CROFT, Nr. Leicester.

Your obedient Servant,

Officer in Charge of Records.

(27305)   Wt.15457/2574   000,000   5/44   A.& E.W.Ltd.   Gp.698   Forms/B.104-82/6.   [P.T.O.

BUCKINGHAM PALACE

The Queen and I offer you our heartfelt sympathy in your great sorrow.

We pray that your country's gratitude for a life so nobly given in its service may bring you some measure of consolation.

George R.I

```
From :   Lieut. Col. G.G.M. Batchelor,
         5th Bn. The K.O.S.B.                    15th April 1945.
         B.L.A.

To    :  Mrs A. Hands,
         29 Kendall Avenue,  Croft,
         Leicester,
```

Dear Mrs Hands

On behalf of all ranks of the 5th Bn. The King's Own Scottish Borderers I write to send you our deepest sympathy in the loss of your son   who was killed in action on the 8th April.

This is an unofficial letter and I presume you will already have received official notification from the War Office. Your son was killed during an attack which this Battalion carried out against stiff opposition. The action was completely successful, due to the gallant actions of all ranks and the enemy were routed. Your son on this occasion, as on previous occasions, carried out his duties in the splendid manner which we have now come to expect from our magnificent soldiers. Your son   was buried on the following day by our Padre, along with his comrades who fell in this action, in a small village called WEESE which lies to the North of OSNABRÜCK.

Again I send you our deepest sympathy in your very great loss.

Yours Sincerely
G.G.M. Batchelor
                                        Lieut Col.
                        Commanding 5th Bn. The K.O.S.B.

Robin Hands

The King's Own Scottish Borderers.

WIDOWS' AND ORPHANS' ADVISORY COUNCIL.

In reply please give Soldier's Number, Name and Battalion.

24th April 1945.

Dear Mrs Hands

    As Colonel of the King's Own Scottish Borderers I desire to express the deep sympathy of all ranks of the Regiment in the great loss you have sustained in the death of your ....Son........ on Active Service.

    If you should find yourself at any time in need of advice, the Widows' and Orphans' Advisory Council will do its best to help you.

    Please write to the Member of the Council of the Battalion of which your ....Son........ was a member.

    Names and addresses are given below.

Yours sincerely,

V.G. Mirtes
Major-General.

1st Battalion.—Mrs. SANDEMAN,
Clifton Lodge,
Totnes,
S. Devon.

2nd Battalion.—Mrs. SELLAR,
Glebe House,
Guilsfield,
Montgomeryshire,

4th Battalion.—Mrs. STEWART CROMBIE,
Eildon Bank,
Melrose.

5th Battalion.—Mrs. McLENNAN,
The Garden Cottage,
Smeaton,
Prestonkirk,
East Lothian.

6th Battalion.—Mrs. BALLANTYNE,
Green Gables,
Peebles.

7th Battalion.—Mrs. STEWART,
Little Corsbie,
Newton Stewart,
Wigtonshire.

9th Battalion.—Mrs. DOUGLAS SCOTT,
Summerfield East,
Hawick.

Depot.—Mrs. BELL,
"Highcliffe,"
Castle Terrace,
Berwick-on-Tweed.

Robin Hands

May. 1945 Price 2½d.

CROFT

The mentioning of Robert Hands killed in action.

PARISH MAGAZINE

Rector: The Rev. J. CASSON, M.A., Canon Treasurer of Leicester Cathedral. Proctor in Convocation.
Churchwardens: Mr. J. Barker and Mr. W. Wass.
Secretary of the Parochial Church Council: Mr. W. Wass.   Sexton: Mr. F. Watson, 5, Pochin Street.
Organist: Mr. J. Barker, A.R.C.O.   Head Master of the School: Mr. W. E. Looker.

SERVICES

SUNDAYS: Holy Communion at 8-0 a.m. and on First Sunday at 11-0 a.m. preceded by Mattins. Morning Prayer at 11-0 a.m.; with Litany on Last Sunday.

Evening Prayer at 6-0 p.m. (see Note).

Holy Days: Holy Communion at 10-0 a.m.

On the greater Festivals and in Lent there are additional Services of which notice is given.

Note.—During the war the time of Holy Communion is adjusted to the black-out, and Evening Prayer is at 3-0 p.m. when black-out is earlier than 7-15 p.m.

Holy Baptism: Any Sunday by arrangement with the Rector.

Churchings by arrangement.

Banns, Marriages, Burials: Particulars should be given to the Rector and the times arranged with him.

Sunday School: 10-15 a.m. and 2-30 p.m. When Evening Prayer is at 3-0 p.m. Sunday School is at 2-15.

Church of England Men's Society: Secretary—Mr. Clifton Bottrill.
Mothers' Union: Enrolling Member—Mrs. W. Wass (provisional).
Girls' Friendly Society: Associates—Miss Casson, Mrs. W. E. Looker.
Society for the Propagation of the Gospel: Secretary—The Rev. H. M. Gorham.

Leicester Cathedral

THE FORM AND ORDER OF SERVICE

in connection with the CIVIC HONOUR to THE LEICESTERSHIRE REGIMENT

SUNDAY, 24th SEPTEMBER, 1944, at 3.30 p.m.

HYMN I.

O GOD, our help in ages past,
　Our hope for years to come,
Our shelter from the stormy blast,
　And our eternal home;

Beneath the shadow of thy throne
　Thy Saints have dwelt secure;
Sufficient is thine arm alone,
　And our defence is sure.

Before the hills in order stood,
　Or earth received her frame,
From everlasting thou art God,
　To endless years the same.

A thousand ages in thy sight
　Are like an evening gone;
Short as the watch that ends the night
　Before the rising sun.

Time, like an ever-rolling stream,
　Bears all its sons away;
They fly forgotten, as a dream
　Dies at the opening day.

O God, our help in ages past,
　Our hope for years to come,
Be thou our guard while troubles last,
　And our eternal home.　Amen.

The hymn being ended, the Provost shall welcome the congregation, saying:

BRETHREN, yesterday the Lord Mayor, City Council and citizens of Leicester, paid honour to the Leicestershire Regiment by conveying officially to the Regimental Authorities the desire that on all ceremonial occasions the Regiment will honour the citizens by marching through the streets of the City with bayonets fixed, Colours flying and bands playing. To-day the Scroll on which that desire is recorded is to be deposited in the Regimental Chapel of St. George in this Cathedral, there to take its place with the other memorials of the history of the Regiment. I therefore bid you welcome to this Service, and call upon you to pray to Almighty God for his blessing upon us all.

W. Thornley & Son, Printers, Leicester.

In Memoriam ✝ Muffled Peal

On April 24th 1945, in 2 hours 33 minutes, on the bells in this tower, a peal of 5,040

Grandsire Doubles.

Frederick Horsewood	Treble	Ernest Morris	4
Gunner F Bailess R.A.	2	William A Wood	5
Frederick Watson	3	Alfred E Warwick	Tenor

Conductor Ernest Morris

Rung muffled to the memory of
Pte. ROBIN HANDS, K.O.S.B.
Chorister and Ringer of this church,
who was killed in Germany on April 8th
1945, six days after his 22nd birthday

Page 290

ALBERT SHENTON

Private Albert Shenton
1st Bn. Leicestershire Regt.
Died Thursday 12 February 1942 age 23
Parents George W and Nellie Shenton of Croft.
Singapore Memorial, Singapore

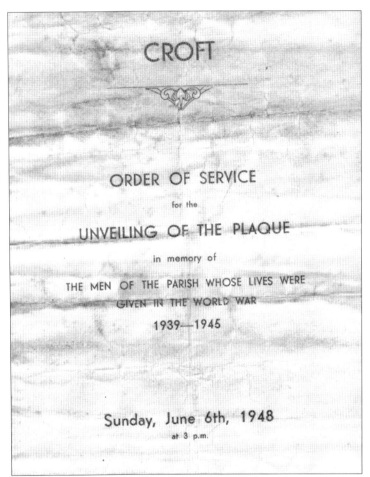

CROFT

ORDER OF SERVICE

for the

UNVEILING OF THE PLAQUE

in memory of

THE MEN OF THE PARISH WHOSE LIVES WERE
GIVEN IN THE WORLD WAR

1939—1945

Sunday, June 6th, 1948

at 3 p.m.

UNVEILING OF THE PLAQUE BY MRS. G. W. SHENTON.

Then the President of the British Legion will read the names on
the Plaque.

PTE. FRED COLLINS	PTE. ROBIN HANDS
6th Lincs.	K.O.S.B.
L/CPL. REGINALD COLLIS	PTE. ALBERT SHENTON
Raiding Support	1st Leics.
PTE. REUBEN DUNCAN	PTE. F. A. THOMPSON
Black Watch	1st Leics.
PTE. LAWRENCE WALE	
Nth. Staffs.	

LAST POST.

SILENCE (1 minute).

Exhortation by the Chaplain.
They shall grow not old, as we that are left grow old,
Age shall not weary them, nor the years condemn,
At the going down of the sun and in the morning,
We will remember them.
Response by Members. We will remember them.
Chaplain. The Legion of the Living salutes the Legion of
the Dead.
Response. We will not break faith with ye.

APPENDIX H

OADBY

OADBY WAR MEMORIAL

The War Memorial in Oadby is situated in the centre of the village on a very busy corner outside Saint Peter's Church, The church is situated on Wigston Road. The memorial commemorates one hundred and eleven men and one woman.

Sister Sybil Gwendoline Richardson was serving with the Queen Alexandra's Imperial Military Nursing Service and died on Saturday 12th February 1944.

Sister Richardson is also commemorated at the Brookwood Memorial Surrey. The memorial commemorates over three thousand men and women of the land forces who died at sea, in the campaign in Norway 1940, as members of raiding parties or as special agents or workers with Allied underground movements and who have no known grave. A seperate panel commemorates the loss at sea of six hundred and thirty nine members of the African Pioneer Corps.

Private C A Fearn	10th Battalion, Lancashire Fusiliers
Private C W Cave	2nd Battalion, Royal Scots Fusiliers
Private L A Ball	2nd Battalion, The King's Own Scottish Borderers
Lance Corporal F Pratt	7th Battalion, The Royal Inniskilling Fusiliers
Private W A Burton	1st Battalion, The South Staffordshire Regiment
Private A Green	1st Battalion, The South Staffordshire Regiment
Private A L Clarke	12th Labour Company, The Black Watch
Private C H Dunkley	11th Battalion, The Sherwood Foresters
Private W E Hames	1st Battalion, The Sherwood Foresters
Private E R Green	4th Battalion, The King's Own Yorkshire Light Infantry
Lieutenant J H Fitzmaurice	6th Battalion, The King's Shropshire Infantry
Private W E Bray	12th Battalion, The Manchester Regiment
Private C Hames	5th Battalion, Seaforth Highlanders
Lance Corporal E Mason	28th Battalion, Canadian Expeditionary Force
Private W O Mellows	13th Battalion, Canadian Expeditionary Force
Private C S Partridge	38th Battalion, Canadian Expeditionary Force
Private T Potterton	43 Cameron Highlanders, Canadian Expeditionary Force
Sergeant Major C E Weston	15th Battalion, Australian Imperial Forces
Private A Goddard	53rd Remount Squadron, The Royal Army Service Corps
Lance Corporal C H H Harrison	The Royal Army Ordnance Corps
Lieutenant H Brice	4th Battalion, The Leicestershire Regiment
Leiutenant A C Clarke	4th Battalion, The Leicestershire Regiment
Lieutenant D C Royce	2nd Battalion, The Leicestershire Regiment
Leiutenant F M Waite	4th Battalion, The Leicestershire Regiment
Sergeant J Cave	9th Battalion, the Leicestershire Regiment
Sergeant J Hall MM	2nd Battalion, The Leicestershire Regiment
Sergeant A Illston	1st Battalion, The Leicestershire Regiment

Sergeant C E Mathews	2nd Battalion, The Leicestershire Regiment
Sergeant H Weston	9th Battalion, The Leicestershire Regiment
Lance Corporal C H Elliott	4th Battalion, The Leicestershire Regiment
Lance Corporal H B Coleman	4th Battalion, The Leicestershire Regiment
Lance Corporal T Granger	1st Battalion, The Leicestershire Regiment
Lance Corporal J P Horner	8th Battalion, The Leicestershire Regiment
Private S T Allen	9th Battalion, The Leicestershire Regiment
Private A Bennett	4th Battalion, The Leicestershire Regiment
Private T Brindley	2nd Battalion, The Leicestershire Regiment
Private H Coleman	2nd Battalion, The Leicestershire Regiment
Private W Fenwick	2nd Battalion, The Leicestershire Regiment
Private H Granger	1st Battalion, The Leicestershire Regiment
Private W Markham	6th Battalion, The Leicestershire Regiment
Private J H Johnson	2nd Battalion, The Leicestershire Regiment
Private J Hammond	6th Battalion, The Leicestershire Regiment
Private J W Hall	6th Battalion, The Leicestershire Regiment
Private J Green	6th Battalion, The Leicestershire Regiment
Private R C G Mould	7th Battalion, The Leicestershire Regiment
Private E G Perkins	11th Battalion, The Leicestershire Regiment
Private W Rowley	1st Battalion, The Leicestershire Regiment
Private F Sturgess	9th Battalion, The Leicestershire Regiment
Private W Sturgess	11th Battalion, The Leicestershire Regiment
Private M Summerland	1st Battalion, The Leicestershire Regiment
Private G E Usher	6th Battalion, The Leicestershire Regiment
Private T R Warner	4th Battalion, The Leicestershire Regiment
Private A Weston	4th Battalion, The Leicestershire Regiment
Private W Weston	9th Battalion, The Leicestershire Regiment
Private G Willcocks	2nd Battalion, The Leicestershire Regiment
Private E W Mathews	2nd Battalion, The Yorkshire Regiment
Private J E Vernon	4th Battalion, The Yorkshire Regiment

Driver R Chamberlain	175th BDE RFA, The Royal Regiment of Artillery
Gunner P A Smith	176th BDE RFA, The Royal Regiment of Artillery
Gunner H Summerland	286th Batty RCA, The Royal Regiment of Artillery
Gunner C L Thornton	231st Batty RCA, The Royal Regiment of Artillery
Gunner L Wakeling	233rd Batty RCA, The Royal Regiment of Artillery
Lance Corporal B Willson	308th Construction Coy, Corps of Royal Engineers
Captain F A Durrad	Royal Air Force
2nd A/M F C Foers	Royal Air Force
2nd A/M C T Gray	Royal Air Force
Private A Tailby	3rd Battalion, Coldstream Guards
Private W Gregory	2nd Battalion, The Royal Scots
Private S C Potterton	12th Battalion, The Norfolk Regiment
Private H Johnstone	10th Battalion, The Lincolnshire Regiment
Sargeant R E Hyslop	2nd Battalion, The Suffolk Regiment
RFN B G Boulter	8th Battalion, The West Yorks Regiment

<u>1939-1945</u>

William A Austin	Royal Air Force
John L Baines	Royal Air Force
Norman Beames	Royal Air Force
John T Berridge	Royal Air Force
Charles Bleackley	Royal Air Force
Harold H Brown	Royal Air Force
Fred R Hardy	Royal Air Force
Douglas Harper	Royal Air Force
Blake Hunter	Royal Air Force
Marcus Hutchinson	Royal Air Force
John R Moran	Royal Air Force
Dennis W Wheeler	Royal Air Force

Victor Beech	Royal Navy
Donald Kew	Royal Navy
Albert W Marston	Royal Navy
Thomas Starkie	Royal Navy
Frank Whitehead	Royal Navy
George Appleby	Royal Navy
Norman Austin	Royal Artillery
Donald Bailey	Northants
Norman J Cooke	RASC
Ernest E Bates	The Leicestershire Regiment
W Douglas Bennett	Royal Artillery
Ronald H Cave	Royal Artillery
Ernest Clarke	Royal Inniskilling Fusiliers
Michael Driver	Royal Artillery
Harold Driver	The Leicestershire Regiment
Philip J Dexter	RASC
Norman J Cooke	The Leicestershire Regiment
Dennis Green	Royal Engineers
Ernest Hamby	Lincolnshire Regiment
E E Harrison	Royal Engineers
W Frank Notley	Royal Artillery
Ian L Rawson	The Leicestershire Regiment
Sybil G Richardson	The Leicestershire Regiment
William Sperry	The Leicestershire Regiment
Samson E Stanley	Queen Alexandra's IM
Jack Steadman	The Leicestershire Regiment
Jeffrey Taylor	Royal Artillery
John Walker	Green Howards
Jack N Wesson	Sherwood Foresters
Eric W Tyler	Bedfordshire Regiment
	The Leicestershire Regiment
	RAF

APPENDIX I

WHETSTONE

TERTIUS SELWYN WARNER

Tertius Selwyn Warner was born on the 17 May 1893. He was the son of Thomas and Agnes Warner living in Whetstone in Leicestershire. He was one of several children having brothers and sisters.

It is known that when Tertius was a young man he was in Canada with his mother and it is thought that they may have been visiting relatives. Tertius and his mother were returning to England via New York in May 1915.

Tertius anxious to return and enlist in Kitchener's Army, booked a second class cabin on RMS Lusitania for himself but his mother was afraid to accompany him as she feared the German threat

to sink the liner was real. Tertius agreed with the view of many other people of the day, dismissing the warnings as propaganda.

On May Day 1915, RMS Lusitania left New York Harbour and was carrying 1,959 passengers and crew and was thought to be transporting small arms for Kitchener's Army. In the early afternoon on the 7 May a few miles off the Irish coastline she was torpedoed by Uboat 20 captained by Kapitanleutnant Walther Schweiger. At Seven Heads Point off the Head of Kinsale 1,198 passengers, including children and crew lost their lives.

Tertius Selwyn Warner's body was never found. His name is remembered on his parents grave stone at Whetstone Cemetery, Leicestershire.

Left: RMS Lusitania

Right: Medal cast by the Germans to celebrate the sinking of RMS Lusitania 7th May 1915

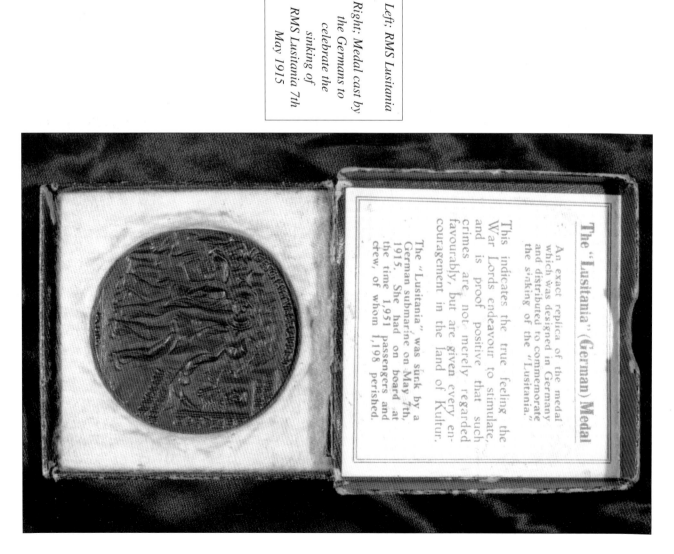

The "Lusitania" (German) Medal

An exact replica of the medal which was designed in Germany and distributed to commemorate the sinking of the "Lusitania."

This indicates the true feeling the War Lords endeavour to stimulate, and is proof positive that such crimes are not merely regarded favourably, but are given every encouragement in the land of Kultur.

The "Lusitania" was sunk by a German submarine on May 7th, 1915. She had on board at the time 1,951 passengers and crew, of whom 1,198 perished.

WHETSTONE WAR MEMORIAL

Saint Peter's Church is situated in Church Nook off High Street in the village and the memorial erected to the men of both world wars is close by. The inscriptions and names of the men are listed as follows.

TO THE GLORY OF GOD AND IN GRATEFUL MEMORY TO THE MEN OF THIS PARISH WHO GAVE THEIR LIVES IN THE WAR 1914-1918

HERBERT A BIGGS	ARTHUR HERRICK	EDGAR PAWLEY
GEORGE W BODICOAT	PERCY HOLDEN	ARTHUR PRATT
EDWARD BOULTER	JOHN HUBBARD	JAS RICHARDSON
HARRY CANNAM	HARRY JOHNSON	CYRIL SHENTON
ALFRED CHARLES	GEORGE W KENNEY	OSWIN SMITH
LONZO CHARLES	ARNOLD KIND	WILFRED SPENCE
AMOS CHARLES	REUBEN KIND	ROBERT E STEVENS
WILLIE COULSON	JESSE LAUNDON	CLIFFORD UPEX
WILLIAM H COULSON	ROBERT MARTIN	ALFRED WALE
THOMAS H ELLIOTT	ARTHUR MAWBY	RONALD WALE
THOMAS FRANKLIN	HORACE MAWBY	OLIVER WARNER
MAURICE C E HALL	FREDERICK NEEDHAM	HARRY WELLS
TOM HALL	WILLIAM NEEDHAM	MAURICE WELLS
SOUTHEY A HALL	TOM PARAMORE	THOMAS WELLS
ARTHUR HENSON	ALFONSO PAWLEY	GEORGE WORSH

ALSO TO THE SACRED AND BLESSED MEMORY OF THOSE WHO LOST THEIR LIVES IN THE WORLD WAR 1939 TO 1945

ALAN ABBOTT	ALBERT H HERBERT	LESLIE C COOPER
WILLIAM RICHARDSON	CALEY L HUNTER	CLIFFORD SHENTON
HECTOR C A GAMBLE	ROBERT H LOUCHLAND	JAMES SMITH
ARTHUR HARROP	BERTIE PHILPS	

WE WILL REMEMBER THEM

FURTHER RESEARCH

Arthur Clifford Shenton	Flight Sergeant 619 Squadron Royal Air Force Volunteer Reserve	Died: Thursday 4 May 1944 Age 22 Courboin Communal Cemetery, Aisne, France	Parents: John Clifford and Hilda Shenton of Whetstone
Andrew Shenton		Injured in January 1940 at Report Centre, Narborough. Died: Friday 13 December 1946 Age 53 at Whetstone	Wife: Ada Maria Shenton 24 Victoria Road Whetstone

APPENDIX J

'I AM NOT GONE'

'MY VILLAGE'

I AM NOT GONE
BY NADINE MURPHY – LINCOLN - NEBRASKA

I am not gone.
Do not think of me as underground
Unless you see me everywhere.
I have joined each seed that dies to be a flower.
So when you plant your garden in the earth
You might think of me.
     In the grave?
I am not there, that is not me!
The Seed has burst and I am free.

I am not gone. I am flying into the sun.
So when you watch the morning in its glory,
The twilight in its quiet beauty,
See my wings flash across the sky and know that I am free.
     In the grave?
I am not there, that is not me.
I am touching your face with the sun.

I am not gone
I am drifting to the sea.
So when you walk beside the ocean
By the deep and restless sea, hear the crying of the gulls and think of me.
     In the grave?
I am not there, that is not me.
I am playing on the farther shore of the boundless sea.

I am not gone
I am sailing into the wind
So I shall sigh through your window in summer
    and blow leaves around you in autumn.
When the wind kisses your hair with laughter you might remember me.
     In the grave?
I am not there, that is not me.
I have unfurled my soul to the wind and I am free.

I am not gone.
I am tiptoeing into the dark to visit the Moon.
Whispering soft goodbyes.
I shall soon fade from sight,
But when the Moon lights a path across dark water
You might think of me,
      In the grave?
I am not there, that is not me,
I am sailing with the moon on the breath of forever

I am not gone.
I am dancing in the storm
Laughing with thunder and lightning leaper
Now when summer storms roll in
With rumbling and fireworks
Do not be afraid, just think of me
      In the grave?
I am not there, that is not me.
I have danced away in thunder and I am free.

I am not gone.
I am part of forever.
In every season, every birdsong,
In flowers, clouds and each rainbow.
I am part of them. They are part of me.
Do not grieve only remember.
      In the grave?
I am not there, that is not me.
The shell is open, the Spirit free.

MY VILLAGE

By Pamela Ward

I speak to thee of railways, not just one but three
Their wondrous grace took village space, their ghosts now speak to me
I hear them in the dead of night rumbling o'er the viaduct's height
Whistles shrill toot past Crow Mill, those mighty engines storm the hill

I speak to thee of churches, O many of all creed
Their services were stirring to serve our hamlet's need
Protestants and Catholics, Methodists and more
Went in hordes to praise their Lord, the wealthy and the poor

I speak to thee of khaki, parading soldiers feet
Stamping to attention and marching through the street
Local band before them shining brass and drums
Twirling mace, no prouder face, to herald Leicester sons

I speak to thee of people all toiling to survive
Of men, machines and masters, who built to make us thrive
Of lowly trades and higher, of gentry and their kin
Residing at Glen Parva Grange, the Knight of Rolleston

I speak to thee of kindness of neighbours standing by
Of children's games, not vandals aims to make the nation sigh
I speak to thee of happy times mingled with some sad
But most of all I speak to thee of life our village had

Changes that have raced with time have not erased those memories fine
Nor dulled our senses to omit the milkman's horse or 'stinking pit'
The smell of tar, the taste of air that belched from chimney stacks up there
The sweetness of the flowers wild that decked the hair of every child

Chimney sweeps all sooty black, the teacher's cane to curb or whack
Trees that lined the one main road that bore the weight of lesser load
The doctor's house and gardens fair, no supermarket standing there
What can I say to make you see how much this village means to me
It's monumental roots still hold those recollections touched with gold
A newer face it may put on: I speak to thee of South Wigston